Angels on Earth

Funded by the Government of Canada
Financé par la gouvernement du Canada | Canada

Demeter Press
140 Holland Street West
P. O. Box 13022
Bradford, ON L3Z 2Y5
Tel: (905) 775-9089
Email: info@demeterpress.org
Website: www.demeterpress.org

Demeter Press logo based on the sculpture "Demeter" by Maria-Luise Bodirsky <www.keramik-atelier.bodirsky.de>

Printed and Bound in Canada

Front cover artwork: Ardith Goodwin, "Guardian Angel," 2013, mixed media/collage, 8 x 10 inches. Artist website: http://ardithgoodwin.com.

Library and Archives Canada Cataloguing in Publication

Angels on earth, mothering, religion and spirituality / edited by Vanessa Reimer.

Includes bibliographical references.
ISBN 978-1-77258-022-8 (paperback)

1. Motherhood -- Religious aspects. 2. Mothers -- Religious life. 3. Feminism -- Religious aspects. I. Reimer, Vanessa, 1986–, author, editor

HQ759.A56 2016 306.874'3 C2016-904647-8

MIX
Paper from responsible sources
FSC® C004071

Angels on Earth

Mothering, Religion, and Spirituality

EDITED BY

Vanessa Reimer

DEMETER

DEMETER PRESS

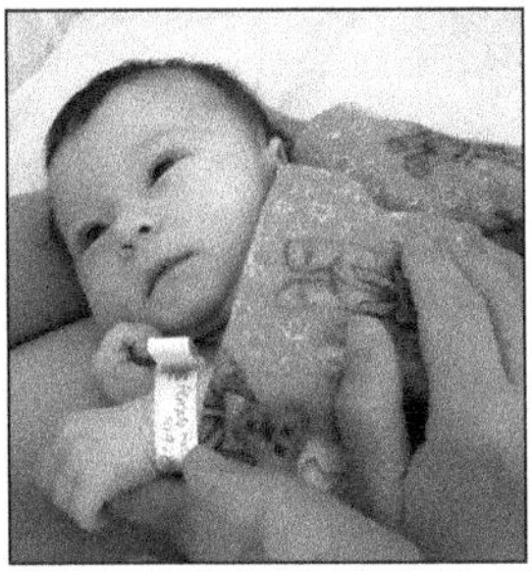

In loving memory of my daughter, Leah.
You will always be my angel.

Also dedicated to my mother.
Thank you for always offering your love, support,
and wisdom when I need it the most.

Table of Contents

Acknowledgements

I would like to begin by thanking Andrea O'Reilly and the entire team at Demeter Press for accepting my proposal for this book and supporting me throughout the editing process. Special thanks to the book's reviewers, whose valuable time and insightful feedback helped improve the manuscript, as well as to Ardith Goodwin for allowing us to feature her beautiful painting, "Guardian Angel," on the book's cover. Finally, I must thank the contributors for their diligence and patience. It is my honour and privilege to include your work in this collection.

Introduction

Contextualizing Spiritual Mothering and Reclaiming Religious Motherwork

VANESSA REIMER

> *"God gave us each an angel and her name is Mom."*
> *"In heaven they are angels. On earth they are mothers."*
> *"Mothers are God's angels on earth."*

WHETHER OR NOT we subscribe to a particular religious tradition or spiritual worldview, many of us are familiar with the above sentiments which extol mothers as celestial beings. Each year they grace the covers of Mother's Day cards, reminding children and adults alike to thank their mothers for the work that they do and the sacrifices they make. In many ways, these phrases highlight the pervasive disconnect between the romanticized lip service that we frequently pay to mothers and the patriarchal ideologies that devalue maternal practice, particularly when women do not emulate the white, slim, able-bodied, heteronormative, and middle-class maternal ideal (Ladd-Taylor and Umansky 2-3). In this sense, they also provide vivid reminders that feminist maternal scholars cannot overlook the crucial role that patriarchal religious traditions have played—and continue to play—in shaping sex, gender, and family norms (Burstyn; Cott; DeConick; Gallagher).

Indeed, Protestant and Catholic Christian traditions have largely established "the structure, meaning, and morality of family life for the great majority of people" (Morgan 35) in Western cultures, as well as among those who have been subject to Anglo-European colonization, slavery, and imperialism. It is thus unsurprising that many feminist scholars—at least those in wealthy, minority world contexts wherein the bulk of feminist scholarship is produced, and wherein Christianity remains the dominant religious paradigm—have addressed religion with a critical voice. For instance, the pioneering maternal theorist Adrienne Rich directly names and problematizes the patriarchal institution of motherhood in her groundbreaking text, *Of Woman Born* (1976). In doing so, she aptly contextualizes oppressive gender hierarchies as operatives of Judeo-Christian patriarchy. Other feminist scholars have similarly addressed how patriarchal ethics are rooted in religious traditions. For example, Marina Warner examines how the contradictory expectations of Christian womanhood manifest in the iconography of the Virgin Mary in *Alone of All Her Sex: The Myth and the Cult of the Virgin Mary* (1976). Mary's supernatural "virgin" pregnancy and birth allowed her to be at once sexually "pure," yet also a mother. Warner argues that all women have subsequently been evaluated—and found wanting—in light of this fundamental paradox that values them for their sexual and reproductive *potentials,* but regards them as deficient and "impure" once these potentials are used.

ANGELS ON EARTH?

In a historical context, the cultural propensity to laud mothers as earthly angels echoes the pervasive Victorian ideology that valorized white, economically privileged women and girls as pure and untainted "angels in the house" (Frost 3; Satter 30). This sentiment is encapsulated by what Barbara Welter calls the "cult of true womanhood," wherein altruism, self-sacrifice, submissiveness, and domesticity are viewed as innate female virtues (48). Furthermore, during this period women were regarded as "naturally" religious (Hardesty 38), and Christian piety was believed to be so innate to girls and women that those who seemingly lacked this virtue were considered "fallen angels" or "no woman at all" (Welter 49).

To that end, by venerating mothers as "angels on earth," it is implied that all women can—and therefore *should*—perform the virtues of piety, selflessness, humility, and servitude in perpetuity. As Paula Caplan astutely notes, this tendency to romanticize motherhood perpetuates the deeply embedded cultural practice of mother-blame (25). Indeed, if it is expected that mothers should constantly embody angelic virtues, it becomes easy to deem them failures when they deviate from these impossible expectations. This also leads to *internalized* mother-blame, wherein women learn to regard themselves as "bad" mothers when they fall short of perfection (Caplan 44-45). In other words, when mothers are lauded as supernaturally righteous beings, they are effectively denied their full and complex *humanity*, and are consequently judged for failing to achieve the unattainable standards that our patriarchal culture has prescribed for them.

OUTLINING THIS TEXT'S GOALS: ADDRESSING RELIGIOUS MOTHERWORK FROM THE "INSIDE"

Although feminist scholars have duly critiqued the oppressive aspects of patriarchal religious traditions, the majority of these voices operate from a perspective that is "outside" religion and spirituality. Consequently, the bulk of such scholarship at best marginalizes—and at worst completely disregards—the importance of religion and spirituality in many women's lives. *Angels on Earth* seeks to contribute to the growing body of feminist motherhood scholarship by addressing how the intellectual, emotional, and physical work of mothering is informed by women's diverse religiosities and spiritualities. In doing so, it further unpacks how religious mothers work to negotiate and resist patriarchal ideologies that devalue their maternal practice, just as it elucidates the empowerment that they derive from their spiritual lives.

As the editor of this collection, I find these goals both political and personal. Like many feminist scholars before me, I was raised in a religious household, and my experiences growing up in a conservative Protestant or evangelical church fundamentally shaped my worldview as a child and young adult. My journey into feminist academe, beginning as an undergraduate student and continuing throughout my graduate studies, has ultimately provided me with the epistemological and theoretical tools to dissect the patriarchal religious ideologies that were always presented to me as incontrovertible "truths." Yet at the same time, I was never able to abandon many of the spiritual beliefs and sacred practices that continue to enrich my daily life. I found myself attending feminist academic lectures and conferences that rightfully critiqued the oppressive aspects of my religious tradition, yet did not provide space for women like me to speak about the *empowerment* we derived from our religiosities.

Furthermore, like many girls and women, my religious experiences while growing up were fundamentally shaped by my relationship with my mother. Many of my earliest memories involve her reading to me from my children's picture Bible and praying with me by my bedside at night. In light of my beliefs, it was easy for me to venerate my mother as an infallible "angel," who seemed to perform the maternal virtues of patience, kindness, and compassion without end. Our relationship became strained when I began to question Christian doctrines that did not reflect my lived experiences or augment my spiritual growth. For a time, I blamed my mother for enculturating me into what I considered to be an oppressive patriarchal religious tradition. Yet as I continued to grow as a feminist scholar, I worked to cultivate a critical understanding of the complex ideologies and structures—both religious and secular—that constrained our relationship. In particular, I began to affirm the valuable work that my mother performed in her children's lives in light of her particular spiritual knowledge. In this way, although my shifting religious-feminist worldview became a point of contention in our relationship, it also opened up space for us to engage in open and authentic dialogue about our epistemologies and experiences. It is my hope that by sharing diverse "insider" perspectives and emphasizing the empowerment that mothers derive from their religiosities and spiritualities, this collection will provoke similar dialogue among girls and women, both within interpersonal and academic spaces.

RELIGIOUS AND SPIRITUAL MOTHERING IN CONTEXT

To be sure, this is not the first volume to explore what mothering looks like in religious and spiritual contexts. Demeter Press has already laid important groundwork in this area with texts such as *Until Our Hearts Are on the Ground*, wherein editors Memee Lavell-Harvard and Jeannette Corbiere Lavall examine how Aboriginal, Indigenous, and First Nations women mother in light of their spiritual traditions. Importantly, this collection also highlights how the colonizing effects of Christian patriarchy have thwarted Aboriginal women's abilities to engage in empowered mothering practices. In *Mothering Mennonite*, editors Kerry Fast and Rachel Epp Buller similarly explore how women mother in accordance with Mennonite traditions and belief systems. Significantly, this collection "situates *Mennonite* and *mother* in the nexus of mothers as transmitters of culture and religion and mothers as re-creators—even creators—of religion and culture" (1). This collection thus elucidates the vital roles that religious mothers play in their families and larger communities; as Fast and Buller note, "Given the centrality of family for the development and maintenance of Mennonite culture and religion, it is evident that Mennonite mothers [bear] a good deal of responsibility as purveyors of Mennonite cultural and religious identity" (3).

These texts establish a vital framework for understanding women's spiritual and religious lives by highlighting how religious traditions do not exist in a vacuum. Rather, they often signify and reproduce diverse aspects of culture and identity. In this way, religion and spirituality can provide key markers of distinction and solidarity for ethnic, cultural, and other minority groups (Becher 2). Furthermore, like the broader patriarchal societies in which women operate, religious traditions often designate women as "natural" caregivers within the domestic sphere (Colaner and Giles 526; Hardacre 132; Mayall 1), and many mothers accordingly act as children's primary religious enculturators[1] (Becher 108, 127; Franks 6; Gerami 32; Levitt 531). Margaret Steel Farrell explores this connection in her personal essay, "My Mother, My Church." Here she recalls how her mother's deep religious commitment fundamentally shaped her childhood experiences: "[My mother and the Church] are so connected in my experience that I cannot talk about one without the other.... My mother was the spiritual and religious cornerstone of our family and organized our lives around her beliefs" (70). Such work demonstrates why feminist maternal scholars must strive to understand the pivotal roles that religion and spirituality play in shaping women's lived experiences.

UNDERSTANDING RELIGIOUS MOTHERWORK

Religious enculturation can be aptly contextualized as a vital aspect of women's daily motherwork.[2] Here Sara Ruddick's three demands that govern maternal thinking are pertinent to consider. Preservation, the first demand, refers to children's physical care and nurturance (21). In contrast, the second and third demands of growth and acceptability are more intricately tied to the mother's peer group and its corresponding values. Since religious enculturation is a central aspect of childrearing within many families, the latter demand of "acceptability" is arguably complicated for religious mothers. This is because they must not only teach their children about broader societal norms and roles, but also help their children learn religious practices that may be devalued in secular contexts.

This task becomes particularly arduous when mothers operate from a standpoint of cultivated ambivalence towards their religious traditions. Feminist theologian Mary Bednarowski defines cultivated ambivalence as a "triple task" in women's religious thought. It includes maintaining a critical distance from one's religious community as well as expanding the possibilities of one's religious tradition by constructing new visions while conserving its core values and insights (20). In this way, religious motherwork presents a unique set of challenges for women who are navigating their own shifting spiritual beliefs and operating at a critical distance from dominant religious paradigms. For instance, in *Appropriately Subversive: Modern Mothers in Traditional Religions* (2002), Tova Hartman Halbertal reflects on the profound dissonance that she experienced while raising her daughter in a predominantly patriarchal Jewish tradition. She specifically recalls confronting the issues of gender-based seating in her synagogue:

> How was I to bring up my daughters to respect and be part of a tradition that I care so deeply about when I know it requires them to pretend that such exclusions, separations—such attempts to make women disappear—have no relevance to their lives? How could I acknowledge to my daughters that they were literally kept behind a curtain for

> reasons that are truly not acceptable to me, yet continue to pass on my faith and tradition? This was my dilemma. (2)

In this way, it is critical to consider not only how mothers navigate the complex ideological systems that shape their religious communities, but also how they actively negotiate and resist oppressive doctrines. The challenges posed by spiritual mothering and religious motherwork are aptly addressed by Andrea O'Reilly's conceptual framework for empowered mothering. She argues that women and their children both stand to benefit when maternal practice is duly understood and affirmed as work and mothers operate from a place of agency, authority, and authenticity (45). Such frameworks offer promising possibilities for religious and spiritual women who find the empowering potentials of their motherwork thwarted by patriarchal ideologies.

RECLAIMING RELIGIOUS AND SPIRITUAL MOTHERING: THE CHAPTERS

Angels on Earth explores diverse aspects of religious and spiritual mothering across various traditions, worldviews, and lived experiences through an empowered mothering framework. The volume's first section addresses contemporary perspectives on spiritual and religious mothering, opening with Sarah-Jane Page's chapter, "Double Scrutiny at the Vicarage: Clergy Mothers, Expectations and the Public Gaze." The author draws from interviews with clergy mothers from the Church of England to illustrate how they are subject to a "double scrutiny," since their success as religious leaders *and* as "good" mothers is perpetually subject to public observation and critique. Next, in "Intersectional Mothering: A Black Baptist Example," Deidre Hill Butler shares interviews with members of the Daughters of Myrtle, a church organization based in Massachusetts, to explore how black women forge critical spaces of support and resistance in their churches and broader communities.

I then analyze how a selection of religious blogs authored by mothers challenges the patriarchal ideologies of "good" womanhood and motherhood that pervade evangelical Protestant subcultures in "Faith-Shifters: Exploring Religious Motherwork in the Post-Evangelical Blogosphere." I argue that these bloggers adopt a post-evangelical discursive framework to challenge Complementarian theology and affirm their motherwork. In the following chapter, "Praying for More: Motherhood in the American Quiverfull Movement," Emily Hunter McGowin similarly explores the theology and "lived religion" behind the contemporary U.S. Quiverfull movement. Her research with Quiverfull mothers elucidates how, despite their commitments to pronatalist ideologies and ideals of male "headship," the lived experiences of Quiverfull families exist in tension with patriarchal precepts.

This section then concludes with Bridget Boland's chapter, "Bridging Sacred Mystery and Medicine: The Role of Doulas in Contemporary Child Birthing," which considers how mothers and their families may benefit from the spiritual support provided by doulas. The author highlights how various doula-supported birthing practices can empower mothers during pregnancy, labour, and delivery, and she encourages birth support professionals to apply these practices in their daily work.

The next section explores how religious mothering has been addressed in historical, religious, and literary texts. It begins with Therese Novotny's chapter, "Mothers of Spiritual Change: Julian of Norwich, Mary Magdalen, and Mother Teresa," which illustrates how these three women performed "the office of motherhood" and challenged patriarchal norms concerning women's roles in the church and broader society. Next, Ann W. Duncan's chapter, "Binding Ourselves to the Truth: Quakerism and the Paradox of Liberated Motherhood," unpacks the feminist view of motherhood that is seemingly at the core of Quaker theology. She further problematizes how Quaker women have found themselves marginalized within feminist movements, since they have not been subject to the sexist oppressions that are commonly associated with Christian patriarchy.

In "Motherhood in Hindu Religion: Glorification without Emancipation," Zairunisha then explores the contrast between Hindu women's lived realities and the accolades that are paid to mothers in religious texts. The chapter further considers how contemporary globalization has triggered a cultural and religious preoccupation with restoring "traditional" patriarchal norms of womanhood and motherhood in India. In the following chapter, "Text Line, Blood Line: Familial Inheritance in Non-Biological Queer Jewish Mothering," Emily McAvan unpacks the challenges of queer Jewish mothering in heteronormative Jewish communities. She argues that dominant understandings of parenting, relationships, and Jewish lineage need to be expanded to recognize the vital contributions that non-biological mothers make in sustaining Jewish families and traditions.

Next, Florence Pasche Guignard explores the connection between religious mothering and Sara Ruddick's three demands of maternal thinking in "Reading Hindu Devotional Poetry through Maternal Theory: Maternal Thinking and Maternal Figures in *Bhakti* poetry of Sūrdās." The chapter explains how a selection of devotional poetry attributed to Sūrdās—a prominent religious and literary figure from early-modern Northern India—constructs divine maternal icons, and then analyzes how these figures exemplify Ruddick's provisions of protection, nurturance, and acceptability. The section then concludes with Elvira Casal's chapter, "Charlotte Brontë's *Villette* as Spiritual Quest for the Mother." Casal explores how the complex relationship that this classic Victorian novel's protagonist, Lucy Snowe, has with Roman Catholic and Protestant traditions is symbolic of her search for a mother figure.

The volume's third and final section shares personal narratives of religious and spiritual mothering to highlight the empowering strategies that mothers employ in their daily motherwork. It opens with "Storytelling as a Way to Reconnect and Co-create Spiritual Contexts: Conversations with Five Muslim Mothers." Here, Rannveig Haga draws from her research with Swedish-Somali and Finish-Somali mothers as well as from her own experiences as a Muslim woman in Scandinavia to emphasize how spaces for spiritual growth can be fostered when women share their personal narratives and co-create new stories.

The next selection of chapters specifically addresses how various tenets of Jewish and feminist mothering coalesce in women's daily lives. Sharon Lang shares how her ever-evolving feminist mothering practices are informed by her Judaism in "'What's a Nice Jewish Girl Like You Doing in a Place Like This?' Reflections on

My Contradictory and Convoluted Journey towards Jewish Feminist Mothering." The author reflects on the challenges that she has encountered as a Jewish feminist mother in a predominantly Christian town, and she further considers how her lived experiences complicate dominant assumptions about the meanings of "being Jewish," particularly what it means to be a Jewish mother.

In the following chapter, "Two Mothers and Two Children" Rosie Rosenzweig reflects on the challenges that she faced when her adult son seemingly abandoned his Jewish roots to become a Buddhist monk. She shares how a trip to meet her son's Buddhist teachers helped her embrace the beliefs that inspired her son's spiritual path, just as it helped expand and transform her own Jewish mothering practices. Next, Rabbi Dr. Haviva Ner-David recounts her menstruation experiences while growing up in an Orthodox Jewish culture in "In Your Blood, Live [With Pride, My Daughters]!" Ner-David dissects dominant patriarchal understandings of women's "purity" and further describes how she challenges these interpretations in her own life by creating new rituals with her daughters.

The volume then concludes with Kathryn Bell's creative non-fiction piece "Joy Unspeakable (or, a Beautiful Day)," which reflects on the simultaneous ambivalence and beauty that constitute daily motherwork. The chapter illustrates how women may draw near to the divine through the seemingly mundane tasks that constitute maternal labour, and it similarly highlights the meaningful spiritual connections that women forge with one another through their motherline relationships.

CONCLUDING THOUGHTS: EMPOWERING RELIGIOUS MOTHERS

Although this volume proudly explores a diverse selection of religious traditions, spiritual worldviews, and lived experiences, it ultimately reflects its minority world context, wherein Judeo-Christian traditions remain most visible and dominant. Even though this does not detract from the importance of the work featured here, it is my hope that future contributions to the growing body of religious feminist scholarship will increasingly reflect the diverse religious and spiritual traditions that women participate in across the globe. This task is particularly crucial given how many religious and ethnic minority women and girls continue to experience violence and discrimination.[3]

To that end, although this collection addresses the myriad of oppressions that mothers encounter in diverse traditions and belief systems, it also offers optimistic possibilities for dismantling patriarchal structures and adopting empowered mothering frameworks. In one capacity, it emphasizes how the specific demands of religious motherwork need to be recognized and named as *work*, and how the particular time, energy, skills, and resources that are required of the many mothers who perform religious enculturation need to be included in academic discussions about motherwork. Too often women's religious and spiritual knowledges are marginalized in feminist research, when in actuality, such epistemologies fundamentally shape many women's maternal practices. As feminist theologian Valerie Saiving famously argues, women experience religion in diverse yet particular ways (23), and their experiences as mothers further shape the religious "ways of knowing" they cultivate throughout their lives. To that end, I hope this volume will encourage readers to affirm women's spiritual epistemologies and religious motherwork, not only as personal sources of empowerment and enrichment, but also as sites of collective growth and resistance.

NOTES

[1]I find it helpful to refer to the pedagogical reproduction of religious beliefs, values, and traditions within families as "enculturation," in contrast to the more frequently used "socialization." While the latter term broadly refers to the process of teaching children about societal norms and roles, as well as preparing them for the responsibilities that accompany adulthood and citizenship within a given society, here enculturation refers to the intergenerational reproduction of beliefs and values that are particular to a religious community. In this way, religious enculturation is a process distinct from socialization because many religious communities—particularly those of cultural and ethnic minorities, as well as fundamen-

talist traditions—understand that they operate outside and often in opposition to mainstream society.

[2]"Motherwork" broadly refers to women's unpaid reproductive and caregiving work (see: Ladd-Taylor). In my own work, "religious motherwork" refers to the unpaid yet vital intellectual and emotional reproductive work that women perform with their children through processes of religious enculturation.

[3]The rampant Islamophobia that has pervaded North American, EU, and UK political and public discourse in recent years is one prominent example of such discrimination. For further reading see Dinshaw; Harris; Nasser.

WORKS CITED

Becher, Harriet. *Family Practices in South Asian Muslim Families.* New York: Palgrave Macmillan, 2008. Print.

Bednarowski, Mary Farrell. *The Religious Imagination of American Women.* Bloomington: Indiana University Press, 1999. Print.

Burstyn, Joan N. *Victorian Education and the Ideal of Womanhood.* New Brunswick: Rutgers University Press. 1984. Print.

Caplan, Paula. *Don't Blame Mother: Mending the Mother-Daughter Relationship*. New York: Harper and Row, 1989. Print.

Colaner, Colleen Warner, and Steven M. Giles. "The Baby Blanket or the Briefcase: The Impact of Evangelical Gender Role Ideologies on Career and Mothering Aspirations of Female Evangelical College Students." *Sex Roles* 58 (2007): 526-534. Print.

Cott, Nancy F. *The Bonds of Womanhood: "Women's Sphere" in New England, 1780-1835.* 2nd Ed. New Haven: Yale University Press, 1997. Print.

DeConick, April D. *Holy Misogyny: Why the Sex and Gender Conflicts in the Early Church Still Matter.* London: Continuum, 2011. Print.

Dinshaw, Fram. "This is What Islamophobia Looks Like in Canada." *National Observer.* Observer Media Group, 22 Nov. 2015. Web. 25 Nov. 2015.

Farrell, Margaret Steel. "My Mother, My Church." *Leaving Fundamentalism: Personal Stories.* Ed. G. Elijah Dann. Waterloo, ON: Wilfrid Laurier University Press, 2008. 69-80. Print.

Frost, Ginger S. *Victorian Childhoods*. Westport: Praeger, 2009. Print.

Gallagher, Sally K. *Evangelical Identity and Gendered Family Life*. New Brunswick: Rutgers University Press, 2003. Print.

Hardacre, Helen. "The Impact of Fundamentalisms on Women, the Family, and Interpersonal Relations." *Fundamentalisms and Society: Reclaiming the Sciences, the Family and Education*. Eds. R. Scott Appleby and Martin E. Marty. Chicago: University of Chicago Press, 1993. 129-150. Print.

Hardesty, Nancy A. *Women Called to Witness: Evangelical Feminism in the 19th Century*. Nashville: Abingdon, 1984. Print.

Harris, Sarah Ann. "Rising Islamophobia in Britain 'Is Creating An Environment of Hate'— Islamic Human Rights Commission Report." *The Huffington Post*, 12 Nov. 2015.Web. 24 Nov. 2015.

Hartman Halbertal, Tova. *Appropriately Subversive: Modern Mothers in Traditional Religions*. Cambridge, MA: Harvard University Press, 2002. Print.

Ladd-Taylor, Molly. *Mother-Work: Women, Child-Welfare, and the State, 1890-1930*. Chicago: University of Illinois Press, 1994. Print.

Ladd-Taylor, Molly and Lauri Umansky. "Introduction." *"Bad" Mothers: The Politics of Blame in Twentieth-Century America*. Eds. Molly Ladd-Taylor and Lauri Umansky. New York: New York University Press, 1998. 1-30. Print.

Morgan, Kimberly J. *Working Mothers and the Welfare State*. Stanford, CA: Stanford University Press, 2006. Print.

Nasser, Shanifa. "Paris Attacks Backlash 'Nothing New,' Canadian Muslims Say, But Public Also Supportive." *CBC News*, 24 Nov. 2015. Web. 25 Nov. 2015.

O'Reilly, Andrea. *Rocking the Cradle: Thoughts on Motherhood, Feminism and the Possibility of Empowered Mothering*. Toronto: Demeter Press, 2006. Print.

Rich, Adrienne. *Of Woman Born: Motherhood as Experience and Institution*. New York: Norton, 1976. Print.

Ruddick, Sara. *Maternal Thinking: Toward a Politics of Peace*. Boston: Beacon, 1995. Print.

Saiving, Valerie. 1960. "The Human Situation: A Feminine View." Eds. Carol P. Christ and Judith Plaskow." *Womanspirit Rising:*

A Feminist Reader in Religion. San Francisco: Harper and Row, 1979. 25-42. Print.

Satter, Beryl. *Each Mind a Kingdom: American Women, Sexual Purity, and the New Thought Movement, 1875-1920*. Los Angeles: University of California Press, 1999. Print.

I.

CONTEMPORARY PERSPECTIVES ON SPIRITUAL AND RELIGIOUS MOTHERING

1.
Double Scrutiny at the Vicarage

Clergy Mothers, Expectations, and the Public Gaze

SARAH-JANE PAGE

IT HAS LONG BEEN recognized that the role of the Christian clergy is at odds with many other occupations. Pastoral ministry blurs the boundaries between public and private life; clergy often live in a house owned by the church, and much of their work in the public sphere is undertaken during the leisure time of parishioners (Mellow; Moore; Peyton and Gatrell). Furthermore, since priesthood is a calling dependent on the idea of constant availability (Robson), clergy are always considered to be on call and available when a crisis looms. This public visibility makes it difficult for clergy to enjoy a private life (Mellow), and it is accompanied by a public accountability and scrutiny that also affect clergy families. As Liz Greenbaker and Sherry Taylor explain: "In no other occupation does public scrutiny focus as intently on the family as it does in the ministry. Every action or deed, their smallest, innocuous statement is watched, heard, and analyzed" (xi). Clergy families therefore experience a lack of privacy as well as a feeling that their personal space is not their own (Davies and Guest).

Clergy families are, generally, expected to model ideals of the good and godly family (Davies and Guest), and when Protestant clergy are men, their wives have been pivotal in ensuring this norm is adhered to (Greenbacker and Taylor). But when the clergyperson is both a woman *and* a mother, the expectations become intensified. Like clergy, mothers as a group are subject to much societal expectation and scrutiny, exercised by various interest groups, including policymakers, medical and school professionals, media outlets as well as other parents who are keen to ensure parenting proficiency (Garey; Gatrell; Jensen). Therefore, when clergy are mothers, they are subject to a "double scrutiny" of an intense and direct nature; the clergy mother is perpetually on display, as she has an active audience—her parish—who evaluates and critiques her performance in creating good future Christian citizens. This chapter, accordingly, addresses how clergy mothers in the Church of England manage this public gaze, especially in contexts when their family life does not adhere to these strict ideals of perfection. It draws from interviews with clergy mothers, most of whom were priests, and a small minority who were ordained as deacons and were awaiting ordination to priesthood. These dynamics will be explored in relation to two themes: the types of scrutiny that the clergy mothers generally experience from parishioners, and how clergy mothers manage these expectations.

MOTHERHOOD UNDER SCRUTINY

The expectations on mothers in neoliberal societies are enormous and multifaceted (Blum); even the behaviour of mothers-to-be is carefully regulated with much advice concerned with eating and other habits (Lowe , Lee, and Yardley). Such expectations stem from the belief that mothers should selflessly put their children before everything else. This idea can be traced back to the historical influence of Rousseau, who viewed children as being inherently good (rather than intrinsically sinful) and recast motherhood as a more involving enterprise in order to cultivate the best possible future citizens (Forna; Miller-McLemore). Aminatta Forna highlights the array of social institutions that support this broader vision of perfect motherhood. She argues that "Motherhood (with a capital letter) is an abstract idea, not a reality. It does not describe how most women do mother.... Yet today, here and now, the Motherhood Myth is being presented as timeless, universal and natural" (259).

This view of motherhood has led to contemporary expectations of intensive mothering, wherein most decisions are made with children in mind, and mothers will go to great lengths to ensure that everything they do is in the best interests of their children's continued development (Hays). Examples of intensive mothering include the expectations that women will breastfeed (*not* bottle-feed) in order to facilitate mother-child bonding (Lee); that they will cultivate continual interaction with children (Hays); and that they will facilitate intellectual development through numerous educational experiences, such as purchasing preschool educational toys (Wall). Although many of these activities can be considered laudable, when connected to the ideology of intensive motherhood, they become part of a chain of perpetual giving, with little thought accorded to the mother's health or sense of identity (Miller-McLemore).

Furthermore, these intensive mothering standards require vast resources of time, money, and energy, and it is mothers (not fathers) who are called upon to enact these expectations. This ironically coincides with mothers' increased participation in paid work; they are therefore less available to mother in this fashion, which stretches their ability to perform intensive motherhood. These personal costs of intensive motherhood are further exacerbated by the perpetual surveillance that mothers are subjected to. As Lee argues, "Intensive mothering ideology ... constructs mothering as an activity that, because of its perceived significance for the development of the child, is too important to be left to mothers alone" (469). For instance, successive governments in the UK have placed the responsibility on mothers to ensure that their children do well in education and go on to undertake fruitful employment, with working-class mothers, who are less able to guarantee such successes, bearing the brunt of censure and opprobrium (Jensen). In this capacity, mothers' practices are evaluated and scrutinized by a range of so-called "experts" in various social institutions (Garey; Gatrell; Jensen).

CONSTRUCTIONS OF MOTHERHOOD WITHIN CHRISTIANITY

Christianity has played its part in perpetuating these narrow and largely inaccessible constructions of motherhood. As Bonnie Miller-McLemore outlines, the Victorian era played a significant role in constructing the image of the unselfish and sacrificial mother, as ministers likened a mother's unconditional love for her children to that of God's love (82-83). Any challenge to this construction, therefore, "undercuts a major religious motif portraying God's own love. Rejecting sacrificial motherhood may seem like a direct assault on God Himself" (83). Within the Church of England specifically, Sean Gill has charted the constitution of various femininities that emerged at this time, consolidated around different church traditions (77). For instance, Victorian evangelicalism emphasized "devotion and self-sacrifice," which found its expression through motherhood. Meanwhile, Anglo-Catholicism advised women to embody the "sweet and gentle" Virgin Mary, whereas the liberal tradition also asserted traditional gender roles.

To that end, the founding of the Mother's Union in 1876 perpetuated the idea that men and women were inherently different, and that a woman's duty was centred on raising her children within the Christian faith. In the twentieth century, debates emerged about women's entry into priesthood; their potential as mothers was used as an explicit reason against their ordination (Furlong; Thatcher). And once women were ordained, these feelings did not disappear. For instance, Anne Dyer, a priest, has detailed how members of her congregation negatively appraised her status as a mother; she further argues that it is easier for women to be accepted as priests if they are single, married but childless, or have adult children (123). She explains how if priests have young children, "The common critique is that we are either neglecting our children or have in some way emasculated our husbands so that they take on an inappropriate portion of the duties of care" (123).

Therefore, clergy mothers are subject to a complex set of expectations. They are not removed from the broader (secular) cultural demands of intensive motherhood (Page, "Altruism"). In addition, as priests, their remit as an intensive mother also includes the expectation to raise "good" Christian children (Miller-McLemore). As mothers, they retain overall responsibility for cultivating "spiritual capital" in their children. This is a term derived from Bourdieu's notion of religious capital ("Genesis and Structure"), with Mathew Guest describing spiritual capital akin to other forms of capital, as "a cultural resource to be acquired and exchanged" (182). For Bourdieu, early socialization is a key moment for the cultivation, development, and transmission of various capitals (Verter). Socialization processes specifically relating to spiritual capital can include teaching Christian values, saying grace at mealtimes, ensuring children know Bible stories, and encouraging theological discussions (Davies and Guest; Guest). Feminist scholars who have examined motherhood in relation to Bourdieu's theory of capitals assert that it is mothers who are given the pivotal responsibility to ensure that their children develop the necessary capitals, lest their motherhood be brought into question (Lawler; Reay). Mothers are measured against their ability to reproduce middle-class values and tastes; for example, aspects of cultural capital are developed through activities, such as children learning to play an esteemed musical instrument (Reay).

Such scholarship has not usually considered how this relates to either spiritual or religious capital. But Callum Brown notes the ways in which Christian piety became associated with mothers during the Victorian era: mothers were seen as essential to children's development of moral Christian values, and evangelical magazines of the era would chastise mothers if they were seen to be failing in their "duty." According to Brown, such expectations did not diminish for mothers in general until the 1960s, with this legacy of pious femininity residually remaining within church contexts. Therefore, Christian mothers have retained the overall responsibility for cultivating spiritual capital, which has become part of the broader remit of intensive motherhood.

For clergy families specifically, it has been noted that even in contexts where the father is the priest, such socialization responsibilities still largely fall to clergy wives (Greenbacker and Taylor). Therefore, even when fathers embody the pinnacle of spiritual capital, a mother's responsibility does not necessarily diminish. Meanwhile, when clergy are mothers, they both embody this culmination of spiritual capital and also encounter expectations specifically *as mothers*. This dual role as priest and mother can result in a questioning of their ability to perform both roles concurrently. As Helen Thorne argues:

> For men, their role as a father has clearer boundaries and, more often than not, is supported by the unconditional availability of a wife.... The time demands of priesthood, which are erratic and often based around the leisure time of the congregation, mean that it is hard to combine priest-

> hood with family life.... Ministry and motherhood are seen as conflicting vocations, each demanding women to be self-giving, available and concerned for others well-being—a situation in which women can only lose. (71)

In this sense, clergy mothers are subject to double scrutiny, not only as mothers but also as priests. As Allison Moore contends, "Expectations of clergy and of mothers and fathers make the reality of male and female clergy lives very different. Clergy mothers challenge both the norms of male clergy and the social messages about mothers" (6). These constructions of motherhood in the context of Christianity raise critical questions regarding how clergy mothers experience scrutiny of their mothering practices and how such scrutiny is managed.

STUDYING CLERGY MOTHERS

This study is based on in-depth interviews with seventeen clergy mothers who are active in the Church of England. All participants had experiences of concurrently being a mother to dependent children (defined as having a child still in school) and being a member of the ordained clergy. The types of clergy roles that they undertook were various, from those just embarking on their ministry in trainee positions, to women who were at senior levels within the Church. At the time of interview, most were already ordained as priests; two were ordained as deacons and were waiting to be ordained as priests. Many were enacting parish ministry. Meanwhile, a minority were employed in a ministry capacity outside the church, in a role such as a hospital, school, university, or prison chaplain. The ages of participants varied between thirty-one and fifty-four. Most of the participants were stipendiary (thus paid), and some were married to other priests. All the women were white and mainly middle class, which fits the profile of religious professionals in the Church of England more generally (Thorne; Walsh). As such, this chapter does not claim to represent all types of clergy mothers, and the remit of this project is further limited by its context in time and space. The identities of participants have been concealed and all have been accorded pseudonyms.

THE CLERGY FAMILY: LIFE IN THE "GOLDFISH BOWL"

Priesthood is an intensely public vocation; clergy are perpetually in the public eye and are recognizable within their communities, as they perform everyday activities, such as supermarket shopping and recreational activities (Mellow). This visibility has implications for priests' homes and family members. Stephanie, a mother of two, explains how family life is complicated by the fact that priests' houses are often owned by the church:

> *We have to get away from the house to be able to do things as a family. [My husband] would love to stay here and spend time at home, but I find it too difficult because the phone's going. The secretary works in the house, and there's no personal space.... It would be really nice sometimes just to be able to stay in your house, do things as a family, get up late. But you can't do it; you've got somebody coming in, and you've got to sort of, almost put on a front for that, and I think those are the things that are difficult during the holiday times.*

Stephanie describes having to "put on a front," which links to Erving Goffman's concepts of the front and back region. Goffman describes the front region as being where "human action play[s] out" (32) and where one performs in public spaces before an audience. Meanwhile, the back region is the space where the person can relax. Ordinarily, one's home would be considered a back region, where individuals can be themselves. But for Stephanie and other priests, this opportunity is revoked by the public nature of the vicarage.

Public visibility is apparent in other spaces, too. When the whole family attended church and the children interacted well with the congregation, this could be enormously beneficial to the clergy mothers, as these quotes illustrate:

> *[Our daughter] is quite an extroverted little girl ... from a small child she's been used to the idea that she goes places with me and everybody knows me, so everybody knows*

> *her. And even now, when we're in town, lots and lots of people will chat away ... So she's very kind of comfortable just talking to people in the street ... and she chats away to them and has this kind of slightly sort of public role you get as a clergy daughter. And she's comfortable with that.* (Rachel, mother of one)

> *We're fortunate, actually, to have two lovely kids who behave and, at the moment, are happy to come to church, and you know, be involved and that's really great. And it will be interesting, no doubt, years down the line to talk to them and say "Well, how was it for you to have two clergy parents?" Because it can't always be an easy thing for them.* (Stephanie, mother of two)

In these quotes, clergy mothers recognize the benefits of having well-behaved children who participate in church life in full. It was not just the case that this made life easier for the clergy mothers; rather, the children's participation also enabled the priests to gain credibility as priests *and* mothers, and facilitated the expectation placed on them to cultivate spiritual capital. Still, participants were keenly aware of the pressures this placed on their children as they coped with what Julie, a mother of two, called "living in the goldfish bowl." She was ordained when her sons were teenagers, and one of the first things that concerned her sons was the potential need to curtail favourite pastimes:

> *[W]hen we moved, [my son] said, "Well does that mean I can't play my music loud?" "No it doesn't; I still play my music loud, so you play your music loud. You do whatever you would have done." But it is different because this [house] is the workplace as well.*

Therefore, life for clergy families proves difficult because there is no clear public-private demarcation between work and family life. Their lives and homes are seen as public property, and this is exacerbated by the fact that the priest's home is also her workspace. Experiencing the "goldfish bowl" and the expectations placed on clergy children to be well-behaved is a common experience in many clergy families (Davies and Guest; Greenbacker and Taylor). But the expectations that are placed on mothers are inherently gendered, as the next section will detail.

CLERGY MOTHERS EXPERIENCING SCRUTINY

By the time participants were interviewed for this project, women's priesthood in the Church of England was well-established—the legislation to allow women's priesthood was approved in 1992. However, when the interviews took place between 2006 and 2007, women were still not allowed to become bishops. (This legislation was passed in 2014.) The debates around women's priesthood and later debates regarding entry into the episcopate were very fraught and protracted (Rees), and most of the interviewees had encountered some negativity during their clerical life. For example, many participants had experienced parishioners refusing to receive communion from them, and some faced resistance from fellow clergy, particularly when such clergy belonged to groups explicitly opposed to women's priesthood, such as Forward in Faith.[11] Despite these negative elements, many of the women were able to live out their everyday lives in welcoming spaces, but with an acute understanding that they could encounter opposition. The interviewees were, therefore, very conscious of the pressure to do a good job, lest it give ammunition to those opposed to women's ordination. It is against this backdrop that clergy women practice their ministry. The context for their ministry is further exacerbated by cultural assumptions about motherhood. As Harriet, a mother of three, explains, "People will automatically think, well if you're young, you'll have a family ... or you won't be as committed.... So I think it is tough. I think it is tough and I think there is discrimination."

As Harriet articulates, assumptions circulate that clergy mothers will not be as committed to their vocation as non-mothers or male priests who are fathers. The presumption is that their attention will be divided between their family and the congregation in a way that would allegedly not occur if the priest were a father (Moore; Zikmund, Lummis, and Chang). To that end, some participants described how they were either dismissed from their posts once they had given birth or were denied the opportunity to do a particular role because they had had a baby. For example, Esther shared that "one of the jobs I considered going to, when he realized that I was pregnant, the chap said, 'Oh no, I wouldn't have someone with a baby.'" Dawn, a mother of one, similarly explains how being a mother was viewed as a burden rather than an asset in ministry contexts: "I was asked a question in interview ... 'What in the last two years has made the most difference to your spirituality?' and I said, 'Becoming a mother.' Again, a really big reaction. 'Well isn't that going to alienate people, if that's what you're preaching?'"

On many levels, motherhood has not been legitimated or validated in ministry contexts (Page, "Femmes, Mères et Prêtres"; "Negotiating Sacred Roles"). Instead, it is constructed as a problem in a way that fatherhood is not. Given these assumptions made specifically about clergy mothers, interviewees also experienced scrutiny of their family lives. As Lois, a mother of two, explains:

> *Since the children have got slightly older, it's really hard to be a priest encouraging people to be at church with their families when it's very hard to take my own family because my husband doesn't come to church. If I bring my children, I can't be there to control them. And so it's quite difficult to work out how to do that and there are some times when I can manage to have them there but I find that quite hard. In fact it's hard to bring my children up within the Christian faith because I can't also be with them. I mean when they were really tiny it was much easier.... People do feel they've got the right to comment on how your children are and to comment to you on what you ought to be doing with your children in a way that they wouldn't to another person in the congregation.*

Lois desperately wanted her children to be in church, but this proved difficult as her husband did not attend. In leading a service, Lois could not personally supervise her children, but since bringing children to church is seen as a mother's duty, her mothering was questioned by parishioners. Congregants felt it was their right to personally interject in Lois's family affairs, making things even more challenging for her. As Moore argues, being a priest is unlike any other job; it is rare for children to be expected to be part of their parents' workplace. But children's church attendance is seen as a crucial aspect of cultivating spiritual capital, and when the mother is the priest, this expectation to demonstrate this element of spiritual capital is heightened and intensified. Although expectations for clergy children to be present in church can be apparent whether it is the mother or the father who is the priest (Davies and Guest), these expectations were specifically gendered, as Dawn, a mother of one, reveals:

> *I suspect that some people yearn for the nice homely wife. Well actually people have said that ... [the previous vicar's wife] used to bring the kids, and if they misbehaved, it was a clip around the ear, and you know, which are kind of indirect ways of saying well, [my husband's] not there; [my daughter's] not there, although I take my daughter to the children's services.*

Dawn's experience is shaped by a clear set of gendered expectations and the disruptions that are perceived to be caused when women, rather than men, are in the pulpit. In addition, just prior to our interview, Dawn had received an anonymous letter from a disgruntled parishioner. Dawn said that although such occurrences were relatively rare, parishioners did make their (gendered) expectations clear in one way or another.

Although mothers are ordinarily expected to undertake the bulk of childrearing, in spiritual contexts, they are also deemed responsible for raising spiritual citizens. When priests are leading services, they cannot directly take responsibility for their child's religiosity in church. This is problematic for clergy mothers who are in the pulpit on Sunday morning and, consequently, rely on the fathers' involvement. For instance, Esther's husband was a Quaker, so he alternated his worshipping practices to facilitate their three children's church involvement:

When they were little, the only way the children could come to church is if [my husband] came with them. So he'd alternate between bringing them to church and being the parent in the pews with two small children ... and going to Quaker meetings. [My husband has] had to worship in an Anglican church—which he copes with very well; he doesn't object to it. But he's not been able to week in week out, you know, worship in Quaker meetings.

Esther's children's presence in church is predicated on her husband forgoing his favoured place of worship. Had he resisted this, Esther's children would have been absent in her church, as detailed in the aforementioned narratives of Lois and Dawn. Fathers are, therefore, implicated much more in their children's faith lives, which proves complicated if the priest is single, if fathers belong to a different faith tradition, or if fathers are not religious. This is also an issue when both parents are priests. For instance, Laura is a hospital chaplain and her husband is a parish priest. Both were running services on a Sunday, and they went to extraordinary lengths to ensure their children attended church. She explains how "On a Sunday we have a babysitter [who] takes the children to [my husband's] church and then they come [to my chaplaincy] for lunch and we all have lunch together."

Clergy mothers with older children expressed feelings of failure when their children no longer wanted to attend church, as Jill, a mother of two, explains:

There is a bit of a sense of being a failure if you're both priests and neither of your children go to church. You think, "Oh what's gone wrong here? Is it church, is it God, or what is it they've taken against." ... The younger one went through a phase last summer, went and printed out a bit of the European Declaration of Human Rights to prove to me that I could not force her to go to church. This is ultimately up to the individual, blah, blah, blah, blah.... But she's back now. She's come back. Not a word was said. She just went back one morning.

Julie, a mother of two, similarly recounts her effort to cultivate an interest in church among her older children:

> *[My children] don't really go to church, and they don't sort of see faith as important. They're at that age where they've turned aside from that, but at least I was here, if there was any discussion or if we needed to talk about anything ... part of my ministry is making sure I give them what I can. [At Christmas] I did ask that the boys come at least once to church which they both did, so that was good. One at midnight and then one [Christmas] morning. Gareth came to both, and that was brilliant.*

Julie attests to establishing a home-life environment that she hoped would cultivate faith development among her sons. When she could, she tried to rekindle interest in church, using key moments, such as Christmas services. But this required ongoing effort.

Natalie's story is even more complex. Her three children had different disabilities, and the way her children had interacted with church services led to accusations that her children detracted from the sacredness of worship:

> *Douglas and Ella are autistic and don't respond terribly well to conventional sets of instructions about how you should behave in any particular place. [What's] interesting is when Douglas decides he's going to get involved ... he likes to be part of the services and knows fairly big chunks of it off by heart. ... He sees no reason why he shouldn't drift across the sanctuary ... and stand right next to me.... On the whole, if Douglas's decided he's going to get involved, I will try and be as gracious as possible about accepting his presence next to me, and he sees no reason why he shouldn't come and stand at the altar. I just go with it.... There's a bit of me that says it's tough if they have trouble with my autistic son standing next to me while I'm presiding. I really cannot see that that makes it any less a holy moment.*

Natalie had experienced very negative attitudes about her

children's behaviour which made some previous parish contexts untenable. She recounted how: "My training incumbent tried to suggest that it was a distraction, and it was [my husband's] job to keep Ella in the body of the church. [Douglas also] said he was getting negative responses from people, and people were being upset by him not being under more control." As such, few allowances were made for her children's disabilities, and, interestingly, Natalie's husband was strategically invoked as needing to take more responsibility, which rarely happened in other situations. Natalie's attempts to keep her children attending church were met with severe censure and constraint.

MANAGING EXPECTATIONS

There were various ways that clergy mothers managed these complex expectations, all of which centred on circumventing the dominant narratives and cultivating new messages about priesthood and ministry, as well as finding acceptable spaces where parishioners were brought alongside the clergy family. Many of the clergy mothers said it was unhelpful to put them on a pedestal and expect perfect behaviour from their children. Instead, they argued that seeing priests in typical family situations—including instances of conflict—could challenge the idea that priests are a class apart as well as cultivate ministry opportunities. As Natalie indicates: "Children ... just don't allow you to do the sort of 'holier than thou' bit, which I think is very healthy. You know, the congregation frequently see me ... less than sort of gentle and polite. They just bring you down to earth all the time." In a similar vein, Laura explains:

> *There is nothing like having children as a real leveller ... whatever images people have of priests as "holier than thou," when people are in the playground [and] see you getting annoyed with your kids like everybody else does, they know that you're simply human too and that's a good thing. ... I can see it makes people think you understand what life is like for them because you actually have to deal with all those same issues about children*

> *doing your head in, what a juggle life can be and I think that's a positive thing.*

As Moore argues, clergy families are usually associated with holiness, especially when it is the father who is ordained, and clear expectations emerge for the clergy family to epitomize this godliness. But as these clergy mothers enact their everyday motherhood publicly, they break down the unhelpful association linking sacredness to the ordained person and their family. Instead they valorize the sacredness of everyday parenthood, and redefine the "chaos" embedded in their caring practices as sacred (Miller-McLemore 16-20). This recalibration allows priests to recast their ministry in a different image, using this as an opportunity to reach out to their congregation.

Despite the public visibility of the clergy mothers, there was also a sense that when they were in welcoming spaces, parishioners could be an enormous source of support when things did not go to plan. As Rachel, a mother of one, recalls:

> *I discovered I was pregnant, which wasn't something at all that we were planning ... but we were delighted ... but then sadly that pregnancy failed. ... I then told everybody because being a parish priest you're a very public person, and, actually, I'm not the sort of person who invents a bout of flu. I find it much easier just to tell people what was going on. Which I did, and the parish were very supportive ... my story... actually touched quite a lot of people; quite a lot of people told me stuff about their lives and people who had a miscarriage sixty years ago or a stillborn child forty years ago and had never really talked about it much ... that was kind of healing for some people. ...The problems I had ... kind of left a tainted history behind me that the parishes will think, "Oh women priests they're a real problem, because you know, all these women's problems." I don't think that's what they'd say if you asked them. I think they'd say they had a good experience with me as an incumbent, and although marred by all of those experiences, you do*

feel, I do feel a public responsibility that I kind of let the side down a bit by having all those problems.

Rachel recognizes that the problems that she faced could be used as ammunition by those opposed to women priests, but she managed to turn it into a ministry opportunity (Page, "Negotiating Sacred Roles") and enabled her parishioners to disclose issues about miscarriage that they had harboured for many years. Rachel's status in the community meant that it was difficult to hide what had happened, yet her openness about her personal life is not something all priests would be comfortable with. However, it did lead to a new level of appreciation for Rachel's ministry to the extent that when she left the parish for another post, her old parishioners articulated, in not so many words, that they preferred her ministry style to that of the new (male) incumbent.

Meanwhile, as the previous section highlighted, Natalie had many difficulties in garnering acceptance in the community for her and her family. In the past, she had to firmly reject the contention that her children with special educational needs were "distracting" in church. But when I interviewed Natalie, she had taken charge of a new church in an economically depressed area, where she and her family had found acceptance:

There are congregations I wouldn't lead—they wouldn't cope ... My family would not fit in the high church context where people were expected to do things properly.... And I would be deeply unhappy about worshiping with a congregation that couldn't cope.... There is a real deep degree of acceptance [here]... in some ways I think my congregation has been quite unique.... We also acquired a significant number of people with learning difficulties, adults with learning difficulties as part of the congregation and I think they've gone hand-in-hand. I think that there's been a strong message that it is acceptable to not fit the norm. To be different and you're welcome as you are ... for a fairly battered, alienated community, the church in which the vicar's son wanders around the place and behaves badly is a much more welcoming place. So I think it's quite

> *a good fit ... we may be focused in a holy building but we need to rediscover the holiness of everybody's lives and the sacred space within each person. And I think this whole bit which fences it off and says it's only for a few select people is just so wrong.*

Indeed, not only was Natalie and her family welcomed, but their presence also encouraged the inclusion of marginalized Christians in the church. Her ministry was a public declaration that church was not for those with "perfect" families but should include everyone, leading her to promote a strong statement about the meaning of sacredness and who was included in this. In doing so, Natalie was able to challenge the past contention that her children were disrupting the sacred.

CONCLUSION

As this chapter has illustrated, clergy mothers are subject to heightened scrutiny in their public roles in their churches and larger communities—more so than male priests or women priests without children. This is largely derived from the cultural expectations that mothers are primarily responsible for cultivating spiritual capital in their families in accordance with Christian precepts and intensive mothering standards. In other words, the cultivation and transmission of spiritual capital are mainly tasked to mothers, meaning that Christian mothers have additional responsibilities in the broader remit of intensive motherhood. Cultivating spiritual capital functions as a dimension of intensive motherhood, but these expectations are heightened for clergy mothers.

As these interviews indicate, it is expected that clergy mothers' children will attend church and be well-behaved. Such spiritual capital entails a very public dimension: it needs to be on display and "proved," often in an embodied way through the physical presence of the compliant clergy child within the church space. But this embodiment of spiritual capital is multi-dimensional, as evidenced by Rachel's daughter who would confidently meet and greet parishioners in the public sphere. Therefore, the skills that need to be on display also tap into other forms of capital that

Bourdieu references, such as cultural and social capital (Bourdieu, "Distinction"; Davies and Guest; Reay). In performing intensive motherhood, Christian mothers have an added burden to encourage children to develop their Christian identity, but for clergy mothers, these expectations are heightened and policed through the watchful eyes of parishioners.

The clergy mothers in this study put great pressure on themselves and did their upmost to cultivate their children's presence in church, even when this meant paying for babysitters for their children to be there. But for older children, for whom mothers had fewer jurisdictions over church attendance, they felt guilty when parishioner expectations were not met, such as when teenagers stopped attending church. These expectations were not only internalized by the clergy mothers themselves, but they were also vocalized by parishioners. Indeed, although all priests (male and female) experience congregational surveillance to a degree (Greenbacker and Taylor), clergy mothers encounter additional layers of scrutiny, as parishioners deem it their right to directly comment on and critique their mothering styles.

Despite the negative experiences that clergy mothers encountered and the scrutiny that they were subject to, there was also a sense that parishes were communities of love and care, and parishioners could actually become hugely supportive in times of crisis. Indeed, sometimes the clergy mothers were able to turn this into a ministry opportunity, such as when Rachel disclosed her miscarriage, which led women to share similar stories with her, or when the presence of Natalie's children with special educational needs actually opened the door to create a much more accepting church space. In doing so, these women worked to challenge and dismantle the contentious expectations placed on clergy families. Miller-McLemore argues that older ideas of sacredness, connected to stillness and silence and embodied *par excellence* in the celibate priest of the Catholic tradition, need to be challenged. The daily routines of motherhood have not been marked out or given much attention within Christianity, and they have certainly not been given sacred status, and this should be rebalanced in order to recover the sacred of the everyday (Miller-McLemore).

Due to their public role and visibility, clergy mothers have a pivotal role in challenging the parameters of sacredness and bringing new perspectives to the fore, thereby challenging oppressive maternal expectations and generating a more holistic and inclusive understanding of Christianity. But because of the specific challenges of concurrently being a priest and a mother (Page, "Altruism"), as well as the way clergy mothers are marginalized within the Church (Page, "Femmes, Mères et Prêtres"; "Negotiating Sacred Roles"), they remain few in number, thus curtailing the potential for change. Indeed, the major remaining barriers relate to the entrenched perceptions of what constitutes being a "good" priest and a "good" mother, and the prevailing view that being a "good" priest is incompatible with being a "good" mother. It is at this definitional level of intensive motherhood and all-encompassing priesthood (what I refer to elsewhere as "intensive priesthood"; Page, "Altruism") that change is needed, and the clergy mothers who participated in this study are the vanguards of new ways of imagining and doing priesthood. But the numbers of clergy mothers remain stubbornly small (also connected to the increasing average age of ordination for both genders; [Peyton and Gatrell]), which may render their broader impact in challenging and changing norms negligible.

Acknowledgements: This research was funded by the Economic and Social Research Council (award numbers PTA-031-2004-00290 and PTS-026-27-2911). I thank the funders as well as the participants, who both made the research possible.

NOTE

[1]Forward in Faith was formed after the 1992 vote approving women's priesthood. It is comprised of individuals who are opposed to women's ordination, in order to unite a variety of groups that were formed prior to the vote. For further reading, see Jones.

WORKS CITED

Blum, Linda. *Raising Generation Rx*. New York: New York University Press, 2015. Print.

Bourdieu, Pierre. *Distinction: A Social Critique of the Judgement of Taste*. London: Routledge, 1984. Print.

Bourdieu, Pierre. "Genesis and Structure of the Religious Field." *Comparative Social Research* 13 (1991): 1-44. Print.

Brown, Callum. *The Death of Christian Britain: Understanding Secularisation 1800-2000*. London: Routledge, 2001. Print.

Davies, Douglas, and Mathew Guest. *Bishops, Wives and Children: Spiritual Capital Across the Generations*. Aldershot: Ashgate, 2007. Print.

Dyer, Anne. "Almost Evangelical." *Anvil* 21.2 (2004): 121-125. Print.

Forna, Aminatta. *Mother of All Myths: How Society Moulds and Constrains Mothers*. London: HarperCollins, 1998. Print.

Furlong, Monica. "Introduction." *Mirror to the Church: Reflections on Sexism*. Ed. Monica Furlong. London: SPCK, 1988. 1-16. Print.

Garey, Anita Ilta. *Weaving Work and Motherhood*. Philadelphia: Temple University Press, 1999. Print.

Gatrell, Caroline. *Hard Labour: The Sociology of Parenthood*. Maidenhead: Open University Press, 2005. Print.

Gill, Sean. *Women and the Church of England: From the Eighteenth Century to the Present*. London: SPCK, 1994. Print.

Goffman, Erving. *The Presentation of Self in Everyday Life*. London: Penguin Books, 1990. Print.

Greenbacker, Liz, and Sherry Taylor. *Private Lives of Ministers' Wives*. Far Hills New Jersey: New Horizon Press, 1991. Print.

Guest, Mathew. "In Search of Spiritual Capital: The Spiritual as a Cultural Resource." *A Sociology of Spirituality*. Eds. Kieran Flanagan and Peter Jupp. Aldershot: Ashgate, 2007. 181-200. Print.

Hays, Sharon. *The Cultural Contradictions of Motherhood*. London: Yale University Press, 1996. Print.

Jensen, Tracey. "Tough Love in Tough Times." *Studies in the Maternal* 4.2 (2012). Web. 17 Sept. 2015.

Jones, Ian. *Women and Priesthood in the Church of England Ten Years On*. London: Church House Publishing, 2004. Print.

Lawler, Steph. *Mothering the Self: Mothers, Daughters, Subjects*. Florence, KY: Routledge, 2000. Print.

Lee, Ellie. J. "Living with Risk in the Age of 'Intensive Motherhood': Maternal Identity and Infant Feeding." *Health, Risk and Society* 10.5 (2008): 467-477. Print.

Lowe, Pam, Ellie Lee, and Liz Yardley. "Under the Influence? The Construction of Foetal Alcohol Syndrome in UK Newspapers." *Sociological Research Online* 15.4 (2010): 2.17 Web. 27 Aug. 2015.

Mellow, Muriel. *Defining Work: Gender, Professional Work, and the Case of Rural Clergy*. Montreal and Kingston: McGill-Queen's University Press, 2007. Print.

Miller-McLemore, Bonnie J. *In the Midst of Chaos: Caring for Children as Spiritual Practice*. San Francisco: Jossey-Bass, 2007. Print.

Moore, Allison M. *Clergy Moms: A Survival Guide to Balancing Family and Congregation*. New York: Seabury Books, 2008. Print.

Page, Sarah-Jane. "Altruism and Sacrifice: Anglican Priests Managing 'Intensive' Priesthood and Motherhood." *Religion and Gender* 6.1 (2016): 47-63. Print.

Page, Sarah-Jane. "Femmes, Mères et Prêtres dans l'Église d'Angleterre: Quels Sacerdoces." *Travail, Genre et Sociétés* 27 (2012): 55-71. Print.

Page, Sarah-Jane. "Negotiating Sacred Roles: A Sociological Exploration of Priests who are Mothers." *Feminist Review* 97.1 (2011): 92-109. Print.

Peyton, Nigel, and Caroline Gatrell. *Managing Clergy Lives: Obedience, Sacrifice, Intimacy*. London: Bloomsbury, 2013. Print.

Reay, Diane. "Gendering Bourdieu's Concepts of Capitals? Emotional Capital, Women and Social Class." *The Sociological Review* 52.s2 (2004): 57-74. Print.

Rees, Christina. "Yes to Women Bishops—Yes to Women?' *Women's History Review* 23.6 (2014): 996-999. Print.

Robson, Jill. "Ministry or Profession: Clergy Doubletalk." *Mirror to the Church: Reflections on Sexism*. Ed. Monica Furlong. London: SPCK, 1988. 106-123. Print.

Thatcher, Adrian. "Families." *The Oxford Handbook of Theology, Sexuality, and Gender*. Ed. Adrian Thatcher. Oxford: Oxford University Press, 2015. 590-607. Print.

Thorne, Helen. *Journey to Priesthood*. Bristol: Centre for Comparative Studies in Religion and Gender, 2000. Print.

Verter, Bradford. "Spiritual Capital: Theorizing Religion with Bourdieu against Bourdieu." *Sociological Theory* 21.2 (2003): 150-174. Print.

Wall, Glenda. "Mothers' Experiences with Intensive Parenting and Brain Development Discourse." *Women's Studies International Forum* 33.3 (2010): 253-263. Print.

Walsh, Clare. *Gender and Discourse: Language and Power in Politics, the Church and Organisations*. Harlow: Longman, 2001. Print.

Zikmund, Barbara Brown., Adair T. Lummis and Patricia M. Chang. *Clergy Women: An Uphill Calling*. Louisville: Westminster John Knox Press, 1998. Print.

2.
Intersectional Mothering

A Black Baptist Example

DEIRDRE HILL BUTLER

THIS CHAPTER EXPLORES black women's visibility through their spiritual enactments in the suburban city of Newton, Massachusetts, where a small black community has thrived since the nineteenth century. By the late twentieth century, many of the black women in this predominantly white city were mothers, and their community activism was rooted in embracing black cultural mothering affinities exercised through their church work. Understanding the womanist consciousness that black mothers use to attain power within community institutions, especially churches, facilitates an overall comprehension of black women's activism. Although other scholars have examined black women's activism in politics, media, and other settings, this chapter's focus on black mothers' roles in one particular Christian Church provides a glimpse of how they negotiate their roles in society more generally. Even though women's leadership has been traditionally relegated to a secondary status in the Black Church, examining the inner workings of church life reveals how black mothers exercise agency and enlist collective networks to pursue their choices in life. As such, by exploring how one group of mothers negotiates social boundaries to acquire visible and elevated status within their church and the local community, this chapter provides a ground-floor view of intersectional mothering.

This chapter draws on interviews that I conducted with members of the Daughters of Myrtle, a women's church organization founded in 1921. Established in 1874, Myrtle Baptist Church is located eight miles west of Boston. The Daughters of Myrtle is not the only women's group working within this principle of community mothering, but it is the only group that matches community mothering with self-care, thus providing a female-centred space for group support and creating their own "homeplace." Not only do members help with church programs, clean houses for indigent members, and raise funds for church infrastructure needs, they also help create a space within the group's agenda for group outings and social activities that just serve them. In doing so, they have turned the community mothering practice inwards to nurture themselves, in addition to reaching outwards into the community. According to Patricia Hill Collins, "other mothering," or "intersectional mothering" for this example, "consists of a series of constantly renegotiated relationships that African American women experience with one another, with Black children, with the larger African American community, and with self. These relationships occur in specific locations such as ... Black community institutions" (118). In this sense, Myrtle Baptist Church—and the Daughters of Myrtle group specifically—serves as a "homeplace" for its members, therein providing space for self and collective care through Christian ministry and mothering.

This Christian-inspired mothering provides the foundation for community-based political activism. According to bell hooks, black women's struggles against racism and sexism infuse their mothering practices inside and outside of their "homeplace" (46). She further explains how "[w]orking to create a homeplace that affirmed our beings, our blackness, our love for one another was necessary resistance" (46). Although racism inevitably shapes black women's thinking, their sense of home, and their modes of parenting, it also motivates them to create sites of resistance. Intersectional mothering inside of a public place, such as the Myrtle Baptist Church, is, thus, a site for resisting racism and sexism as well as for elevating black women's community status. It also affirms the spaces of leadership that women develop through black church ministries and community service work. Myrtle women, and particularly the Daughters of Myrtle group, accordingly redefine themselves as community workers for their church and community.

Such a womanist practice extends sociologist Katrina McDonald's contention that black activist mothering—another name for intersectional mothering—is a form of black women's activism deriving from a conjunction of empathy for other black women who suffer similar social disadvantages and of African American norms of solidarity, responsibility, and accountability (774). Through activism black women redefine the role of mothering, therein mingling social reform, motherhood, and religious teaching. As activist mothers, Newton's Black Baptist women are engaged in an ongoing process to reshape black womanhood and embolden their community.

PERSPECTIVES ON INTERSECTIONAL MOTHERING

Sons and daughters view their activist mothers at Myrtle Baptist Church as community service agents. The late Mr. James Spikes, son of the founder of the Daughters of Myrtle and husband to a former member, shared in his interview memories of the work performed:

> *Well, they would have programs, and they would have speakers come on the programs. Their principal job, besides taking care of the communion and stuff like that, would be helping with families, take care of girls that needed female assistance of women, who had had children, and they would go into the houses and take care of the houses and clean the houses up and prepare meals and everything. They [the club women—deaconesses, willing workers, Sunday school workers, of the church and Daughter of Myrtle members, and many Daughter of Myrtle members had multiple memberships] felt it was their personal duty.*

The women also taught black history, which always delivered a social reform message of racial uplift and community solidarity. Mrs. Lee Hill remembered during in her interview how the Daughters of Myrtle ordered copies of the *Carter G. Woodson Journal* from the Association for the Study of Negro Life and History in the late 1930s and early 1940s. The journal was shared among members, and they spread its message of academic research on topics relating to black experiences to their Sunday school classes and through other activities. In this sense, at Myrtle Baptist Church, the Sunday school provided a window through which black children from "the village" could connect to the wider black community.

Intersectional mothering, thus, provided an alternative, autonomous space of leadership for women at Myrtle Baptist Church during its first generation. The fifty or so women who made up the core of black women's community workers in Newton grappled with racial and gender limitations within their suburban context. Newton women decided it was best to address local social limitations rather than connect to regional or national club movements. Even though their struggles were similar, rural, urban, and suburban black women did not wrestle with the lack of visibility as one united front. Instead, they developed similar but separate actions in their local places.

Black women in Newton also chose not to forge institutional links with urban women, perhaps because of their economic status, although Boston was home to a growing middle-class black community. Most black women in Newton worked as domestics, even if they did live in their own homes. Domestic work provided Newton's black activist women with steady but hardly lucrative employment. Therefore, in terms of economics, the black community workers in Newton in the 1920s and 1930s were working class, or at least lower middle class. However, because they lived in Newton, black women were considered middle class by urban blacks, even though their lived experiences were not dissimilar to those of urban black women. Sharon Harley argues that less financially stable black women took up membership in churchwomen's groups because participation in those groups elevated one's status within the community and granted more visibility (336). Hence, Myrtle's intersectional mothers chose from a seemingly complex duality of status levels. On the one hand, these women seemed to see their activism as a means to attain the social status of respectable women who were worthy of community acknowledgment and an elevated status. On the other hand, they also chose to balance teaching the community's children with nurturing each other and building a community space for status elevation.

THE DAUGHTERS OF MYRTLE

Candace Haywood migrated to Newton from rural North Carolina as a teenager in 1928, and she was invited to join the Daughters of Myrtle in 1938. One could not just join the Daughters of Myrtle—potential members had to be invited. As Mrs. Haywood explained,

> *When I first joined I was the only young person of my group, and I was sure that the others would be joining. They told me that they had been watching me and seeing what I was doing and they had decided [I] could qualify to come into their group. Membership in the Daughters of Myrtle was set aside for just a select few.*

Reverend Howard Haywood, former pastor of Myrtle Baptist Church and lifelong church member, is the son of an early member of the Daughters. He shared similar sentiments,

> *I would think that at one point that people would say that the Daughters of Myrtle was an elitist organization. Everybody was not welcome into the Daughters of Myrtle. They [other church members] said those people [Daughter of Myrtle members] think they are better than anybody else.*

There was no competition between organizations. Most Daughters of Myrtle members belonged to other church groups, which is what made them attractive to the organization in the first place. Co-ordinating community bazaars demonstrated how members exercised their leadership talents. Most of the members were also leaders in other church organizations prior to joining the Daughters, and many maintained those high-profile positions after membership. Choosing the highest profile black female leaders in the church who exemplified strong community workers brought prominence to the organization. However, the Daughters of Myrtle always had a special place in the hearts of the church community: it was the only group where the mission was to serve the community and the church. However, there was also an unspoken expectation that members should serve each other. The organization evolved into a women-centred space for aid and support. The Daughters, accordingly, became the most visible church-related group because their activities constantly tied community and church together. This was not a backstage, silent helper organization; instead, it grew to be well known inside and outside of the church.

James Spikes's mother and aunt were founding members of the Daughters, and his wife was also a member. He remembered the organization sponsoring two large community fundraisers a year: "They would have a ... spring fair and a fall fair. They would make different tapestries and napkins for the fair, and they would sell that. They had a lot of trinkets and things. They would also have chitlin' suppers or pig's feet suppers or chicken suppers at the church." He further shared how

> *Those women used to prepare such fabulous meals [for the May sales], like turkey and stuffing, and all the fixings. They had desserts and they had ice cream, and one of the ties to the church for my brother and myself was freezing the ice cream. My mother used to make sherbert. And it wasn't sherbert, it was more lemon ice cream because she put like three quarts of milk and a pint of cream and whipped it up. Of course, we had the pleasure of stirring. But that was done at home, next door, where we lived then.*

The May sales were annual events that allowed the community to see the organization in action. Their best baked goods went on sale, and members made enough from the sale to contribute to the church budget. However, the May sale meant more to the community. A spring ritual allowed Myrtle Baptist Church to reach out to non-members and reinforce broader suburban community links. When I interviewed three second generation members, they explained that the May sales had a special place in their hearts. Lillie Jefferson, the former church historian and secretary, said, "I miss the May sales. Because those were always fun." "Yeah, the ice cream and lemon sherbert," responded Candace Haywood. Lillie then went on to say, "Usually when we had a dinner the dessert was gingerbread and whipped cream or lemon cake or plain cake with lemon sauce—that was one of the standards."

Daughters of Myrtle 2015, courtesy of Myrtle Baptist Church website

Daughters of Myrtle members also enlisted their families for support. Family members wanted to support their community mothers who were sustaining the church, a much beloved community institution. This established a cycle of community involvement that worked its way through the efforts of the Daughters of Myrtle. For instance, Lillie Jefferson discussed how the organization gave large donations toward the purchase of a new organ: "When things needed to be refurbished we were the first to say 'let's get the money to do this.'"

The Daughters of Myrtle provided a supportive environment for its members, and this became the lasting meaning for the group. Members chose women like themselves, and in this sense, the organization is an example of "homeplace," a space where people work to affirm black women's racial and gendered selves, thereby providing a place to love one another. Candace Haywood put this process into perspective:

> *When you heard [a] member of the* DOM *[was sick] or having a baby or whatever, you just put your things down and go to her house and you didn't ask her what can I*

do, you just went right along and you did what you saw needed to be done. And that's the way they did all the time. I remember, I think it was Trustena [Edwards] said, "You know, we're just like sisters."

Even male members of the community commented on the support system that Daughters of Myrtle members created for themselves. Mr. James Spikes recalled how members would aid sick mothers:

When there were families who were having problems, like the mother or something was sick, some of the Daughters would constantly take food over, they'd fix meals, and they'd go over to the house, and stay with the sick person. I guess sometimes, someone would spend the night. 'Cause in those days, up here, the families didn't spend the night in the hospital.

Elaine Nichols Thomas joined the Daughters of Myrtle in 1988 as a second-generation member. Elaine's mother and aunts were active during the first generation of the organization. The impression that she received about the work they did largely centred on the service they provided to the church community. Similarly, Katie Haywood, a third-generation member and wife of former Reverend Howard Haywood, pondered why the group structure allowed only certain women during its first generation:

They'd work in wealthy white people's homes during the day because none of them were [traditionally] educated and that is what they did for a living ... but [the group] was their chance to put out their best, and the funny thing is my Aunt Tinks [Helen Lomax, founding DOM member], there was always a joke about her because she was always very prim and proper. And my mother [Helen Evans, a second-generation DOM member] used to tease her because she said that she acted like the woman that she worked for, you know. But that is where she learned her airs. So, they got to be the elegant ladies of the Daughter of Myrtle.

During our interview, Reverend Haywood remembered another story about his mother's inner strength, something he still marvels at today years after her passing:

> *One day a guy, the same age as one of my brothers, came over one time to bring clothes to my mother and called my mother Julia. And I got so mad. Why he thought he could call my mother by her first name, you know. And it kind of, you know, it just bothered me. She [Mrs. Haywood] knew who she was. You could call her anything you want, you know. She could tell me, yeah, he can call me Julia, but his mother can't do without me. That kind of stuff didn't bother them [Daughters of Myrtle members]. They just shrugged that stuff off.*

That is how it looked to Reverend Haywood as a youngster. His mother commiserated with other group members, and they redefined themselves through working together to serve the church community and create a visible identity. This does not disguise the subtle forms of discrimination that Daughters of Myrtle members suffered, but it acknowledges that these women created a space of resistance through serving themselves, the community, and one another that helped them cope with social limitations. Reverend Haywood believed his mother was just a very humble lady trying to give and do whatever was necessary:

> *A lot of other people that I thought were the people that were more had more; she [my mother] was just a worker. But she also kind of reflected the real spirit of the Daughters of Myrtle, you know. And the women, many of them had difficulties in their life, losing their husbands early, bringing up the children and not only bringing up their children, but being very much a mother figure for many of the children in the community. All of them had that kind of similar trait. I used to tell people there were a lot of people in the Daughters of Myrtle that people called Aunt something. And a lot of them, I always thought they were my aunts. I always thought they were my mother's sisters.*

> *And I was always amazed at that kind of a relationship, even though they were very different women, there was something about them that brought them together. And, obviously, it was the Spirit of God.*

These intersectional mothers rarely compartmentalized their social reform work, and they often used similar strategies to address the same dilemmas. Daughters of Myrtle members fostered the community mothering ethic by sponsoring programs that shared their club's purpose with the community. For example, The Mother and Daughter Teas, which started in the 1940s and 1950s, provided members with a space to socialize young women into the ways of refined womanhood. The best linen and china were placed on the tables, and a small lunch was served. Mothers brought their daughters, and if a member did not have a daughter, she borrowed one from the community. Long-time member Mrs. Lee Hill recollected how "Daughters of Myrtle members used [to] have tablecloths and tea sets and things and they would be matching linen tablecloths and matching napkins and fine china." A member from the organization would speak about topics, such as edifying the mother-daughter relationship as well as the need for higher education and stronger family values. These speakers largely preached to the converted, and the teas, thus, had a double mission: to inform attendees about black women's contributions to the local community and broader society and to reaffirm the ongoing process of black women working together for a common goal. The teas became a place where local black women were honoured for their contributions to community efforts. They became a staple in "homeplace" development, and the Daughters worked together to create this space, which affirmed their black female heritage and supported the relationships that they built as a public act of opposition to the dominant negative stereotypes about black women.

By the late 1970s to the 1990s, these teas evolved into Annual Anniversary Banquets, which focused solely on celebrating the history and legacy of the Daughters of Myrtle. The grand luncheon meals were first held in the Agape Room, the activity room in the church, for five dollars a ticket. The difference between the tea and the banquet was that the focus on the mother-daughter relationship was minimized to emphasize a broader community connection. This method brought the Daughters into the mainstream of the church and community calendar; no longer was "the grand meal" solely a woman-only event. Plus, the program had more agenda items and speakers so that attention strayed away from a focus on linen and china.

By the 1970s, the Daughters of Myrtle group was composed of two sets of members, mostly daughter and mother combinations. The younger members had a different vision of how the group should undertake its mission. Leahora Hill's niece, Elaine Thomas, joined the organization in 1988. As a child, she thought the Daughters of Myrtle was just a group for her mother and aunts, but, soon, she found herself as a young married professional woman wanting female support on everyday issues. Elaine's generation went to college and had careers inside and outside of traditional fields for black women, yet the third generation of Daughters of Myrtle members desired female support through their church affiliations as well. Elaine recalled how

> *We were all getting married at that point, a bunch of us were starting to get married and stuff, but all of us had been back and forth with college, too. And a lot of us weren't really settled back in Newton because we had gone off, you know. I didn't graduate from college [University of Massachusetts at Amherst] until 1978, and, at that time, when I graduated, I was getting married, trying to get my job situation squared away, you know. You left that to my mother and her sisters and that age group, not us. And I think one person joined and then I joined. I ended up being an officer soon after joining.*

Penneye Williams, a senior financial analyst with the Polaroid Corporation in Cambridge, Massachusetts, who is similar in age to Elaine, had elder cousins in the Daughters. Penneye recalled tensions between the older and younger members. Since the younger set had experiences in groups working for black women's issues, or they had participated in professional organizations, they had more knowledge about group dynamics. Penneye observed:

> *What I do find interesting in the Daughters, and I've experienced it both in the sorority [Delta Sigma Theta Sorority, Inc.] and another organization at Polaroid, is the difference between the younger and older members of the organization. What you hear a lot of the times is, we always did it like this. And many young women get frustrated. It's like, well, if you don't give me a chance ... what is the future going to look like?*

However, members were able to reach compromises in light of such changes. For instance, the Anniversary Luncheon eventually became so large that it was moved outside of the community to a hotel, and ticket prices increased from fifteen to twenty dollars. More seasoned Daughter of Myrtle members wanted the event to stay the same price and location. However, the luncheon committee convinced the older members that the event was a heritage celebration as well as the group's major fundraiser. With the success of the first few Anniversary Luncheons, it became evident to all members that, although the event structure had changed, the tradition of celebrating local accomplishments of Newton's oldest black women's group had not.

DISCUSSION

This chapter has highlighted how black women living in a suburban place created and sustained supportive and community-minded intersectional mothering practices. Creating the Daughters of Myrtle enabled members to thrive on their own terms and create modes of visibility in church ministries as well as to foster their own forms of social connectedness. In one capacity, they perform church and broader community work in conjunction with black middle-class etiquette, which reinforces the class distinctions within Newton's black community and exemplifies an ethic of black female middle-class collective consciousness.

Stephanie Shaw and other social scientists present the concept of collective consciousness as a process of mixing individual and community social responsibility "to enhance individual development in a manner that regularly demonstrates, frequently demands, and often yields individual postures of collective consciousness and social responsibility" (6) through visible service measures. This chapter reveals how the Daughters of Myrtle work within this rubric. Furthermore, as the first Auxiliary of the Myrtle Baptist Church, whose initial mission was to prepare a dinner for a Northern Baptist Convention, the Daughters of Myrtle are part of a larger discourse framed by Evelyn Brooks Higginbotham's 1993 text, *Righteous Discontent*. Higginbotham focuses on the National Baptist Convention, the largest religious movement among black Americans, from 1880 to1920. She shows us how women were largely responsible for making the church a force for self-help in the black community. In this way, the Daughters of Myrtle provide a mother-centred example of the larger activism that occurred within black culture and consciousness during the twentieth century, and which continues to thrive today.

CONCLUDING THOUGHTS

The Daughters of Myrtle are still active as the premiere women's group at Myrtle Baptist Church in West Newton, Massachusetts. Under the leadership of Rev. Tamara Sheard, the group hosts an array of activities, including fostering connections with college students, supporting local shelters, participating in the Mississippi Salvation Army's Adopt-an-Angel initiative, and reaching out to the sick and shut-in members of the community ("Daughters of Myrtle"). Annually, they host informational and sponsored events, such as the Community Health Fair, the Anniversary Luncheon, and the weekly Collation. The group still holds true to its original mission of supporting church ministries while sustaining a space for intersectional mothering, self-care, and activism.

On the whole, in addition to their vital community work and activism, the Daughters' emphasis on self-care, ultimately, became the beacon for their particular brands of black-suburban Baptist mothering and womanhood, as they always took time for group retreats and relaxation. This chapter illustrates how Daughters of Myrtle members operate as intersectional mothers in etching out visible spaces of leadership and status for themselves in a larger world, in which they go unnoticed or are diminished. By striving to comprehend the complex relationships and social lives of Daughters of Myrtle members, this research renders their lives visible.

WORKS CITED

Collins, Patricia Hill. *Black Feminist Thought: Knowledge, Consciousness, and the Politics of Empowerment.* New York: Routledge, 1991. Print.

"Daughters of Myrtle." *Myrtle Baptist.* N.pub. n.d. Web. 2 March 2016.

Harley, Sharon. "For the Good of the Family and Race: Gender, Work, and Domestic Roles in the Black Community, 1880-1930." *Black Women in America: Social Science Perspectives.* Eds. Michelene R. Malson, Elisabeth Mudimbe-Boyi, Jean F. O'Barr, and May Wyer. Chicago: Chicago University, 1988. 336-349. Print.

Higginbotham, Evelyn Brooks. *Righteous Discontent: The Woman's Movement in the Black Baptist Church, 1880–1920.* Cambridge: Harvard University Press, 1993. Print.

hooks, bell. *Yearning: Race, Gender, and Cultural Politics.* Boston: South End Press, 1990. Print.

McDonald, Katrina Bell. "Black Activist Mothering: A Historical Intersection of

Race, Gender, and Class." *Gender and Society* 11.6 (1997): 773-795. Print.

Shaw, Stephanie. *What a Women Ought to Be and to Do: Black Professional Women Workers During the Jim Crow Era.* Chicago: University of Chicago Press, 1996. Print.

3. Faith Shifters

Exploring Religious Motherwork in the Post-Evangelical Blogosphere

VANESSA REIMER

MUCH HAS BEEN WRITTEN on the cultural significance of religious blogs in the past decade, especially as their growing popularity among readers has coincided with the continued decline of Catholic and Protestant institutional church attendance in North America (Campbell; Cheong, Halavais, and Kwon; Corrigon, Morgan, Silk, and Williams). In a similar vein, the proliferation of "mommy blogs" has been explored by feminist researchers, particularly in light of their potential to foster empowering representations of motherhood and cultivate meaningful connections among mothers (Friedman; Lopez; Morrison; Powell). However, much less has been written on the significance of religious blogs authored by mothers and, particularly, by those who write from a standpoint of cultivated ambivalence[1] towards their religious communities—a phenomenon that is critical for feminist scholars to consider, since patriarchal religious traditions and institutions continue to marginalize and delegitimize women's voices (Bammert 155; Gallagher 215; Steiner-Aeschliman and Mauss 248).

This chapter, accordingly, explores how mothers use the blogosphere's fluid and dynamic space to share their experiences of religious motherwork and critique their conservative Protestant or evangelical Christian subcultures. In doing so, this chapter illustrates how these bloggers employ a post-evangelical discursive framework to navigate their shifting religious beliefs and construct their religious motherwork as an act of resistance to the Complementarian theological paradigm that pervades North American evangelicalism. It concludes by considering how the act of blogging can be empowering for mothers as they cultivate their particular religiosities and engage in daily motherwork.

CONTEXTUALIZING EVANGELICAL SUBCULTURES

Contemporary North American evangelicals can be aptly contextualized as operating within distinct religious subcultures,[2] with particular beliefs and practices that demarcate "in-group" status and distinguish them from other religious groups. In accordance with their fundamentalist[3] roots, many evangelicals conceptualize themselves as a persecuted minority group, whose beliefs and values are perpetually threatened by secular cultural forces. To that end, these religious subcultures largely strive to cultivate group solidarity by rejecting all forms of scepticism, compromise, and doubt among members (Gerami 29).

Along this trajectory, canonized texts that enforce patriarchal gender hierarchies are continually affirmed within many evangelical subcultures simply because of their biblical precedence, and the primacy of this imperative is illustrated by the pervasiveness of Complementarian theology within contemporary evangelicalism. This theological movement emphasizes the importance of universal male "headship" and female "submission" in all domestic and public spheres in accordance with select biblical proof-texts.[4] In this sense, Complementarian theology constructs the maintenance of "traditional" gender roles as a central locus for resisting secular forces—namely feminism, "homosexuality," and all forms of "liberalism"—that seek to eradicate Christianity's cultural and political influence. In light of its pervasiveness among evangelical subcultures, this theological paradigm has particularly vital implications for evangelical women who are mothers.

THE EVANGELICAL MATERNAL ETHOS

The evangelical maternal ethos[5] is informed by evangelical doctrines, the internalized demands of maternal thinking, and the deeply entrenched cultural practice of mother-blame. To begin, this ethos is rooted in an evangelical prosperity gospel paradigm, wherein salvation is understood to be an individualized, purposeful commitment (Castells 22), and it is believed that God rewards the morality, virtue, and devotion of individual believers with visible success,[6] including financial, physical, and spiritual well-being.[7] It is also informed by the dominant belief that children are born with innately sinful natures,[8] so their childhoods must be shaped by intensive religious enculturation[9] and strict discipline.

Since Complementarian theology designates women as "natural" caregivers within the domestic sphere (Colaner and Giles 526; Hardacre 132), mothers, consequently, assume the role of children's primary religious enculturators (Franks 6; Gerami 32; Levitt 531). In this capacity, religious enculturation is a key aspect of evangelical women's daily motherwork.[10] Here Sara Ruddick's three demands of maternal thinking provide a useful conceptual framework: whereas the first demand of preservation refers to children's physical care and nurturance, the second and third demands of growth and acceptability are more intricately tied to the mother's peer group and its corresponding values (21). Since religious enculturation is a central aspect of childrearing within evangelical subcultures, it can be argued that the third demand of acceptability is exacerbated for evangelical mothers. This is because they must not only teach their children about broader societal norms and roles but also ensure that their children internalize and perform evangelical doctrines that are believed to directly oppose the larger "secular" society.

Complementarian theology, thus, compels mothers to model patriarchal ideals of femininity in their families and reproduce these values in their children. This theological framework propagates discourses of "righteous femininity," wherein the extent to which women perform patriarchal precepts provides a primary measure of their individual devotion to God *and* their dedication to the evangelical subculture as a whole. This resolution is further compounded by the evangelical prosperity gospel paradigm, which enables—if not directly promotes—the cultural practice of blaming mothers for all that is perceived to go wrong in their children's growth (Caplan 44).Within this intricate discursive framework, mothers who are truly moral and dedicated to their families will be "blessed" with children who grow into acceptable Christian adults. Likewise, mothers whose children do not internalize and perform these precepts may be subject to blame and judgment, both as mothers and as women of faith.

Of course, the potential for resistance lies at the core of every power relationship (Foucault 82). To counter the patriarchal ideologies that continue to pervade North American evangelical traditions and institutions, evangelical feminists have long argued that the Bible actually supports an egalitarian approach to gender relations and that gender equality is a natural extension of the Christian faith (Gallagher 226, 230). In this sense, it is critical to consider women's capacities to appropriate, negotiate, and reject evangelical doctrines that do not reflect their religious knowledge or lived experiences. It is equally pertinent to explore how women may cultivate such resistance through the physical, intellectual, and emotional labour that constitutes their religious motherwork.

BLOGGING AND THE EVANGELIZING IMPERATIVE

Accordingly, this chapter explores how evangelical women use the blogosphere's fluid and dynamic space to resist oppressive religious doctrines and renegotiate the meanings of "good" womanhood and motherhood. Broadly speaking, evangelicalism mandates that individual Christians must accrue converts for "the body of Christ" by sharing God's truth with everyone they meet. In addition, the desire to be politically and culturally influential has been a key defining characteristic of evangelicalism from its very onset, with its revivalist discourse of being "in" but not "of" the world (Cochran 7). In a contemporary North American context, this imperative is, perhaps, most visible in evangelical leaders' astute appropriation of media technologies in their efforts to expand their church communities in the capitalist marketplace and share their teachings with mass audiences (Gallagher). In this capacity, media consumption has become a fundamental aspect of religious life (Corrigan et al. 11).

Propagating evangelical doctrines through internet platforms, such as blogs, serves as a modern manifestation of the evangelizing imperative. Indeed, as Lorne Dawson and Douglas Cowan posit, "The Internet is changing the face of religion worldwide. This is a simple but very important claim" (1). Religious blogs in particular have seen significant growth in the past decade (Joonseong 97), which has generated widespread concern regarding the legitimacy and authenticity of religious bloggers' authority (Corrigan et al. 4) as well as the extent to which such bloggers challenge "traditional" forms of religious authority (Campbell 251). Heidi Campbell argues that the question of the internet's impact on religious authority is a complex one. Although some blogs do critique religious leaders, structures, and texts, Campbell's research reveals that many Christian bloggers affirm traditional religious authorities and doctrines more often than challenge them (270-272). Karine Barzilai-Nahon and Gad Barzilai similarly argue that religious communities tend to use the Internet and other media technologies to affirm traditional beliefs rather than to challenge them (26-27).

POST-EVANGELICALISM AND BLOGGING AS RESISTANCE

The potential for women to challenge patriarchal evangelical doctrines through their blogging practices warrants critical investigation. To explore these possibilities, I conducted a feminist critical discourse analysis (Naples 28; Weiss and Wodak 5, 14) of four popular religious blogs, which are authored by evangelical women who are mothers. Importantly, I selected blogs that operate within a post-evangelical discursive framework. Initially coined by Dave Tomlinson, this term refers to "people who struggle with the restrictions in evangelical theology, spirituality, and church culture—yet who still want to journey with the Christian faith."

The selected blogs primarily explore the authors' personal contentions with dominant evangelical doctrines. Even though the selected bloggers identify as Christian, they consider themselves to be outsiders from their evangelical subcultures and, consequently, from the institutions of "good" womanhood and motherhood (Rich 37), which are central to Christian patriarchy. I purposefully selected entries that address how these bloggers navigate their fluid and ambivalent religious beliefs as well as how they understand and perform religious motherwork in light of their shifting religiosities. In this way, the selected blogs challenge patriarchal ideologies that laud the importance of the maternal role while devaluing women themselves within a Complementarian gender hierarchy.

POST-EVANGELICAL "WOMEN OF VALOUR"

None of the selected bloggers addresses the pervasiveness of Complementarian theology, as well as her post-evangelical stance on the matter, as directly as Joy Bennett, a freelance writer and editor who is based in Ohio. In her now defunct blog, *Joy in This Journey,* she contends, "*Women are subordinate but not inferior. The weaker sex. Created equal in value while called to a role of lower (or no) authority.*" Evangelica Christians call these ideas about women (and men) 'complementarianism' or the complementarian view of gender roles" ("The Achilles Heel of Complementarian Theology.") She goes on to explain that "I'm an insider, having been immersed in complementarian theology from birth. I know it inside and out. I'm also an outsider. I've stepped back from this theology to consider alternative interpretations. I am not blindly following but can see and describe the strengths and weaknesses of all the views." In a similar post, she critiques the underlying hypocrisy that drives Complementarianism, therein challenging the movement's mandate that men and women are "separate but equal":

> Despite vigorous assertions that the church and the world supports women and sees them as equal and valuable, the truth is that rules like this only apply to men. When I am proactive ... I get my head patted, my hand slapped, or horror of horrors, called a "feminist." (As if that's a bad word. *Of course I'm a feminist.* Your point?). ("Great Things Come to Those Who Act")

In this regard, reclaiming or renegotiating the meaning of the term "feminist" provides a key discursive strategy for challenging Complementarian ideals of "good" womanhood. Sarah Bessey, a freelance writer and editor who is based in British Columbia, dedicates considerable space in her blog to problematizing how feminism is unjustly demonized within her evangelical subculture. To counter the pervasive assumption that embracing feminism is a concession to the "secular world," Bessey validates her feminist identity by constructing it as a natural outflow of her Christian beliefs: "My first allegiance isn't to feminism," she explains. "My first allegiance is to Jesus and his Kingdom. Following Jesus changed my feminism, not the other way around" ("In Which I Choose to Be a Feminist"). She also problematizes the anti-feminist rhetoric that pervades evangelicalism by reclaiming feminism as a positive social force: "I'm a Jesus-following, joy-filled feminist. My eyes are full of God's daughters, worldwide, making space for goodness, mercy, justice, wholeness" ("In Which I'm No Angry Feminist").

Similar to Bennett, Bessey also draws from her lived experience to critique Complementarian doctrines of "good" womanhood: "I can't tell you how many women I hear from who are trapped in abusive or unhealthy or broken homes but feel unable to leave because they simply have no way to support themselves or their children," she contends. "Their lives are still dependent on the good will of a man. ... The consequences of this damaging theology are legion but lately I've been reminded afresh just how much of a price women pay when they are kept powerless" ("Have Your Own Truck").

Kathy Escobar, an ordained pastor who co-leads an "eclectic faith community" in Colorado, wages similar critiques on the sexist beliefs and practices that pervade evangelical subcultures. She particularly addresses the existence of "white privilege, male privilege, straight privilege, and economic privilege" ("Privilege") in evangelical institutions, just as she names and problematizes patriarchy as a "deeply grooved pattern of male-dominated leadership that damages women ... [and] is strongly embedded into our culture whether we acknowledge it or not" ("The Problem of Patriarchy"). Jessica Bowman, a freelance writer who is currently based in British Columbia, also recounts the Complementarian theology which pervaded her evangelical subculture while growing up in the southern United States. Throughout various posts on her blog, *Bohemian Bowmans,* she critically addresses evangelicalism's narrow views on women's reproductive rights ("Pro-Life Christians") and marriage equality ("Dear Chick-Fil-A"). She also critiques Complementarian gender norms: "I'm really not sure when I first started questioning this conservative, patriarchal interpretation of the Christian life," she explains. "While no one was claiming that our calling as Proverbs 31 women was easy or even fair, it couldn't be argued with. It was our lot in [Eve's] curse" ("Feminism Schfeminism").

In this respect, the bloggers' rejection of Complementarian gender roles is pointedly expressed in their critiques of how the "wife of noble character," described in Proverbs 31, is lauded as the ideal of contemporary womanhood in their evangelical subcultures. For instance, Escobar argues that "evangelical Christianity has created a lot of divided women ... who love God but aren't sure God really loves us just-as-we-are because we've been bombarded with teaching about our depravity and eve-nature and how we need to be more like Proverbs 31" ("Ex-Good Christian Women").

In addition to critiquing the problematic ways that Proverbs 31 is interpreted and applied in evangelical subcultures, the selected bloggers also work to reclaim the meaning of this text. Rachel Held Evans, a fellow post-evangelical blogger, dedicated a series of posts in 2012 to reclaiming the term "woman of valour" by contextualizing Proverbs 31 as a "blessing, not a to-do list,"[11] in accordance with the passage's significance in Jewish traditions. This reclamation of Proverbs 31 was taken up by Bennett as she defended Evans against her Complementarian critics ("Nine Must-Read Books by Christian Women"), as did Bessey, who stated in a 2013 post that "Ever since Rachel wrote about the true meaning of 'woman of valour' of Proverbs 31, I've used that phrase in all corners of my life" ("In Which I Add 'Ish Gibor Chayil!' to Our Lexicon").

POST-EVANGELICAL "MOTHER OUTLAWS"

In addition to critiquing evangelical precepts of "good" womanhood, the selected bloggers also construct themselves as "outlaws" (Rich 195) to the evangelical institution of motherhood. In contrast to the ideology that "good mothers" must reproduce the patriarchal social order in the next generation of "true" Christians, these bloggers reclaim the meaning of religious motherwork as they navigate their own shifting beliefs and worldviews. For instance, Escobar challenges the Complementarian belief that raising children within a heterosexual marriage covenant constitutes a woman's primary life purpose, just as she problematizes the belief that caring for "biological" children is the only authentic way to mother:

> Having children often becomes the ultimate pinnacle of womanhood, especially Christian womanhood. This pushes an awful lot of women to the margins and dishonours all that we were created to be beyond making babies. Women are … strong, tender, wise, beautiful, compassionate, creative, powerful, brave, messy. Kids, no kids, single, married, gay, straight, rich, poor, educated, uneducated, divorced, widowed, young, old—it makes no difference. ("There Are Lots of Ways to Mother").

Bessey similarly contests the Complementarian expectation that "true" Christian women are innately maternal and find enjoyment in all aspects of motherhood. She reflects on the ambivalence that shapes her motherwork each day as well as on her need to individuate herself within the maternal role: "Mothering is very, very hard work," she explains. "It's constant. It's tiring. Mothering will expose the parts of your heart that you can keep politely hidden from general society." She further contends that "I enjoy mothering because I don't expect to find my worth and my value here. … It's so vital for me to find these pockets of my own personhood in the midst of the daily work of life together to ensure that I enjoy mothering" ("In Which These Are My Practices of Mothering").

To that end, Bessey also draws from her lived experience to problematize the evangelical belief that devout Christians will be blessed with good health and visible prosperity. For instance, after discovering that she was unexpectedly pregnant, she confesses that "I have three [children] and this is my eighth pregnancy. Those kinds of odds can mess with a woman." She further shares how

> Over these weeks, I felt like a fragmented woman, believing and unbelieving all at once. … I don't believe I can control God through prayer or through faith, I don't believe God is waiting for me to "prove" that I have enough faith or know enough Bible verses to argue the points. … Still I wonder about faith and the nature of prayer, I still hold

> my understandings loosely. … After all, if I say that God performed a miracle this time [if my baby survives], what does that mean for my other babies, the ones I never got to hold except in my folded-up tea towels? I can't forget them. ("Flutters of Faith")

In sharing the challenges that she has encountered while caring for her now deceased oldest daughter, Bennett similarly challenges the prosperity gospel paradigm which informs the evangelical maternal ethos: "I've always been a capable person with the full calendar and resume to prove it. But ever since our oldest daughter was born with life-threatening complications, it was like having someone press my nose into the mud of my personal weakness and hold it there." She goes on to explain how

> Once I started looking for it, I discovered that this thread of I-don't-need-help independence weaves through the American national identity and it influences how Christianity enters and merges with that national identity. … This American-Christian halfbreed teaches that we can do anything if God is on our side. … It idolizes independence. And it culminates in the false gospel, "*God won't give you more than you can handle.*" …American Christianity told me that the perfect Christian, woman, wife, and mother was someone who could handle everything herself. … But by telling me "God won't give you more than you can handle," this false gospel also taught me that my failures were my fault. If I couldn't handle something, it was because I was a bad Christian. ("Independence")

In a similar vein, Bowman encourages her readers to speak about their lived experiences in an effort to debunk oppressive parenting ideologies, such as the evangelical belief that children are innately sinful and in need of strict discipline: "Christians are often in opposition [to grace-based parenting], especially the authoritarian heavy, pro-spanking, spare-the-rod-spoil-the-child types," she contends. "Which is why I think it's SO important for more Christians to speak out about not only having veered off the authoritarian path to pursue a more gentle method of discipline, but that it was their Christian faith that laid that burden and conviction on their heart to begin with" ("Gentle Christian Parents"). She also contests the belief that "true" Christian women will find ultimate joy and fulfilment in the maternal role. She calls on her readers to be patient and compassionate with themselves when they struggle with mothering:

> [When assessing my worth and success as a mother] I discount all of the times when I was patient, loving, or kind. And all I can see are the times when I'm quick tempered, tired, and frustrated. I start to think that 100% of my relationships with my children are made up of these negative moments. Yes, I fail. Everyone fails. ... There has never been a perfect mother in the history of the world. ("I'm a Failure as a Mother")

Along this trajectory, since mothers are expected to reproduce "acceptable" children for their evangelical subcultures by modelling and instilling biblical values, performing religious enculturation proves challenging for the selected bloggers as they navigate their shifting religiosities. For instance, Bennett reflects on how her personal faith struggles have made her day-to-day mothering experiences more complex. In a post that is addressed as a letter to her children, she confesses:

> When you talked about your doubts, I heard you speak my own words back to me. ... In my mind's ear, I hear angry preachers yelling "God hates you" and "babies are vipers in diapers" the way you heard them. I'm instantly haunted by all those arrogant churchy words I absorbed for so many years about the depravity of humans, our spiritual deadness, and God's wrath and hatred of sin and sinners. I taught you about a wrathful God who hates the human beings God made and condemns them to eternal judgment unless they submit to him. No wonder you fear making the wrong choice. No wonder you don't believe that Jesus loves you. I have been so caught up in untangling

> the lies I have believed about myself and God that I didn't see how you were tangled up in them too. ("I Taught You to Be Afraid")

Escobar similarly recounts how difficult it was to navigate her "faith shift" while mothering her children. She confesses: "I wish I had just [told my children] the truth: 'I am going through a really weird season in my faith where I am struggling with God and the church, but I am going to be okay. We're going to be okay.'" She further elucidates the joy and enrichment that she now derives from engaging in open and authentic dialogue with her children as they discuss their shared questions and doubts:

> *It's good to loosen our grip on these things, defuse power struggles, and let our kids participate in their faith development in a more organic way....* It's so hard to parent through a faith shift! It's scary, and my heart hurts for all of the suffering many parents have endured wondering if their choices were going to damage the kids. It's important to let go of perfectionism and control when it comes to this important task. We will mess things up. We will make mistakes. We will feel afraid. But in the end, the best we can offer is modeling our own authentic faith. ("Faith Shifts")

CONCLUDING THOUGHTS AND FUTURE DIRECTIONS

This brief chapter has explored how a selection of post-evangelical bloggers challenges the dominant Complementarian theological paradigm which shapes tenets of "good" womanhood and motherhood within evangelical subcultures. By drawing from their own lived experiences to debunk the ideologies that pervade Christian patriarchy, these women problematize the evangelical maternal ethos. Furthermore, by directly naming and contesting the expectations that govern Complementarian evangelical doctrines, these bloggers construct the religious motherwork that they perform in light of their personal "faith shifts" as acts of resistance.

In this sense, this chapter raises significant questions about the potentials for religious women to use the blogosphere's fluid and dynamic space to forge meaningful connections with one another and speak authoritatively about their knowledge and experience. To be sure, this potential should not be romanticized: although internet technologies may extend the geographical and interpersonal boundaries of religious communities, the abilities to access and produce web content are always mediated by structures of economic class, race, and gender as well as particular technical, social, and cultural skills (Lövheim and Linderman 125). To that end, it can be presumed that the privileges associated with the selected bloggers' shared status as white, educated, cisgendered, able-bodied, married, and heterosexual women who reside in North America contribute to the size of their evangelical readerships. This status also likely provides them with a degree of authoritative "legitimacy," despite their gender identities and their post-evangelical standpoints. It is, therefore, critical for future studies to investigate how blogs authored by women who are marginalized by intersecting identity markers—and particularly those who do not reside in the West, given the exponential growth of evangelicalism in the global South[12]—problematize and negotiate Complementarian evangelical doctrines.

Even so, it is critical to acknowledge how online spaces may provide opportunities for women to speak authentically about their lived experiences and problematize their patriarchal religious subcultures. For instance, in Bennett's final post before closing her blog in 2015, she reflects on her experiences starting *Joy in This Journey* while caring for her oldest daughter's special needs and coping with the spiritual abuse that she experienced in institutional church. In this way, authoring a blog has provided invaluable opportunities for her personal growth, both as a mother and as a woman of faith:

> Back [when I started this blog] in 2004/2005, I desperately needed to connect with people, and with myself. Our oldest daughter was critically ill, in and out of the hospital so often I kept a bag packed by the door. ... We were dealing with things like feeding tubes and heart arrhythmias, seizures and occupational therapy, IEPs and wheelchairs. No one else I knew had any of that in their vocabulary. ... The

> blog gave me a place to process this unexpected parenting journey. The act of writing helps me organize my thoughts and corral the worst case scenarios I concocted with such ease. … This blog has been invaluable. It introduced me to some of my best friends and served as therapy as I worked through the most challenging and painful years of my life. ("Closing Time")

It is clear that the post-evangelical blogosphere has the potential to provide empowering opportunities for woman "faith-shifters" to foster community, share their personal narratives, and affirm their religious motherwork. This chapter thus presents auspicious possibilities for future research that seeks to understand and connect with the many "women of valour" whose invaluable knowledge and labour are transforming religious institutions and communities across the globe.

NOTES

[1]Feminist theologian Mary Bednarowski defines cultivated ambivalence as a "triple task" in women's religious thought. It includes conserving a tradition's core values and insights while maintaining a critical distance from it, as well as imagining new possibilities for moving forwards. For further reading see her 1999 text *The Religious Imagination of American Women* (20).
[2]For further reading on subcultural identity theory and its relevance in understanding contemporary North American evangelicalism, see Christian Smith's 1998 text *American Evangelicalism: Embattled and Thriving.*
[3]Although fundamentalism is a fluid and contentious term, it can be initially traced to the conservative evangelical movement that transpired throughout the late nineteenth and early twentieth centuries in Britain and North America (Castells 21; Sandeen 106). Broadly speaking, Christian fundamentalism as theological praxis is distinguished by its reliance on literal biblical exegeses as well as its resistance to societal changes that undermine "traditional" beliefs and practices (Bauer 228, 237; Gerami 27-28; Hardacre 129; Sandeen 103).

[4]For a definitive evangelical-Complementarian manifesto, see John Piper and Wayne Grudem's edited collection *Recovering Biblical Manhood and Womanhood: A Response to Evangelical Feminism.*
[5]For further reading, see my article "Guardians of Virtue: Historicizing the Evangelical Maternal Ethos and Exploring the Empowering Potentials of Religious Mothering."
[6]As with any discourse that enjoys dominant status in a given cultural context, North American evangelicals may adopt and reject various aspects of the "prosperity gospel." Popular evangelical authors and speakers, such as Joel Osteen and Joyce Meyer, are often regarded as proponents of this paradigm, whereas others, such as Francis Chan, refute it. On the whole, this research reveals that the prosperity gospel paradigm is often endorsed in practice if not always in theory by dominant evangelical precepts.
[7]In this capacity, the evangelical prosperity gospel paradigm similarly supports the pervasive North American ideology that social mobility can be attained by any individual through virtuous hard work and sacrifice.
[8]For a contemporary evangelical perspective on children's innately depraved spiritual natures, see Michael and Debi Pearl's 1994 manual *To Train Up a Child.* It should be noted that this text and its corresponding ideologies do not encapsulate the beliefs of all evangelical Christians; however, it does reflect a prevalent childrearing discourse within evangelical circles, and it remains a popular text among evangelical parents.
[9]I refer to the pedagogical reproduction of religious beliefs, values, and traditions within evangelical subcultures as "enculturation," in contrast to the more frequently used term "socialization." Although the latter term broadly refers to the process of teaching children about societal norms and roles, enculturation refers, here, to the intergenerational reproduction of beliefs and values that are particular to a given culture or subculture. I contend that religious enculturation is a process distinct from socialization within evangelical subcultures because these groups tend to argue that mainstream secular society deliberately undermines their religious worldview. In this sense, evangelical subcultures acknowledge aspects of mainstream socialization ("this is what the secular society wants you to do") so that such values can be

repudiated through religious enculturation ("this is what God wants you to do").

[10]I employ the term "motherwork" in accordance with Molly Ladd-Taylor's text *Mother-Work: Women, Child-Welfare, and the State, 1890-1930*, referring to women's unpaid work of reproduction and caregiving. I similarly use "religious motherwork" to refer to the intellectual and emotional reproductive work that women perform with their children through processes of religious enculturation.

[11]See Rachel Held Evans's "Women of Valor" blog series.

[12]For further reading, see the edited collection *Evangelicals Around the World: A Global Handbook for the 21st Century.*

WORKS CITED

Bammert, Gaye M. "Narrating the Church." *Journal of Feminist Studies in Religion* 26.2 (2010): 153-174. Print.

Barzilai-Nahon, Karine and Gad Barzilai. "Cultured Technology: The Internet and Religious Fundamentalism." *Information Society* 21.1 (2005): 25-40. Print.

Bauer, Janet L. "The Mixed Blessings of Women's Fundamentalism: Democratic Impulses in a Patriarchal World." *Mixed Blessings: Gender and Religious Fundamentalism Cross Culturally*. Eds. Judy Brink and Joan Mencher. London: Routledge, 1997. 221-256. Print.

Bednarowski, Mary Farrell. *The Religious Imagination of American Women*. Bloomington: Indiana University Press, 1999. Print.

Bennett, Joy. "Closing Time." *Joy in This Journey.* WordPress, 30 Jan. 2015. Web. 3 Mar. 2015.

Bennett, Joy. "Great Things Come to Those Who Act Unless You're a Woman." *Joy in This Journey.* WordPress, 1 July 2012. Web. 3 Mar. 2015.

Bennett, Joy. "I Taught You To Be Afraid: A Letter to My Children." *Joy in This Journey.* WordPress, 16 Mar. 2014. Web. 20 Mar. 2015.

Bennett, Joy. "Independence: The False Gospel Destroying American Christianity." *Joy in This Journey.* WordPress, 15 July 2014. Web. 20 Mar. 2015.

Bennett, Joy. "Nine Must-Read Books by Christian Women." *Joy in This Journey.* WordPress, 16 Nov. 2012. Web. 20 Mar. 2015.

Bennett, Joy. "The Achilles Heel of Complementarian Theology." *Joy in This Journey.* WordPress, 30 June 2014. Web. 20 Mar. 2015.

Bessey, Sarah. "Flutters and Faith." *Sarah Bessey*. N.p., 22 Oct. 2014. Web. 20 Mar. 2015.

Bessey, Sarah. "Have Your Own Truck: On Empowering Our Children." *Sarah Bessey*. N.p., 27 May 2015. Web. 20 Mar. 2015.

Bessey, Sarah. "In Which I Add 'Ish Gibor Chayil!' to Our Lexicon." *Sarah Bessey*. N.p., 16 Feb 2013. Web. 20 Mar. 2015.

Bessey, Sarah. "In Which I Choose to Be a Feminist in The Way That Jesus Would Be a Feminist." *Sarah Bessey*. N.p., 25 July 2013. Web. 8 Mar. 2015.

Bessey, Sarah. "In Which I'm No Angry Feminist." *Sarah Bessey*. N.p., 7 May 2012. Web. 8 Mar. 2015.

Bessey, Sarah. "In Which These Are My Practices of Mothering." *Sarah Bessey*. N.p., 8 Aug. 2011. Web. 8 Mar. 2015.

Bowman, Jessica. "Dear Chick-Fil-A, I Just Want to Eat More Chicken." *Bohemian Bowmans*. N.p., 26 July 2012. Web. 10 Apr. 2015.

Bowman, Jessica. "Feminism Schfeminism." *Bohemian Bowmans*. N.p., 25 Feb. 2013. Web. 20 Mar. 2015.

Bowman, Jessica. "Gentle Christian Parents." *Bohemian Bomans*. N.p., 12 Mar. 2013. Web. 20 Mar. 2015.

Bowman, Jessica. "I'm a Failure as a Mother and So Are You." *Bohemian Bowmans*. N.p., 18 May 2011. Web. 10 April 2015.

Bowman, Jesseica. "Pro-Life Christians: You're Doing It Wrong." *Bohemian Bowmans*. N.p., 3 May 2013. Web. 10 Apr. 2015.

Campbell, Heidi A. "Religious Authority and the Blogosphere." *Journal of Computer-Mediated Communication* 15.2 (2010): 251-276. Print.

Caplan, Paula. *Don't Blame Mother: Mending the Mother-Daughter Relationship*. New York: Harper and Row, 1989. Print.

Castells, Manuel. *The Power of Identity (The Information Age: Economy, Society, and Culture Vol 2)*. Oxford: Blackwell, 1997. Print.

Cheong, Pauline Hope, Alexander Halavais and Kyounghee Kwon. "The Chronicles of Me: Understanding Blogging as a Religious

Practice." *Journal of Media and Religion* 7.3 (2008): 107-131. Print.

Cochran, Pamela D. H. *Evangelical Feminism: A History.* New York: New York University Press, 2005.

Colaner, Colleen Warner, and Steven M. Giles. "The Baby Blanket or the Briefcase: The Impact of Evangelical Gender Role Ideologies on Career and Mothering Aspirations of Female Evangelical College Students." *Sex Roles* 58 (2007): 526-534. Print.

Corrigon, John, David Morgan, Mark Silk, and Rhys H. Williams. "Electronic Media and the Study of American Religion." *Religion and American Culture* 16.1 (2006): 1-24. Print.

Dawson, Lorne L. and Douglas E. Cowan. "Introduction." *Religion Online: Finding Faith on the Internet.* Eds. Lorne L. Dawson and Douglas E. Cowan. New York: Routledge, 2004. Print.

Escobar, Kathy. "Ex-Good Christian Women." *Kathy Escobar.* N.p., 31 May 2012. Web. 8 Mar. 2015.

Escobar, Kathy. "Faith Shifts: What about the Kids?" *Kathy Escobar.* N.p., 17 Nov. 2014. Web. 8 Mar. 2015.

Escobar, Kathy. "Privilege." *Kathy Escobar.* N.p., 13 July 2012. Web. 8 Mar. 2015.

Escobar, Kathy. "The Problem of Patriarchy and Living the Solution." *Kathy Escobar.* N.p., 24 Oct. 2012. Web, 8 Mar. 2015.

Escobar, Kathy. "There Are Lots of Ways to Mother." *Kathy Escobar.* N.p., 11 May 2013. Web. 8 Mar. 2015.

Evans, Rachel Held. "Woman of Valour Blog Series." *Rachel Held Evans.* N.p., 3 Sept. 2012. Web. 25 Sept. 2015.

Foucault, Michel. *The History of Sexuality: An Introduction (Vol. 1).* New York: Random House, 1976. Print.

Franks, Myfanwy. *Women and Revivalism in the West: Choosing "Fundamentalism" in a Liberal Democracy.* New York: Palgrave, 2001. Print.

Friedman, May. *Mommyblogs and the Changing Face of Motherhood.* Toronto: University of Toronto Press, 2013. Print.

Gallagher, Sally K. *Evangelical Identity and Gendered Family Life.* New Brunswick: Rutgers University Press, 2003. Print

Gerami, Shahin. *Women and Fundamentalism: Islam and Christianity.* New York: Garland, 1996. Print.

Hardacre, Helen. "The Impact of Fundamentalisms on Women,

the Family, and Interpersonal Relations." *Fundamentalisms and Society: Reclaiming the Sciences, the Family and Education*. Eds. R. Scott Appleby and Martin E. Marty. Chicago: University of Chicago Press, 1993. 129-150. Print.

Joonseong, Lee. "Cultivating the Self in Cyberspace: The Use of Personal Blogs among Buddhist Priest." *Journal of Media and Religion* 8.2 (2009): 97-114. Print.

Ladd-Taylor, Molly. *Mother-Work: Women, Child-Welfare, and the State, 1890-1930*. Chicago: University of Illinois Press, 1994. Print.

Levitt, Mairi. "Sexual Identity and Religious Socialization." *The British Journal of Sociology* 46.3 (1995): 529-536. Print.

Lopez, Lori. K. "The Radical Act of 'Mommy Blogging': Redefining Motherhood through the Blogosphere. *New Media & Society 11* (2009): 729-747. Print.

Lövheim, Mia, and Alf G. Linderman. "Constructing Religious Identity on the Internet." *Religion and Cyberspace*. Eds. Morten Hojsgaard and Margit Warburg. New York: Routledge, 2005. 121-137. Print.

Morrison, Aimée. "Suffused by Feeling and Affect: The Intimate Public of Personal Mommy Blogging." *Biography* 34.1 (2011): 37-55. Print.

Naples, Nancy. *Feminism and Method: Ethnography, Discourse and Activist Research*. New York: Routledge, 2003. Print

Pearl, Michael and Debi Pearl. *To Train Up a Child*. Pleasantville, TN: NGJ Ministries, 1994. Print.

Piper, John and Wayne Grudem, Eds. *Recovering Biblical Manhood and Womanhood: A Response to Evangelical Feminism*. Wheaton, IL: Crossway, 1991. Print.

Powell, Rebecca. "Good Mothers, Bad Mothers and Mommy Bloggers: Rhetorical Resistance and Fluid Subjectivities." *MP: A Feminist Journal Online* 2.6 (2010): 37-50. Print.

Reimer, Vanessa. "Guardians of Virtue: Historicizing the Evangelical Maternal Ethos and Exploring the Empowering Potentials of Religious Mothering." *Journal of Motherhood Initiative for Research and Community Involvement* 5.1 (2014): 275-290. Print.

Rich, Adrienne. *Of Woman Born: Motherhood as Experience and*

Institution. New York: Norton, 1976. Print.
Ruddick, Sara. *Maternal Thinking: Toward a Politics of Peace*. Boston: Beacon Press, 1995. Print.
Sandeen, Ernest R. *The Roots of Fundamentalism: British and American Millenarianism 1800-1930*. Chicago: University of Chicago Press, 1970. Print.
Smith, Christian. *American Evangelicalism: Embattled and Thriving*. Chicago: University of Chicago Press, 1998. Print.
Steiner-Aeschliman, Sherrie, and Armand L. Mauss, "The Impact of Feminism and Religious Involvement on Sentiment toward God." *Review of Religious Research* 37.3 (1996): 248. Print.
Tomlinson, Dave. "Post Evangelical." *The Bad Christian Manifesto*. WordPress., n.d. Web. 20 Apr. 2015.
Tomlinson, Dave. *The Post-Evangelical*. London: SPCL, 1995. Print.
Weiss, Gilbert, and Ruth Wodak. "Introduction: Theory, Interdisciplinarity and Critical Discourse Analysis." *Critical Discourse Analysis: Theory and Interdisciplinarity*. Eds. Gilbert Weiss and Ruth Wodak. New York: Palgrave Macmillan, 2003. 1-34. Print.

4. Praying for More

Motherhood in the American Quiverfull Movement

EMILY HUNTER MCGOWIN

DEBORAH AND DAN OLSON (not their real names) live in a midsized city in the U.S. Midwest. Although she had planned to have a career in public school teaching, Deborah never went back to the classroom after giving birth to their first child. She always wanted a large family, but it was only after they had difficulty conceiving that they decided to forgo birth control entirely. Now, they are open to as many children as God gives them, even though Deborah has had six "very difficult pregnancies." One of their children has an autoimmune disease that calls for major dietary restrictions, frequent doctor visits, and lots of worry. Because they live only on Dan's income, the Olsons consider finances a "constant problem." Yet Deborah says, "I would welcome another baby." In fact, she finds the prospect "thrilling." The only worry that she has is the toll that it would take on her body and the possibility that she may be prevented from caring for her family because of injury or surgery. Deborah Olson is pushed to her limit. She is concerned about the consequences of another pregnancy, yet she is eager for more children. And she is not the only one.

In her book, *Quiverfull: Inside the Christian Patriarchy Movement*, Kathryn Joyce describes the screen names of many mothers in the Internet chat rooms that she explored. Many called themselves "Praying for More" or something similar (161). This name is illuminating, not just because it describes well the Quiverfull mother's constant openness to having more children but also because it accurately describes the movement's general approach to motherhood. The Quiverfull movement's lived religion—that is, the way their Christian faith is practised in daily life—means that mothers birth and nurse children well into their forties, and they do this while serving as the household cook, maid, and administrator as well as the children's primary educator from preschool through to high school, and sometimes beyond. Thus, the Quiverfull mother is always, in a sense, "praying for more"—not only for more children, but also for the perseverance to carry on.

Yet as this chapter will argue, "praying for more" has another, less explicit valence within the lives of some Quiverfull mothers. I researched the lives of Quiverfull mothers through in-depth interviews from the fall of 2012 to the spring of 2015. My aim was fairly simple: to allow Quiverfull mothers to tell the stories of their life's work in their own words. I discovered that many families experience significant tension within their patriarchal discourse because of the expanded practice of motherhood at work in the Quiverfull subculture. That is to say, the "more" offered by Quiverfull motherhood sometimes strains and modifies the patriarchal model that the larger movement fervently promotes. This phenomenon is not unique to Quiverfull families; a number of scholars—including Judith Stacey, R. Marie Griffith, Brenda Brasher, Sally Gallagher, and Julie Ingersoll—have used ethnographic research to show that the experiences of women within patriarchal sectors of evangelicalism often defy tidy explanation (Stacey; Griffith; Brasher; Gallagher; Ingersoll). Despite appearances to the contrary, the construction of gender remains hotly contested within evangelical Protestantism, both in public and private settings. In this sense, this chapter is not promoting a novel thesis but expanding the scholarly field of vision to include data from a previously unexamined subculture within American evangelicalism.

I begin this chapter with a brief discussion of the origin and meaning of "Quiverfull" and an explanation of how I use the term, along with a summary of the ideal of motherhood offered by elite Quiverfull practitioners. Drawing on my ethnographic findings, I then present a general description of what the lives of Quiverfull mothers look like "on the ground." Finally, I conclude by discussing how the experiences of some Quiverfull mothers evidence tension with the movement's guiding patriarchal discourse. These experiences suggest that, in some cases, the overarching

Quiverfull patriarchal ideology is subverted by the mother-led nature of their daily lives.

WHAT IS QUIVERFULL?

As a social and cultural phenomenon, Quiverfull is an ideologically inflected subgroup that developed within the networks and organizations of the Christian homeschooling movement in America over the past thirty-five years. The neologism "Quiverfull" has its origin in the language of Psalm 127:3-5: "Children are a heritage from the Lord, offspring a reward from him. Like arrows in the hand of a warrior are children born in one's youth. Blessed is the man who fills his quiver with them. They will not be put to shame when they contend with their opponents in court" (New International Version Translation). This psalm and the "full quiver" principle are featured in *The Way Home: Beyond Feminism, Back to Reality*, a book by homeschooling pioneer Mary Pride. Pride treats motherhood and reproduction as part of woman's divinely ordained profession. Just as Sheryl Sandberg urged working women in 2013 to "lean in" to their careers, Pride urged Christian moms in the 1980s to "lean in" to stay-at-home motherhood, not just for their own happiness but also for the advancement of the Kingdom of God. In 1990, Rick and Jan Hess promoted the intentional "filling" of one's "quiver" with their book *A Full Quiver: Family Planning and the Lordship of Christ*. Over time, couples within the Christian homeschooling movement who followed these teachings began to use the word "Quiverfull" to describe their families. By the time Kathryn Joyce published her book *Quiverfull* in 2009, the word had been in use for about fifteen years.

But what exactly qualifies a family as Quiverfull? Although the lived religion of these families includes many things, three practices are central: homeschooling, pronatalism, and patriarchy. Homeschooling refers to the practice of educating one's children in one's home rather than in traditional brick and mortar schools. The mothers in private family homes conduct the vast majority of Christian homeschooling, even when they work with other families in co-operative programs. Pronatalism refers not simply to a willingness to have children or the desire for a large family but the intentional effort to have as many children as possible. Patriarchy, of course, is a term used in many ways in many different contexts and disciplines today. In reference to Quiverfull, however, patriarchy is a term practitioners openly embrace; it refers to their practice of "male headship" and belief in a gender-based hierarchical arrangement in the home, church, and broader world. Generally speaking, Quiverfull men are supposed to "lead," and women are supposed to support and follow male headship. Of course, many evangelical families in America practise one or two of these things without being Quiverfull; as such, a helpful way to conceptualize this discourse is to imagine that homeschooling, pronatalism, and patriarchy are circles in a Venn diagram. It is at the centre where all three circles overlap, and the lived religion of Quiverfull can be found.

THE QUIVERFULL CONSTRUCTION OF MOTHERHOOD

This section considers how motherhood is constructed within the movement's literature and draws on sources authored by cultural elites—that is, the people with the most cultural influence through their organizations, publications, and status. For the Quiverfull construction of motherhood, two interrelated elements are central: 1) the dual role of wife and mother (and they are, indeed, inseparable) is fully constitutive of womanhood, and 2) because of their role as wives and mothers, women exist primarily for the purpose of helping men.

To begin, Quiverfull writers assert that God has commanded motherhood from the creation of humanity. God's directions to the first humans to "be fruitful and multiply" (Genesis 1:28) are understood to be applicable to all people, at all times, and in all places. Thus, married couples must seek to have children, and women are commanded to become mothers. Moreover, the command to motherhood is assumed to be a command to *prolific* motherhood, which follows the belief that God has complete control over the reproductive process (Hess and Hess 23). In the words of the Botkin sisters, "As Christian women, we should pray to have several children and not limit God in how He wants to bless" (Botkin and Botkin 292). Although the inability to conceive is acknowledged as a reality for some women, the state of "barrenness" is unambiguously considered a "curse" (Campbell 45; Hess and Hess 102). In addition, the salvation of women is tied directly to their obedience to prolific motherhood. As Pride says, "[By] persevering in our God-given role—childbearing—with a godly attitude, we will be saved. ... [H]aving babies and raising them is our role, and we show we belong to God by persevering in it" (Pride 41-42; DeMoss 171). Quiverfull elites, thus, cannot conceive of a Christian woman who does not fulfill the divine command to "be fruitful and multiply."

Of course, motherhood is not only divinely commanded but also a biological given. To be a woman is to be biologically designed for motherhood. As Nancy Campbell writes, "Women have been physically created by God to mother. God gave them the gift of womb and breasts. These are the most distinguishing characteristics of woman" (105). Since women's bodies were designed to mother, then only "real" women are mothers. Pride says it simply: "Childbearing sums up all our special biological and domestic functions.... Childbearing *is* woman's 'peculiar function'" (Pride 41-42). Although it is occasionally acknowledged that not all women will be married or bear children, "the exceptional circumstance ought not to redefine the ordinary, God-ordained social roles of men and women as created" (Phillips, Sproul Jr., and Lancaster). Moreover, women who do not become wives and mothers are to remain under the authority of their fathers, assist their mothers, and serve their families at home. In this capacity, even single women are defined in terms of mothering (Botkin and Botkin 219-220).

If motherhood is constitutive of womanhood because it is divinely commanded and biologically given, then motherhood is also the primary means by which women participate in Christian dominion over the earth. Among the most ardent Quiverfull proponents, motherhood is conceived as the Christian woman's "battle station" in the war against Satan and the debased American culture (Joyce 137). Even the adopted descriptor "Quiverfull" is a military metaphor. Mothers, therefore, give birth to, shape, and sharpen their children as "arrows" for spiritual combat (Campbell 81). The Botkin sisters conclude their book with the following description of motherhood: "Woman's hope and future is fulfilled through *motherhood....* We should think ahead, not only to our children but to our grandchildren and great-grandchildren, aspiring to be a mother of thousands of millions ... for the glory of God" (292-293).

Closely connected to the idea that motherhood is constitutive of womanhood is the Quiverfull conviction that women were created to be men's helpers. To be clear, Quiverfull elites do not simply argue that wives are helpers to their husbands, but that *all* women exist to help all men. In this sense, women do not have a purpose apart from their relationships to men. This reasoning is based primarily on literalist readings of Genesis 2 where the woman, Eve, is understood to be the perfect complement to the man, Adam. Of course, affirmations of male-female complementarity abound in Protestant, Catholic, and Orthodox theology, but the conclusions Quiverfull teachers draw from this idea are quite different. Jennie Chancey and Stacy McDonald write: "In all of her tasks, [a woman] seeks to further [her husband] as a man. His work of dominion is her work; she embraces his vision as her own as she promotes and enhances his life pursuits" (Chancey and McDonald 32). The Botkin sisters make this point even more forcefully: "[A] woman's life will always be tied into a man's life, whether she is married or not. This is a basic feature of womanhood, and women are to be dependent upon men's protection and leadership" (Botkin and Botkin 34).

Because of their inherent role as man's complement, Quiverfull elites conclude that all women are excluded from the exercise of authority over all men. Vision Forum, a recently dissolved organization that promoted the Quiverfull way of life, stated in their declaration on Biblical patriarchy because "Adam's headship over Eve was established at the beginning, before sin entered the world," male leadership applies in the home, the church, and society. Thus, "A God-honoring society will ... prefer male leadership in civil and other spheres as an application of and support for God's order in the formative institutions of family and church." Moreover, "[I]t is not the ordinary and fitting role of women to work alongside men as their functional equals in public spheres of dominion" (Phillips, Sproul Jr., and Lancaster). Thus, a necessary corollary of the assertion that women are, by nature, dependent on and completed by men is that women are barred from participation in "public spheres of dominion" (Phillips, Sproul Jr., and Lancaster). Because women were "created with a domestic calling," all women everywhere are designed by God to serve men by working within the home (Phillips, Sproul Jr., and Lancaster). This means that motherhood is the only way by which a woman may exercise "dominion" over the earth and contribute creatively to the world around her.

To summarize, Quiverfull elites see motherhood as fundamentally constitutive of womanhood. Due to God's design, to be a woman is to be a mother, even for women who never marry or bear children. Because of their God-given role as wives and mothers, women are universally understood to exist for the purpose of helping men. Therefore, among the most vocal Quiverfull proponents, women have no self or purpose apart from the men they serve, whether it be their fathers, husbands, brothers, or sons. Becoming a mother is the chief end of womankind, and the work of motherhood is relegated to serving the family's patriarch within the private sphere.

QUIVERFULL MOTHERHOOD IN PRACTICE

It is one thing to understand what Quiverfull elites say about motherhood, but it is quite another to see how it is practised in real life. In what follows, I offer five general characteristics of motherhood as it is experienced on the ground. As I said above, these generalizations are based on two and half years of ethnographic research with Quiverfull mothers. Of the many informants I worked with, three mothers were especially enthusiastic and willing to make themselves available for monthly in-depth interviews. Their stories are key in the analysis that follows. (Their names and some minor details of their stories have been changed to protect their anonymity.) Despite the depth such regular conversations provided, it is important to recognize that my participants do not constitute a sociological "sample" in any sense. Thus, what follows is a small window into the lived experience of some Quiverfull mothers, but it should not be viewed as representative of the movement as a whole.

What does it look like to be a Quiverfull mother? First, Quiverfull mothers are pregnant or nursing—or both—for up to three decades. Because they choose to forgo any kind of birth control to limit or space their children, Quiverfull mothers who are healthy and fertile can have children from their early twenties, when most of them are married, into their late forties. In this mode of motherhood, women's bodies are devoted to reproduction and infant care for up to thirty years. In the words of one mother: "[H]aving many children means that you never really stop having babies and it's just a way of life. It was just normal to me to have a baby on my hip or in my arms."

Of course, the consequences of the pronatalist commitment for women's bodies are significant. The stories of the moms featured in *Three Decades of Fertility: Ten Ordinary Women Surrender to the Creator and Embrace Life* contain lengthy explanations of the detrimental physical consequences that come with repeated childbearing: debilitating back pain, sciatica nerve pain, varicose veins, pubis-symphysis dysfunction (the movement or misalignment of the pelvis), hernias, adrenal fatigue, hormone imbalances, multiple miscarriages, depression, anxiety, and more. Some women continue to welcome pregnancy and childbirth despite being warned by medical professionals against it. In these stories, it is clear that the bodily work of repeated pregnancies can exact a heavy toll.

The second characteristic is that Quiverfull mothers approach motherhood as their only vocation, and caring for and educating children is their primary work for the majority of their adult lives. In theory, motherhood is not something that they can do alongside some other form of work; however, because of the financial strain of supporting a large family on the father's salary alone, some mothers take on occasional jobs. One of the mothers I interviewed cleans a home every week, and another teaches piano lessons on the side. Others sell cosmetics or homemade goods. But even in these cases, motherhood is viewed as a full-time job requiring all of one's attention and resources. When mothers are forced to work for pay, there is a general understanding that the more paid work they do, the less adequate they are as mothers. The accompanying unstated implication, of course, is that fatherhood is not a full-time job in the same way, and that men's work beyond the home does not affect their ability to father.

The third characteristic is that motherhood is, to some extent, professionalized. Most of the women that I interviewed do not see themselves as "just" stay-at-home moms but homeschooling moms, which is motherhood of a different sort. On the one hand, all mothers teach their children, from tying shoes to potty training to table manners. On the other hand, homeschooling mothers assume the task of being the primary educator of their children from preschool through high school. If they seek to approach the subjects taught by most public schools, homeschooling mothers will teach their children reading, writing, literature, mathematics (from long division to calculus), history (state, American, European, and world), geography, sciences (biology, chemistry, physics), government, economics, art, and music. In addition to the many subjects of study, there are also numerous educational pedagogies from which to choose: Montessori, Waldorf, classical education, unschooling, and more. Not all homeschooling mothers undertake all of these subjects, nor do all mothers develop a distinct pedagogy. But all of my informants spend countless hours preparing for their children's schooling, especially as they reach the higher grades. And they are teaching multiple ages at once: the kindergartener learning to read is working alongside the junior high student doing geometry. The mothers who approach this work with seriousness—which is most of them—end up pursuing homeschooling as a kind of professional vocation.

The fourth characteristic of Quiverfull motherhood is that the mother's body and work is the de facto centre of the household due to the practices of pronatalism and homeschooling. Although it is not uncommon in American life for the mother to be central to the family, this centrality increases in intensity in the Quiverfull family. The mother is pregnant or nursing most of the time and requires regular assistance from her husband and older children. She is responsible for everyone's education. She orders their days, determines their workloads, delegates their assignments, and dispenses their grades. She administers the housework, plans their voluntary church work, and organizes their extracurricular activities. And even though Quiverfull families strongly endorse the father as the "spiritual leader" of the family, it is usually the mother who provides regular religious education through Bible reading, prayers, and discipline of various kinds throughout the day. Thus, despite their devotion to patriarchy, many Quiverfull homes are functionally mother-centred.

Finally, the fifth characteristic of Quiverfull motherhood is, because of the mother-centered nature of the household, the older children and father are regularly—although not always—called upon to assist in household responsibilities. This seems particularly true of families with six or more children. In these situations, children are required to learn a degree of self-sufficiency from early on. Older children learn to cook, clean, and help care for their younger siblings. Similarly, younger children learn to respect older siblings as authority figures, for good or ill. Fathers are often required to do more than they would normally do in either a two-income household or a typical stay-at-home mom situation. With the mother occupied most of the day with her children's education, the household work becomes something that requires sharing if it is to get done. Certainly, not all Quiverfull fathers assist in this way, but all of my informants save one confirm their husbands' active involvement in household chores.

QUIVERFULL MOTHERHOOD AND PATRIARCHY

With a general picture in place of motherhood in the "full quiver," I will spend the rest of this chapter reflecting on the interaction between the performance of motherhood and the patriarchal ideology that is central to the Quiverfull discourse. My research suggests that two characteristics of Quiverfull motherhood described above can strain Quiverfull patriarchal discourse into incoherence: 1) motherhood is often professionalized through the practice of homeschooling, and 2) the "professional" mother often requires the help of others in the household. As I said above, the focus here is necessarily limited and these women's experiences cannot be generalized to represent the movement a whole. But their experiences do suggest that there is significant complexity to Quiverfull motherhood as it is practised in daily life.

Because the work of homeschooling gives mothers something that very much resembles a career, the "professional" homeschooling mother can acquire a degree of expertise and cultural respect. In her essay on homeschooling as religious practice, Colleen McDannell says, "Teaching becomes their profession. They no longer see themselves as simply housewives or mothers. They have found an occupation that is fully acceptable within their religious and cultural milieu" (210-211). This dynamic is born out in the lives of my informants. As the designated expert on the education of her children, the mother requires the respect and deference of her husband, even as she asserts her subservient role within the family.

In addition, there is also a sense in which the homeschooling endeavour domesticates—and perhaps even feminizes—the Christian patriarch. Men are expected to be the financial providers and spiritual leaders of the home, yet part of that expectation includes providing material assistance and moral support to their wives. And oftentimes this support is required not only in the work of education but also in the maintenance of the household. This can serve to tie some Quiverfull men closely to the domestic sphere, which encourages them to become adept in the feminized space of the home (McDannell 211). Thus, for some families, the discourse of patriarchy works itself out in surprisingly non-patriarchal ways.

Deborah, whom was introduced at the beginning of this chapter, is a mother of six and a strong proponent of patriarchy. For her, patriarchy begins with gender essentialism. She says,

> [Men] are different. They're made differently with different thoughts and wants and desires. And women, vice versa. Women do things differently, have different thoughts, wants, and desires. And I believe their roles are different. God created them to be different.... The story of creation makes it clear that the Lord expected woman to be an aid to the husband.... [I]t seems pretty clear to me that God made [men and women] like a puzzle to fit together. Of course, that makes it challenging to deal with. We're very different creatures.

Despite both being made in God's image and consisting of the same basic substance, men and women are so distinct, she argues, as to be "very different creatures." The distinction between the sexes is spelled out in terms of roles: men are meant to lead and women are meant to help.

When Deborah speaks in more detail about her marriage, though, her strident commitment to patriarchy becomes muddled. Dan has struggled throughout their marriage to control his temper. His anger is often expressed in loud outbursts and yelling, which he learned from his family. Deborah says that early in her marriage "it was very hurtful for me and I was crushed at first." They tried a few forms of counselling, but, eventually, she made it clear to him that such behaviour was simply "unacceptable." She relates the turning point in the following way:

> [A]t the end of the day I was just kind of snide about it: "My Bible says the fruit of the Spirit is self-control. Sink yourself deeper into his word and into his Spirit, and if you are there, then there is no way you'll be screaming at your wife and children." I think he was like, "Oh goodness, I've got a hard one now." [Laughter.] And I wasn't willing to make excuses for him. But now I think he's thankful that I was persistent in that mindset.

When I suggest to Deborah that her account of that struggle seems at odds with the doctrine of wifely submission, she laughs knowingly and replies:

> Submission is such a hard subject.... I'm passionate and intense and very opinionated and very bold and very wordy. My husband is not. He's a quiet guy.... [E]arly in marriage, submission was very difficult for me because I felt like I had a husband who hadn't arrived yet at adulthood. I felt like he hadn't even arrived yet as a Christian. I really wanted a God-centred marriage, and he just wanted me. [Laughter] We just had to grow into a pattern that ultimately became more pleasing to the Lord. Me learning where and when to tone it down and praying that the Lord would convict his heart because I could not be his Holy Spirit.... It's amazing the interaction between he and I now compared to then. It will be fifteen years this fall. There are a lot of areas where I don't say anything and he just chooses and does it. It took a lot of pruning on my part and growing on his part.

Deborah sees gender roles as fixed patterns of behaviour and activities that are the same for all people regardless of personality. Even though she is "passionate," "opinionated," and "bold," she has had to go through "a lot of pruning" in order to learn to defer to Dan's leadership. Their growth in their prescribed roles has allowed their marriage to become "more pleasing to the Lord." But if Deborah's forceful handling of Dan's anger problem does not seem like submission, she disagrees, saying, "[I]n no way would I define submission as a person without an opinion or a person led by a leash. I believe it has to do with me respecting the authority that the Lord gave Dan as the head of our home.... But I don't think the Lord would have given Adam a helpmeet that couldn't help him."

The result of Deborah's conviction that Adam's "helpmeet" is supposed to "help him" is that she has a significant amount of authority and influence within the marriage. When asked to describe the man's spiritual leadership, she says:

> I believe that man is placed as leader of the home whether we want him to be or not. He's still the leader regardless. Dan and I have struggled in the past, and I have said that to him, "You're the leader whether you want to be or not." God has placed me in [the role of mother]. It's not up to me to decide that. It's not that the man should be in charge of all of it. I'm the teacher in my home. I'm just naturally gifted and it's easier for me to communicate and teach.... When I say, "Men should take the lead," I mean they're ultimately responsible for [all that happens].

Although she is very much invested in the doctrine of male headship, the way Deborah articulates her conviction makes it clear that she is comfortable with the leadership that she exercises: "I'm the teacher in my home," she says. "I'm just naturally gifted." In the education of their children, Deborah is the leader and, in a very real sense, he is the "helpmeet." Also, Deborah frames Dan's headship as a role weighted with moral responsibility, not just for himself but also the rest of the family. She says, "[Dan's] the head of our home whether [or not he] does the right thing, which is why when he's doing the wrong thing we will suffer for it. I tell him, 'If you're not doing the things the Lord wants you to do, then we'll be suffering because of it.'" The rhetoric here is striking: the onus to behave rightly is placed squarely on her husband's shoulders with the added threat that his family will suffer if he is negligent in his duties. This parallels her resolute insistence that Dan deal with his anger management problems. Clearly, Deborah leverages both her work as a mother and the doctrine of male headship to obtain desired behaviour from her husband.

Another example comes from the experience of Carley Miller and her husband, David, who are also from the Midwest, and have seven children aged two to thirteen years. Although she, too, holds to Christian patriarchy, Carley describes patriarchy in caretaking rather than authoritarian terms. She explains: "Like a shepherd. They should lead gently. I wouldn't really put controlling in there at all. Like a gentle shepherd that follows the Lord." Carley also moderates her affirmation of male headship with the concept of mutual accountability to Christ. She says, "I think if a woman is married that the husband should be the head and the wife should be submissive, but I also think that each of us is an individual and accountable to Christ." For Carley, then, the doctrine of male headship is tempered by the equality of both sexes before Christ.

One of the results of this moderated patriarchal vision is that Carley also describes her marriage as a "partnership," and she admits that their partnership often defies traditional gender roles. She says:

> [David] does lead our house. We try really hard to bounce ideas off [each other]. I don't feel like he's the only one who makes the decisions, but I think we know that there's an underlying [expectation] that if he needed to put his foot down that I respect that. I think with the amount of children we have, some of the things that some people say men can't do—like do dishes and wash clothes and wash hair—those go by the wayside. We need both of us to make our house function. I've had a bout recently with a [chronic condition] and in survival mode David has done way more dishes than I have over the past year. And we know several families like that. It's not just a special case for us. We have good friends who, when you walk in the

> house, you know that he is pulling as much weight as she is and vice versa.... It's unspoken. There is no, "Honey, can you help me?" It just gets done.

Even as Carley asserts from the outset that David is the leader, it is clear that the work of homeschooling a large family leads the Millers to a pragmatic approach to gender roles. Because of Carley's first priority to educate seven kids, what matters is that household chores get done rather than who does them.

Although Deborah and Carley's narratives reveal how the lived experience of Quiverfull motherhood can lead to tensions within the practice of patriarchy, there are other times when these tensions lead to a rupture. Renee and Gary Tanner are in their mid-fifties and live in a small town in the Southwest. Renee married young and was captivated from early on by the Quiverfull vision for motherhood. She says, "I met Gary at seventeen and married him at eighteen.... [The Quiverfull way of life] gave me something big and exciting and a purpose. It gave a purpose to the male-female roles. It gave me something to do with my brains and talent." Over the course of twenty years, Renee gave birth to eleven children, now ranging in age from five to twenty-five.

Today, Renee recognizes that the amount of work expected of her was extraordinary, calling it the equivalent of "two or three full-time jobs." Despite the fact that Gary owns his own business, which allows him some flexibility, all of the responsibility for the home and children's education fell to her. She says, "Most all of it was on my shoulders.... [Some] men take on teaching responsibilities with their kids but most of the men in my generation didn't do anything. In our situation and with our personalities, I'm the one who does all of it. I was the only one thinking about it and working on it." Faced with the gargantuan task of caring for and educating eleven children with very little spousal support, Renee, eventually, let go of her belief in patriarchy. For her, time and experience proved that the Quiverfull ideal was unworkable. She explains:

> I started out thinking that patriarchy was the way to go.... But the men I see in my age group in the homeschooling movement aren't involved and aren't close to their chil-

> dren.... My husband didn't want to be the leader. [He'd say,] "Why should I do that? Why is all that my responsibility?" I probably would have been into patriarchy, but my husband wasn't one of those men. He just didn't do any of those things that patriarchs were supposed to do.... I mean, what woman doesn't want an amazing man who is godly, kind, strong, has all the answers, and leads the family? Anybody could stay pregnant and serve at home—heck, even serve him!—willingly. [Laughter.] But that didn't work out for me.

Rather than see the support and service of the patriarch increase through the expanded work of Quiverfull motherhood, Renee saw it break down. The leadership that she exercised in her maternal duties in the home actually decreased Gary's patriarchal presence. The literature of Quiverfull elites gives significant emphasis to the leadership of fathers and the significance of the father's role in the instruction of children. But according to her testimony, Renee's situation is not unique within the movement as a whole. She says, "I don't think it's uncommon nationwide for women to be more passionate [about Quiverfull] and the men to just go along with it." In Renee's experience, the women were the active, passionate leaders, whereas the men were more or less along for the ride. Regardless of her perspective on the larger movement, however, it is clear that the patriarchy of Quiverfull could not withstand Renee's lived experience of motherhood. The mother-centred nature of her daily life eventually compelled her to jettison patriarchy in favour of a more egalitarian vision of gender relations.

CONCLUSION

As different as the above narratives of Quiverfull motherhood are, they all reveal the instability of gender in American evangelical practice—a phenomenon already documented by a number of other scholars. My research expands this perspective by showing that notions and practices of patriarchy vary widely, even among the most ideologically conservative evangelicals. Because of the expanded practice of motherhood at the centre of the Quiverfull movement, many families unwittingly modify the patriarchal ideal to bring it into harmony with the mother-centred nature of their lived religion. This "domesticated" patriarchy is expressed mainly in terms of service and sacrifice—actions that have been traditionally associated with women—and male headship becomes functionally symbolic. In at least one case, patriarchy was entirely abandoned within the crucible of Quiverfull motherhood.

Nevertheless, it is important to state that not every Quiverfull family displays the tensions and modifications to patriarchy evidenced in my research. The negotiated gender dynamics on display in the lives of Renee, Carley, and Deborah occur within marriages that do not include patterns of manipulation, exploitation, or abuse. Moreover, neither partner suffers from mental illness. There are a growing number of women, mostly in online communities, who are speaking out about their abusive and oppressive experiences within Quiverfull families. None of my informants shared these experiences, but each of them could think of one or more families that they know who have unhealthy or abusive patriarchal home environments. It is vital, therefore, to keep in mind that although some Quiverfull marriages defy patriarchal gender roles, there are plenty of others that seek strict conformity to these ideals with treacherous results for women and their children.

In conclusion, this chapter has sought to contribute to the growing body of literature on motherhood in various religious contexts by focusing on the lived experience of mothers in the American Quiverfull movement. Quiverfull lived religion—centered as it is on homeschooling, pronatalism, and patriarchy—results in a radically expanded practice of motherhood. Indeed, women's bodies and prolific work in the home are crucial to maintaining their way of life, and their performance of motherhood often creates tension with their conception of male headship. Although sweeping generalizations are inappropriate at this point, it is clear that, despite the extremity of their ideological commitments, Quiverfull practitioners share with their American evangelical neighbours a tendency to modify gender norms based on the specific needs of their context. The practice of motherhood is one important arena where these renegotiations are taking place within the American Quiverfull movement.

WORKS CITED

Botkin, Anna Sofia and Elizabeth Botkin. *So Much More: The Remarkable Influence of Visionary Daughters on the Kingdom of God*. San Antonio, TX: Vision Forum, 2005. Print.

Brasher, Brenda. *Godly Women: Fundamentalism and Female Power*. New Brunswick, NJ: Rutgers University Press, 1998. Print.

Campbell, Nancy. *Be Fruitful and Multiply: What the Bible Says about Having Children*. San Antonio, TX: Vision Forum, 2003. Print.

Chancey, Jennie, and Stacy McDonald. *Passionate Housewives Desperate for God*. San Antonio, TX: Vision Forum, 2007. Print.

DeMoss, Nancy Leigh. *Lies Women Believe and the Truth that Sets Them Free*. Chicago, IL: Moody Publishers, 2002. Print.

Gallagher, Sally. *Evangelical Identity and Gendered Family Life*. Piscataway, NJ: Rutgers University Press, 2003. Print.

Griffith, Marie R. *God's Daughters: Evangelical Women and the Power of Submission*. Berkeley and Los Angeles: University of California Press, 1997. Print.

Hess, Rick, and Jan Hess. *A Full Quiver: Family Planning and the Lordship of Christ*. Brentwood, TN: Wolgemuth & Hyatt, 1990. Print.

Ingersoll, Julie. *Evangelical Christian Women: War Stories in the Gender Battles*. New York: New York University Press, 2003. Print.

Joyce, Kathryn. *Quiverfull: Inside the Christian Patriarchy Movement*. Boston: Beacon Press, 2009. Print.

McDannell, Colleen. "Creating the Christian Home: Homeschooling in Contemporary America." *American Sacred Space*. Eds. David Chidester and Edward T. Linenthal. Bloomington and Indianapolis: Indiana University Press, 1995. 187-219. Print.

Phillips, Douglas, R.C. Sproul Jr., and Philip Lancaster. "The Tenets of Biblical Patriarchy." *Vision Forum Ministries*. Vision Forum Ministries, n.d. Web. 2 Dec. 2010.

Pride, Mary. *The Way Home: Beyond Feminism, Back to Reality*. Westchester, IL: Crossway Books, 1985. Print.

Stacey, Judith. *Brave New Families: Stories of Domestic Upheaval in Late-Twentieth Century America*. Berkeley: University of California Press, 1990.

5.
Bridging Sacred Mystery and Medicine

The Role of Doulas in Contemporary Child Birthing

BRIDGET BOLAND

DOULAS STAND AT THE crossroads where the primordial magic of birth as a sacred rite of passage for mother, father, and baby intersects with the miracles of modern medical technology and interventions. The Greek word *doula* translates as "female slave" but, now, commonly refers to a woman who supports a mother through childbirth (Mander 113-133). Historically, women have acted as guides and aids to birthing mothers in most cultures throughout the world. These women have usually been relatives or members of the same community.

In 1992, Doulas of North America, one of the first doula training and certification organizations, was founded (Askren). A doula's job in contemporary Western society includes educating clients on pregnancy and birth, advocating for informed and empowered medical choices and decisions, offering emotional support, and providing comfort measures including massage, breathing techniques, and suggestions on positions for labour and delivery.

Western culture has recently seen a growing awareness of childbirth as a profound life experience. As a result, the role of doulas is expanding to include spiritual and energetic support. It is pertinent to note that in the U.S., where I practice, doulas are often hired by private clients who pay out of pocket for their services, so they are more popular among middle- and upper-class parents ("Doulas, a Mom's Best Friend"). However, some doulas offer discounted or pro bono care to indigent women. Hospital- and community-based programs also make doulas available to clients who are unable to afford private services (Ballen and Fulcher 304-311).

Doulas work within a wide variety of religious and spiritual traditions. The spiritual and energetic practices that I describe in this chapter come primarily from my training in Indigenous Peruvian shamanism. This chapter, thus, serves to educate readers about doula practices as well as to encourage those already working in the field to consider adopting some of the less common spiritual and energetic practices described herein. As a practising doula, Forrest Yoga teacher, and shamanic energy medicine practitioner for nearly fifteen years, I have come to believe that comfort measures and advocacy are just the beginning of what doulas can and should provide for their clients. I feel that as the understanding of pregnancy and birth evolve, doulas should "hold sacred space" or create a safe energetic "container" for the birthing family. The parents' and baby's souls participate together as conscious creators at conception as well as during childbirth. Shamans act as intermediaries between the natural and spiritual realms. They provide healing from psychic and/or soul wounding as well as opportunities for clients to access higher realms of conscious awareness. Shamanic and energetic processes—including conscious conception ceremonies, illuminations, decoupling, and soul retrievals—offer parents, babies, and their extended families tools for profound transformation. To explore these tools, this chapter draws from my experiences working with expecting mothers, their partners, and family members. All of the men and women mentioned in the chapter are my clients. Their names have been changed out of respect for their privacy.

THE HUMAN ENERGY FIELD, OR *AURA*, AND THE *CHAKRAS*

The human body is infused with energy running through pathways known in Chinese medicine as *meridians*, and in the yogic tradition as *nadis*. The body also sits within a magnetic energy field called an *aura*. The auric field contains multiple *chakras*, which are vortexes or funnel-like portals, wherein energy and information are exchanged between the human energetic and physical bodies and the life force energy in the surrounding environment (Brennan). Most modalities reference seven primary *chakras* on the human body: the first at the perineum; the second two inches below the navel; the third at the solar plexus; the fourth at the centre of the chest near the heart; the fifth in the throat; the sixth between the eyebrows, also called the "third eye"; and the seventh on the crown of the head.

From the moment of conception, the developing baby and its energy body are embedded within the womb of the mother's physical body and field. Energetic "cords," somewhat similar to the physical umbilicus, intimately connect the mother's energy to the child's long after the child is born and the umbilical cord is cut. Just as nourishment and other substances that the mother ingests permeate the blood barrier between her and her child, research shows how pregnant mothers' thoughts and emotions may seep into the growing baby's field (Davis et al.). Although no mother can be expected to be free of anxiety, fear, or stress throughout gestation, research suggests that it is in both the mother's *and* the baby's best interests to identify and work to minimize such emotions during this time. As emotional support persons, doulas are well-suited to provide beneficial energetic processes for optimal gestation and birth time.

ENERGETIC PRACTICES FOR CONCEPTION: CALLING THE BABY IN

When a mother is ready to welcome a child, performing a ceremony to "call the baby in" can be a powerful aid to conception. The most crucial time for optimizing the health of a baby is before or during conception (Baker). A doula can facilitate this short and easy ceremony by meeting with the mother and other prospective parents in their home. Lighting a candle and smudging the room with cedar or sage opens sacred space by clearing the environment of stale, lingering energy, and provides a clean container for the ceremony. It also signals to spiritual entities—such as spirit guides, deceased ancestors, and angelic beings—that a ceremony is taking place and spiritual support is requested for the family members. The doula can then invite prospective parents to sit on a yoga mat or blanket spread out on the floor or even on their bed. The woman wishing to become pregnant sits within her partner's legs so that her back is against her partner's chest. The partner then places his or her hands on the woman's abdomen, over the uterus, and the woman also places her hands on her lower belly. The doula can guide mother and partner through a visualization process, which encourages them to connect to the baby's spirit and to let the baby know that they are ready to welcome him or her into their lives. The doula can invite the couple to visualize the egg and sperm coming together any time that they try to conceive and to invite the baby's spirit to come into the fertilized egg. The couple can do this repeatedly during intercourse and also while sitting quietly together.

This powerful visualization process works whether the child is conceived naturally or with fertility services. My clients Susan and Chad recently chose to engage in this process a few days before Susan went in for in vitro fertilization. They reported that it helped them feel connected to each other as well as to the spirit of their hoped for baby. They also felt comforted as they prepared for the procedure as well as during the following two weeks before learning whether the procedure was successful.

Another wonderful way to "call a baby in" is to create a prayer bundle. My clients Dan and Linda chose this ceremony when they decided they wanted to become pregnant. We used a small baby blanket and other supplies—including flower petals and small bright candies, such as M&M's and Skittles, to represent the sweetness of life, cotton balls for the clouds and sky, salt for the tears and sadness of life, dried lentils, beans, and rice for the sustenance that comes from the earth, and sequins and confetti for a sense of celebration. I laid the blanket out on a table, and Dan and Linda sat in front of it. I invited them to pick up small handfuls of the various items and blow their deepest hopes, desires, and wishes for a baby into the objects and then to scatter them onto the baby blanket. The bundle took on a powerful energy of its own as it was built. Once the bundle felt finished, I folded the edges of the blanket over to hold in all the objects and tied it closed with a ribbon. Dan and Linda then buried the bundle in the earth beneath a tree. Couples can also burn these bundles in a ceremonial fire, allowing their prayers to be received by the earth, which births all into being.

PREGNANT WITH POSSIBILITY: DECOUPLING, ILLUMINATION, AND SOUL RETRIEVAL

Pregnancy and parenthood are often accompanied by a wide range of emotions, from awe to fear. Doulas can use various tools for handling these emotions, including the following: "decoupling," which quiets the fight-or-flight response of the central nervous system; "illumination," a technique for clearing stagnant energy out of physical and energetic bodies; and "soul retrieval," a deeper clearing and recapitulation process to help clients feel present and empowered throughout this extraordinary time.

Decoupling

Mia was thrilled when she discovered that she was expecting her first child. But along with her delight came intense dread. Her sister's baby had been stillborn—what if her infant would suffer the same fate? And if her baby was born healthy, how would she cope with the guilt when her sister had endured such a painful loss? At just eleven weeks pregnant, Mia was caught in a double bind. It seemed to her that no matter how her pregnancy and birth experience went, she would end up feeling badly. Her fears and lack of control over the outcome manifested as extreme anxiety, sleeplessness, and periods of deep sadness, which she confided to me during her first doula consultation.

I suggested that we start with the fear releasing process of decoupling. The process quiets the adrenal glands, which produce the stress hormones cortisol and adrenaline. It also soothes the central nervous system. Many people are in a state of fight-or-flight much of the time because of busy lifestyles and the stress levels that accompany them. When the body's fight-or-flight mechanism is activated even at a low level, it can impede the benefits of other energetic processes. Performing decoupling allows the other healing practices to be more effective. I have found that decoupling works effectively if done for at least five minutes, with thirty minutes producing optimal results. Many clients become so relaxed that they fall into a sleep state. A thirty minute session has been likened to a typical night's sleep in terms of its rejuvenating effects.

To begin Mia's session, I asked her to lie face up on the massage table. I connected my energy field to hers and asked for the ability to help her ease her worries in our session. Then I placed my right hand under her lower back, just above the sacrum, where the adrenals nestle against the kidneys. My left palm slipped up between her shoulder blades at the back side of the heart *chakra*. I invited Mia to breathe in deeply through her nose and out through her mouth. I quieted my mind and felt for the subtle but strong rhythmic beating of her heart. Once I sensed her heartbeat, I sent its reassuring energy down her spine in waves to soothe her adrenals and quiet her central nervous system.

Illumination

The process of "illumination" is a wonderful way to clear out old emotions so that they no longer affect present-day experiences. After I decoupled Mia for twenty minutes, I could sense from her body's relaxed state that her energy field was more open. I asked Mia to notice where her body was responding to her mixed emotions, particularly her dread and fear. Mia pointed to her heart, then after a moment pointed just below her navel as well. I used a pendulum to confirm that her second and fourth *chakras* were being affected by the strong negative feelings she associated with pregnancy and motherhood. I offered Mia a small amethyst stone to hold in her hand. I then invited her to call up the feelings related to pregnancy and childbirth in her body and to release them by blowing them into the amethyst. In this practice, the stone acts as a "container" to hold feelings without being harmed by them; unresolved emotions in the human energy field can lead to illness and disease.

Once Mia felt she had blown as much of these emotions out as possible, I took the stone back. I opened the second and fourth affected *chakras*, and then laid the stone over the fourth at the centre of her chest. I moved to the top of the table and gently cradled Mia's head with my hands to encourage a steady flow of energy down from her crown *chakra* at the top of her head through all the lower ones. I asked her to concentrate on releasing from her body and energy field any and all memories and feelings related to her double bind. The energy was released in waves as she breathed deeply. At one point she started to cry, which is another form of energetic release.

After about fifteen minutes, Mia's breathing slowed, as did the waves of energy moving off her. I removed the stone from her heart, poured golden healing light energy into the second and fourth *chakras*, and then rewound them closed. I invited Mia to sit up. She reported feeling lighter and brighter than prior to the illumination. Most importantly, for the first time, she felt that it was possible to enjoy her pregnancy and look forward to her birth time. The dread and fear were no longer hampering her joy anymore.

Soul Retrieval

"Soul retrieval" builds on the illumination process. It is a visualization tool for identifying deeply held fear-based beliefs meant to preserve safety or survival. These limiting beliefs are often created when people are very young and remain throughout adulthood. Life experiences sometimes offer "spontaneous" soul retrievals—epiphanies about life and how to operate in it, which empowers one to change and grow. Soul retrievals can also be performed as an energetic process. Several weeks after the illumination session, Mia chose to schedule a soul retrieval to help her discern any deep-seated beliefs that may be hampering her ability to fully enjoy becoming a mother.

In soul retrieval, I sit quietly with my client and journey into the client's unconscious using a visualization technique. Once there, I ask to see any limiting beliefs or "contracts," such as fear, that are holding the client back. Examples of such contracts include "I'm not loveable unless I'm successful" or "I'm never enough" or, in Mia's case, "Life is a no-win situation." Limiting beliefs are often concerned with survival. Pregnancy can create a heightened vulnerability in the mother. She may experience mixed feelings about being pregnant or have a partner who is not happy about the pregnancy. Health complications may make her fear for her own life or the life of her unborn child. Similarly, her life situation at the time of pregnancy—including her economic status, bodily healthy and ability, and the availability of supportive relatives and friends—can trigger valid fears and anxieties.

To help her understand where the limiting belief came from, I shared the contract with Mia, and she observed the feelings that it arose. She then contemplated whether to "edit" the contract or to nullify it and create a new one that better represented her soul's truth. Ultimately, she chose to release the old contract and write a new one: "Life is full of limitless possibilities and I savor being alive."

The soul retrieval process helped Mia cultivate a more empowering belief about her ability to have a joyous, peaceful birth, which eradicated any fears that were not cleared by the illumination. Within a week or so of doing the soul retrieval, she reported feeling much more at ease about her birth time with no lingering doubts or worries.

BIRTHING CONSCIOUSLY: LABOUR AND DELIVERY

Energetic techniques can induce labour and make it both shorter and easier. I often see women at around forty-two weeks of gestation who wish to avoid a medical induction. To energetically "induce" labour, I have the mother lie on her side on the massage table. I feel into the baby's energy field, as well as the mother's, and ask both for permission to encourage the birth process to begin. If I sense that both are in alignment with this plan, I lightly shake a rattle around the mother's body to open up her energy field. Then I move down to the first *chakra* and use the rattle to unwind it counter-clockwise, which "opens" the *chakra*. I visualize a stopper or plug in a filled bathtub and imagine that I am pulling the stopper out of the drain. I encourage the energy around the first *chakra* to swirl down and out, which draws the baby down as well, while I dilate and efface the cervix. I then perform the same technique in the second *chakra*. If the mother has been feeling very tired, I will sometimes move up the body and clear all seven *chakras*, which cleanses her field and gives her an energetic boost. Most women feel refreshed and rejuvenated after a seven *chakra* clearing. One recent client reported that she had not felt so energized since becoming pregnant. Other women reported feeling the energy swirling and draining downwards. Cramping and contractions can begin as early as minutes after this process, and often within twenty-eight to forty-eight hours of the energy work.

I use my energy tools—a rattle, a large crystal, cleansing spirit water, essential oils—during labour, too. Unwinding the first and second *chakras* is helpful throughout birth time, particularly when labour stalls or if contractions grow unbearably painful. Some mothers also find it helpful to blow the intensity of their contractions into a small stone or crystal. If the baby is in any position other than head down, I use the rattle to encourage the child to shift into the optimal position for birth.

Decoupling is also an essential childbirth tool. It can counter the rising adrenaline and cortisol that the mother's body produces in labour. Decoupling is particularly helpful around "transition," when the cervix reaches seven centimetres in dilation and the new mother is more susceptible to the fight-or-flight response and its accompanying fear and discouragement. Quieting the central nervous system can aid the mother in staying centred and calm at this critical juncture. Decoupling and illumination can also reduce the need for pain management medications such as analgesics and epidurals.

LIFE SUPPORT: POSTPARTUM TOOLS FOR MOTHER AND CHILD

Just as energetic practices can aid in pregnancy, labour, and delivery, these tools can also help with postpartum recovery, as the birth canal, pelvic floor, genitals, and perineum can all be adversely affected during vaginal births. Some women experience tearing or require episiotomies, which damage the tissue. Others report a lack of sensation or numbness in the pelvic region after giving birth, and this is even more common when an epidural is administered. Illumination can, therefore, aid in clearing any residual "trauma" from the birth and encourage the nervous system to fully operate again after being numbed by the medication.

In the event of a Caesarean birth, women sometimes report feeling as if something is out of place in their abdominal cavity after the surgery. This is a sign that the organs are not sitting within their energetic imprints or templates in the energy body. A small bit of energetic "rearranging" done with a rattle or the doula's hands usually puts things back into their proper place easily and painlessly. A seven *chakra* illumination is also wonderful for clearing both the mother's and baby's bodies of the lingering anesthesia used for the surgery as well as for aiding the incision to heal completely.

On the whole, as a critical awareness of the profound ramifications of pregnancy and childbirth expands in contemporary Western culture, so should the role and skills of doulas. Beyond basic comfort measures and emotional support, new parents can benefit from the energetic arts that have long been used in the birthing process throughout the world. As this chapter has highlighted, birth-support professionals with these skills can be a great help to families during conception, pregnancy, labour, and delivery as well as during the postpartum period. In sharing knowledge about such practices and striving to make their services more widely accessible, doulas may also affirm the sacred roles that women have performed—and continue to perform—as birth assistants and caregivers in diverse spiritual and religious contexts.

WORKS CITED

Askren, Hana. "Doula Comeback Tied to Gaps in Modern Birth Care." *Womens eNews*. N.p., 18 Aug. 2012. Web. 2 February 2014.

Baker, Phil. "The Face of Fear." *Radio New Zealand National*. Radio New Zealand, 29 Mar. 2013. Web. 2 Feb. 2014.

Ballen, Lois, and Ann Fulcher. "Nurses and Doulas: Complementary Roles to Provide Optimal Maternity Care." *Journal of Obstetric, Gynecologic and Neonatal Nursing* 35.2 (2006): 304-311. Print.

Brennan, Barabara. *Hands of Light: A Guide to Healing Through the Human Energy Field*. Ealing: Bantam Press, 1988. Print.

Davis, Elysia, Laura Glynn, Christine Schetter, Calvin Hobel, Aleksandra Chicz-Demet, and Curtis Sandman. "Prenatal Exposure to Maternal Depression and Cortisol Influences Infant Temperament." *Journal of the American Academy of Child and Adolescent Psychiatry* 46.6 (2007): 737-746. Print.

"Doulas, a Mom's Best Friend During Labor, Grow in Popularity|Mission Local." *Missionlocal.* N.pub. 22 Febr. 2010. Web. 2 Feb. 2014.

Mander, Rosemary. "Supportive Care and Midwifery." *The Doula.* Hoboken: John Wiley & Sons, 2001. Print.

II.

RELIGIOUS MOTHERING IN HISTORY, THEOLOGY, AND LITERATURE

6.
Mothers of Spiritual Change

Julian of Norwich, Mary Magdalen, and Mother Teresa

THERESE NOVOTNY

IN THE LATE MIDDLE AGES, one Christian writer refused to think of "mothering" in terms of a mutually exclusive male or female dichotomy. Julian of Norwich (1342-1416) was a mystic, whose writings described "Mother Jesus" or the Jesus who took on "the office of motherhood" (Julian of Norwich 595).[1] Three specific components of this transformative idea are that Jesus, though male, still acted like a mother to create, nourish, and protect humanity. Unfortunately, her concept was largely neglected for centuries. Instead, the Christian tradition has cast the leading roles for women as servants, and this tradition has offered few models for women who are active agents of change. Usually, female labour supports a male-dominated society while women perform good works and multiple acts of self-sacrifice. Even the physical processes of pregnancy, childbirth, and lactation are often conceptualized as things that happen to a woman rather than physical processes that she actively performs. Moreover, in a nurturing role, a mother is expected to give so much of herself that nothing remains of her own identity. She risks falling into an empty void, without recognizing her inherent value to herself or to others in her community (Saiving 37). In contrast, in order to fulfill the role of spiritual mothers, women need to perceive themselves—and be perceived by others—as active participants and agents of change.

Mothering is an active, thoughtful process. Across cultures and throughout centuries, mothering usually includes three categories of tasks: protecting, nurturing, and training children for social acceptability (Ruddick 51).The maternal work of caring for children includes an ongoing list of continuous tasks: assessing emotional well-being, gauging psychological needs, maintaining a shelter, preparing food, monitoring nutrition, providing safety, attending to the needs of the vulnerable, and teaching members of the family and extended social networks. When all goes well, daily work rolls smoothly. In contrast, when the need to protect a child conflicts with an urge for independence, maternal work involves nuanced thinking with immediate and long-term consequences in the balance. Maternal thinking requires cool judgment, rapid assessment, and appropriate action. Moreover, maternal practices unfold in the messy, daily business of caring, even though they may be based on abstract values supported by society. Consequently, the vigilant "mother" watches and asserts herself as an agent of change. Furthermore, in contrast to some stereotypes, maternal work can be performed by biological and non-biological mothers and by men and women alike. The acts of pregnancy, labour, and lactation, which are tied to the female body, are only performed for a brief time in a child's life, compared to the entire span of years wherein a child needs mothering (Ruddick 46).[2] Mothers, then, can engage their intellectual and spiritual capacities to help raise children, which gives direction in the family and the extended community.

Despite a mother's seemingly powerful control over children's behaviours, mothers may feel powerless, especially if they are women. Some may live inside a limited authority system, in which they are denied the necessary economic and political tools to exercise their own agency. This imbalance of power propels mothers to effect social change to help themselves and others, and to teach their children to do so. Such an effort to navigate social networks and advocate for their children can be considered as a spiritual enterprise, even if such work lacks any affiliation with organized religion, simply because it motivates individuals to work toward a greater good. The work of mothering, which includes emotional and psychological nurturing, can prompt mothers to be spiritual agents of change. When mothers seek the best in themselves, not only can they help their children, but they can tap the potential to become self-fulfilled and spiritually mature. Their motivation to nurture, protect, and train their children often elevates their own self-actualization.

Accordingly, this chapter discusses three women who opened new and radical paths to spirituality: Julian of Norwich, Mary Magdalen, and Mother Teresa. In recognizing God's affiliation with them, each became an agent of change. They performed acts of nurturing and protecting but with a distinct perspective that they gained while achieving an active and integrated spiritual life. Consequently, they did not base their actions on male approval or male benefit; instead, they challenged spiritual traditions while carving out spaces for women's agency. In this capacity, these women used their creative and nurturing capacities to weave transformative change within their cultures, thus empowering themselves and others. Their mothering was not limited to biological abilities but also included the intellectual, intuitive, organizational, and interpersonal abilities to nurture. Julian's language of the feminized Jesus builds a scaffold on which to discuss the other two; Mary Magdalen nurtures, protects, and announces Jesus's resurrection to the others; and Mother Teresa nurtures, protects, and creates an international organization for the poor while founding a new religious order to do her work.

JULIAN OF NORWICH

Julian of Norwich casts the framework of spiritual mothering in her two texts, which are the first written by a woman in the English language. *The Showings,* written in 1373, provides an account of her sixteen visions of Jesus's passion, and she spent nearly twenty years revising and contemplating her experience. Her second text, *The Revelation of Love,* which will be discussed in this chapter, expands on concepts in her first text: it asks questions about the meaning of sin and redemption as well as about Jesus's abundant forgiveness and his role as mother to the world. Through her writing, she carved out a new definition of the female religious experience that speaks to the modern world as much as it did the medieval.

Julian's life as an anchoress limited her physical space, yet it allowed her to cultivate a mature spiritual self. Born in 1342, she settled in Norwich sometime after her thirtieth year, where she remained until her death in 1416. Her true name is unknown, as is her family history. Living as an anchorite, she was sealed in an enclosed cell adjacent to St. Julian's Church with limited access to conversations and contact with others. Although anchorites lived in solitude, their isolation did not remove them from a spiritual and even social context of community, which allowed for the sharing of ideas or an openness to the outside world. In England, anchorites were usually lay women, who often lived outside a cloister prior to their enclosure (McAvoy 10-11). Norwich, the second largest town in England after London, was an economic and religious hub, which housed four mendicant orders and a cathedral, several thriving craft guilds, and a textile centre. In a century of social disruption, including peasant uprisings, outbreaks of the plague, and the Hundred Year's War, Julian's anchorhold allowed her the luxury of space and time to pray, write, and meditate, which was often unavailable to other lay women. The anchorhold also gave her access to advisors, ongoing informal religious instruction, and spiritual direction. Moreover, anchoresses perceived themselves as being partnered with other women who were "spiritual sisters" in prayer, religious practices, and ecclesiastic status. It was the nuns, even more than the monks, who were actively engaged in developing instructional materials in English to be shared and used amongst each other (Bell 75-75). Although they lived in solitude, they were able to foster spiritual community and share their ideas with the outside world.

Julian's writings introduced discussions of scripture and church teaching into the vernacular, and became accessible to women, even if they could not read Latin. Given the church's acknowledgement of female personal devotion and prayer, her own words were accepted as having authorial credibility, since they came directly from God in her vision. Julian's contemporaries, Bridget of Sweden and Catherine of Siena, were similarly esteemed for their special connection to God through visions. The institutional church, thus, recognized the direct connection between God and the visionary, and credited them with receiving the words of God without a mediating priest, cleric, or spiritual advisor. Some of Julian's ideas were revolutionary, and to avoid falling outside the realm of church teaching, she employed careful rhetorical and theological strategies to explain the meanings of her visions.

While working within the Roman Catholic spiritual tradition, Julian of Norwich challenged a male-centric view of Jesus. Julian emphasized a Jesus who physically shared a body with Mary before birth. This pre-birth connection between the two so strongly empowered Mary that the church, even today, is uncertain about how to discuss this type of transformative space. For Julian, the connection between Jesus and Mary continued to grow in a reciprocal and interconnected evolution throughout Jesus's life and beyond his death. In her view, Jesus took on the role of motherhood and, thus, became "our Mother Jesus." Julian established the notion that women are more than mere vessels to be filled by God; rather, they are essential parts of a divine process of redemption, and are thus intertwined in the salvation of the world. In this way, Julian describes the shared embodiment of Jesus and Mary. Moreover, Mary embraced and played an active part in the work of nurturing, protecting, and preparing Jesus for life in the Jewish culture. Without Mary's repeated and varied performance of maternal work, including pregnancy and labour, Jesus would not have physically matured or socially interacted with humanity.

In this capacity, the "office of motherhood" is a concept that evolves throughout Julian's text *Revelation of Love*. It is introduced with a common natural object, a hazelnut, which, like all objects made in creation, is nurtured and protected. The comparison introduces connections that will unfold throughout her text, as the hazelnut provides a metaphor for all that is created by God, small though it is. It is only a "ball" that could suddenly have "fallen to nawght," but it is significant to God because He made, loved, and protected it (Julian of Norwich 300). Julian then connects the hazelnut to "our Mother Jesus," therein comparing the properties of motherhood to those of the God who loves the hazelnut. The same three traits are repeated when Jesus is compared to a woman: "oure very Moder Jhesu" takes on the office of motherhood, to "beryth us" to "fede us" and to "systeynth us" (Julian of Norwich 595-596).[3] Julian explains that Jesus, clothed in the human condition, gives birth to salvation for humanity through his suffering. Like a mother, he feeds his people with the sacrament and his flesh and blood, and he sustains humanity with comfort and support.

As part of the "office of motherhood," Julian emphasizes the protecting and nourishing physical attributes of Jesus's mothering. The message of salvation occurs in two levels. On one level, Jesus acts as a mother who literally saves her child through feeding and caring for it. On another level, Jesus saves his children from God's wrath, even enduring death to save them from an everlasting hopelessness. He inserts his power into the most powerless situation of all. His agency continues after his death in a metaphorical transformation of his body. Just as a mother feeds her child with her own milk, "oure precious Moder Jhesu, he may fede us with hym selfe and doth full curtesly and full tendyrly with the blessyd sacrament" (Julian of Norwich 596-597). The work of the mother is, thus, connected to physical nurturing and care but also to the emotional labour of love and concern. The mother ushers in a physical person but anticipates the child's diverse needs, including the spiritual and emotional. According to Julian, Jesus comforts his people as a mother does her children.

Julian further forges the concept of motherhood from the metaphors linking Jesus's body to the female body. One dominant metaphor refers to Jesus's side wound in chapter twenty-four of *Revelations of Love*. In chapter sixty, she pushes this metaphor to the edge of orthodoxy and suspends it over both old and new meanings. She initially uses the image of the open wound in Jesus's side to reference traditional scriptural attributes of the physical wound Jesus received when the soldier placed a lance in his side to assure his death. Julian, however, assigns increasingly feminine attributes to the same wound as she continues throughout her text. For example, the "wound" refers to a container for blood and water: "hys ...worthy blode and hys precious water" (Julian of Norwich 395). Next, it refers to a breast, as "the moder may geve her chylde sucke" (Julian of Norwich 596), and then to his milk ("mylke") used to feed his children. Julian does not make the metaphorical leap in one move; rather, she accumulates meanings and rhetorical amplifications of images to produce new concepts of "our Mother Jesus."

Moreover, Julian places Jesus's feminine nature at the centre of creation. His feminized body gives birth to the space that opens up salvation, and Julian's language creates a means to articulate this transformation. Julian describes Jesus as the feminized agent of change, and in describing this act, she suggests that all women share this capacity. Her texts describe Jesus's labour in creating the space of rebirth; his death and resurrection change a desolate world into one that is reborn. In this way, his suffering on the cross is a labour of birth. Envisioning the side wound as both a physical form of torture and a source of new life suggests the original tension of the metaphor. Both interpretations are sustained at one time, and the unusual relationship between the two spins a new space for imagination and language. Julian mediates between new meanings of the word "wound"; in chapter sixty, she even returns to the initial image of the side with blood and water flowing out, as it would after birth, to make sure that she has woven the thread back to chapter ten. The tension and gaps between the multiple meanings of the "wound" build a new construct of "motherhood" and God. Through his body, Jesus will bring forth his children, the church, and forge a path for humanity to avoid God's everlasting wrath. Jesus needs his feminine attributes to actively change the world and bring about hope for humanity to engage in forgiveness and rejuvenation. In this way, her writings create a space to contemplate Jesus as the feminized agent of change.

Julian's writings allow her listeners to participate in the "forthbringing" or birthing of a new idea. After describing the open wound of Christ and its feminine attributes of nourishment, she describes how the wound can lead to a "forthbringing" or birth: "For though it be so þat oure bodily forthbryngyng be but lytle, lowe and symple in regard of oure gostely fort brynggyng ... our lord doth it in hym.... Thus he is our moder" (Julian of Norwich 599). Julian places Jesus as the one "by whom it is done"(Julian of Norwich 599). The biological role of women, then, is no longer coincidental or tangential; it is absolutely central to the creation and sustenance of life. In this way, Julian subverts a male-centric view of Jesus and asserts Jesus's feminine agency, as well as her own.

On one hand, some feminist theologians argue that the female matriarchal language and symbols attributed to Jesus still support a Christian viewpoint that is inherently and essentially sexist (Fiorenza 84-92; Daly 53-68). The argument may follow that Julian is still trapped into using language and symbols that inevitably choke female access to power and refer to God the Father, the male authority figure. In the end, then, the masculine language in Julian's writing still stresses the sovereign and absolute authority of a patriarchal religious system. Contrary to this view, however, Julian takes the historical male person of Jesus and recognizes his maternal thinking and even his maternal labour, creating an image of Jesus that transcends gender. Her words are based in scripture, but her vision and meditation upon it links maternal actions as essential and necessary to salvation. Jesus's maternal work establishes a foundation for women to view themselves—and for others to view them—as agents of change.

MARY MAGDALEN

Mary Magdalen situates the feminine in the centre of the Gospel narrative. A woman physically and spiritually connected to the body of Jesus, she performs tasks even his closest apostles avoid. She witnesses Jesus's crucifixion and his appearance after being placed in the tomb. Her exact relationship to Jesus has been the subject of much heated speculation and scholarship (Bourgeault 1-29). She has been associated with the woman in scripture who brings the alabaster jar and cleanses Jesus's feet, but none of the gospels identify her by name. Regardless, her story has been connected to the "sinner," the "prostitute," the "demonized," or the "other" for centuries. Despite her "problematic" past, her intimate place with Jesus at his passion and crucifixion, as well as her closeness to him during his journey to Calvary, solidifies her as a model of spiritual faithfulness. Although she says few words in scripture, her insistent and consistent presence in the gospels makes her Jesus's spiritual companion. By her actions and deeds, she negotiates an active and participatory place for women. Although she is often with Mary, Jesus' mother, she assumes other parts of the "office of motherhood." Like Jesus's mother, Mary Magdalen witnesses crucial events in Jesus's life, but she also intuitively grasps their significance and is "fed" by them. Eventually she "feeds" and "sustains" the other apostles by going to them with news of Jesus's appearance after he was placed in the tomb. This concept of "feeding" her own spirituality and being "fed" or "sustained" by it is crucial for the intuitive step that she takes when she recognizes the risen Jesus after his death.

Mary Magdalen's story throughout history is a complex one. By the early Middle Ages, she was a saint, whose legend served multiple purposes to diverse audiences. Her life narrative was a combination of the lives of three women in the Bible: first, Mary of Bethany, the sister of Martha; second, Mary Magdalen, the woman of the gospels who prepared Jesus's body after death; and third, the unnamed sinner who washed Jesus's feet (Reames). Although she was not identified as a prostitute in the gospels, the various stories and legends make that claim. The vague details of her life has allowed preachers to assign qualities of misconduct to her, all in an effort to teach about a woman's place in society and the problems associated with prostitution. Textual evidence of her story is found in the *Old English Martyrology* (c. 900), the *South English Legendary*, John Mirk's sermon written for her feast day, and the Digby play, *Mary Magdalen*. The widespread proliferation of this material by the fourteenth century suggests that her story was recognized across Germany, France, England, and the Low Countries. Her following in France was helped by the location of her pilgrimage shrine, which was also on the route to St. James Santiago in Compostalla. The various themes of her legend appealed to a variety of audiences. For women, she represented faithfulness to the end. To the monk, part of her story told of her choosing the better side by listening to Jesus rather than attending to the household. Preachers identified with her efforts to spread the gospel to Europe. For those who fed the hungry and cared for the sick, she represented compassion. By the fourteenth century, she offered hope for the sinner who was redeemed, and she represented an illustration of God's love and forgiveness as well as Jesus's intimate connection with humanity, including women. In this way she served as a symbol of renewal and restoration.

In scripture, Mary Magdalen stands boldly for the marginalized, particularly women among Jesus's entourage. According to scripture, she was marginalized in her community because she was a "sinner" and was overcome by demons. In Luke (8:2) and Mark (16:9), she enters the group who follows Jesus as he passes through cities and villages.[4] Despite her reputation as being possessed by demons, or perhaps because of her cure from them, she continues to travel with Jesus. Luke thus writes: "And the twelve were with him, and also some women had been healed of evil spirits and infirmities: Mary, called Magdalene, from whom seven demons had gone out, and Joanna, the wife of Chuza, Herod's steward and Susanna and many others, who provided for them out of their means" (Luke 8:2). Although blind men and paralytics are the recipients of Jesus's healing powers, many of them are never heard from again in scripture. In contrast, Mary Magdalen remains with Jesus, as she carves out a space within his inner circle of followers. Jesus travels with "The Twelve," all male companions, but other disciples gather to hear him, as evident in the miracle scenes, such as the feeding of the crowd with the loaves and fishes. As such, her sense of comradery and evolving commitment to and identification with his work, especially the miracles and healings, keep her moving with him. She is not an image of passivity but is an active participant in Jesus's story.

Even inside the inner circle, Mary Magdalen's commitment is stronger than most of the apostles' in performing the nurturing work of mothering. As she travels with Jesus, she sustains him physically and spiritually. She performs the conscientious labour of inserting women into Jesus's story of suffering, death, and transformation. Particularly at the crucifixion, she does not run; instead, she remains committed to Jesus. She follows, nurturing and hoping to protect him, and, in some ways, helps him to shape and perform his ministry in its final stages. According to Mark 15:40, she cares for his daily needs, which would have included preparing his food and assisting him: "There were also women looking on from afar, among them were Mary Magdalene, and Mary the mother of James the younger and of Joses, and Salome, who, when he was in Galilee, followed him and ministered to him; and also other women who came up with him to Jerusalem."

To perform this ministry, Mary Magdalen learns to intuit the power of Jesus's words and actions. She is, thus, willing to perform the "office of motherhood" for him, to understand him, and to provide solace for him. Intellectually and intuitively, she might have also been one of the first women to understand the significance of the crucifixion and resurrection. In the beginning of the gospel stories, she witnesses the passion, but at the end, she has the capacity not only to witness Jesus's suffering but also to announce and explain the risen Jesus to others. To take that step, she had to understand the significance of his suffering and rising or else she might have run in fear as the apostles did. She performs the emotional labour of mothering by stepping outside of the self and into another world that contained a nearly unimaginable possibility: life after death. At the end of the gospels, her role is essential to understanding the resurrected Jesus. All four gospels state that she was among the first witnesses to the resurrection, either alone or in a group. What did she expect to see? In Matthew's account, the three women meet an angel who tells them to look for Jesus outside the tomb. When they go, they see Jesus in a living body: "So they departed quickly from the tomb with fear and great joy, and ran to tell his disciples. And behold Jesus met them and said, 'Hail!' And they came up and took hold of his feet and worshiped him. Then Jesus said to them, 'Do not be afraid; go and tell my brethren to go to Galilee, and there they will see me" (Matthew 28:8-10). When they find Jesus, they are all physically drawn to him and embrace him. They meet with a mixture of fear and joy. Jesus asks them to be recognize the significance of the event. He asks the women to help unfold the next part of the scriptural narrative. For them to proceed unafraid, and with "great joy," they have to have a transcendent understanding of the resurrection as a transformation of life and death. In this way, Mary Magdalen becomes an agent of change; she does not wait for other signs or for approval from those in authority but rushes to communicate her knowledge to others.

Like Julian of Norwich, Mary Magdalen challenges and subverts traditional expectations of life and death. The apostles hide in the upper room after Jesus's crucifixion, perhaps out of shock, grief, and fear. They understand the implications of Jesus's death, and that it might lead to their own, yet Mary Magdalen recognizes that his crucifixion could have led to something beyond death. Jesus had been tortured, crucified, and buried, so how could he be alive after such a grueling ordeal? As a result of her spiritual maturity, Mary Magdalen comprehends the significance of this moment and does not waiver in her convictions. Even when she is met with ridicule and hesitancy from the apostles, she insists on her account of seeing the risen Jesus, which appears in Mark 16:9: "Now when he rose early on the first day of the week, he appeared first to Mary Magdalene, from whom he had cast out seven demons. She went and told those who had been with him, as they mourned and wept. But when they heard that he was alive and had been seen by her, they would not believe it." As an agent of spiritual formation, Mary Magdalen gives birth to the meaning of Jesus's life and ministry, which opens the world to concept of life after death. Jesus's appearance to the women helps them to understand how a death and life are connected. Earthly suffering is not an end to life; it can lead to growth, transformation, and a newly formed sense of personhood.

MOTHER TERESA

Mother Teresa of Calcutta gave birth to a religious order whose mission was to serve the poor and foster a radically intimate connection with them. Her own actions spoke loudly to a life dedicated to the "office of motherhood," particularly nurturing and protecting the poor and sick. Her single-minded conviction and dedication to this work gave birth to a recognition of the oppressed at the end of the twentieth century. Although she was not the first or only person to recognize the poor and oppressed, her mission shed light on extreme poverty in parts of the world that were often left unnoticed. Her work also happened during a time when global awareness of oppression became increasingly evident as travel and media technologies helped spread information. She made it hard to ignore the intense poverty she saw. Her early promise to Jesus was "not to refuse him anything" (Kolodiejchuk 38) and this led her to actively serve the poor with unprecedented vigorousness. Her pace stunned those who lived with her, since she often worked through the night and woke before dawn. According to those she visited, when she travelled "she would sometimes arrive at midnight, but would still wake at 4:40 in the morning to be in the chapel" (Kolodiejchuk 324). Given the intensity of her labour, which involved feeding, bathing, nursing, holding, and lifting the poorest, Mother Teresa was an agent of change.

Mother Teresa's mission began with a traditional introduction to nurturing and serving as a teacher, but it transformed rapidly. In 1933, she made her profession of vows for the Loreto Sisters at the age of twenty-three and taught at St. Mary's High School for Girls in Calcutta, where she learned Bengali and Hindi fluently. She continued to teach there, and in 1946, she experienced a powerful second call while riding a train from Calcutta to the Himalayan foothills. After this experience, she wanted to bring "Christ into the unhappy holes of the slums of Calcutta's poor-later on the other places" (Kolodiejchuk 73). She received initial resistance from the Archbishop Périer, who had concerns about her safety and wondered how a new mission would affect her existing order, the Loreto Sisters. She continued to press for permission but had already decided that this was her chosen work. After finally receiving approval from the local archbishop, she travelled for the first time to Calcutta's slum with the general goal of aiding the unwanted and unloved. She started an open-air school and a home for the destitute and dying, which served the needs of those who had nobody else to care for them. Her mission led her to form her own order, the Missionaries of Charity, which provided a space in the slums for hospices, hospitals, and shelters.

Mother Teresa's actions gave birth to an organization founded on unprecedented contact with the poor in India. In the same ways that Julian of Norwich challenged the traditional patriarchal understandings of Jesus and Mary Magdalen challenged traditional beliefs about death, Mother Teresa defied dominant views of the poor by locating Jesus in their faces and bodies. In 1983, she wrote a litany answering the question "Who is Jesus to me?" Her responses illustrate an active response to the oppressed, whether to "feed," "protect," or "embrace" them (Egan 459). In this way, her dedication to the poor required the physical and emotional labour of mothering. Her insistence on caring for the physical needs of people who would otherwise be considered untouchable characterized her calling.

To that end, Mother Teresa chose unconventional ways to challenge traditional notions of gender, social class, ethnicity, and religious affiliation. She was insistent that her sisters in India, China, and other parts of the globe speak the native language and dialect of the people that they served. Despite strong lines distinguishing religious groups from one another in India, she did not distinguish between Muslim, Catholic, Buddhist, or Hindu. Her own garb subverted the traditional Roman Catholic clothing most nuns wore, which reflected her affiliation with the marginalized people of India. In August of 1948, she left for India with a blue and white sari, and brought only five rupees with her. Her role as a "mother" meant entering their space to live, dress, and eat. She thereby left her "self" to enter a life of nurturing and caring for others. Her insistence on sustaining the poor physically and spiritually remained decades later when she wrote an open letter to Mr. Morarji Desai, prime minister of India in 1978, addressing the Freedom of Religion Bill. In her letter, she defended the rights of all religious adherents:

> Do not destroy the freedom our country and people have had, to serve and love God according to their conscience and belief. Do not belittle our Hindu religions saying that our Hindu poor people give up their religion for "a plate of rice." To my knowledge, I have not seen this being done though thousands have died in our hands beautifully in peace with God. (Egan 486-487)

The Catholics who followed her message might have been surprised that she supported anyone who could bring a person closer to God. In Oslo, when she received the Nobel Prize, she was asked what she thought of herself. She replied, "I am an Albanian. My citizenship is Indian. I am a Catholic nun. As to my calling I belong to the whole world"(Egan 413).

Mother Teresa's radical commitment also led her to extreme actions. She was reckless in her determination to feed and nurture the poor. At one point she left St. Mary's Entally, the boarding school that housed and fed three hundred girls, because they had no food. This occurred in August 1946 during the Hindu-Muslim conflict that left five thousand dead in the streets, later labelled "The Day of Great Killing." She had been warned not to go out into the streets, but she went anyway. She later described the scene and her actions:

> Then I saw the bodies on the streets, stabbed, beaten, lying there in strange positions in their dried blood. We had been behind our safe walls. We knew that there had been rioting. People had been jumping over our walls, first a Hindu, then a Muslim.... We took in each one and helped him to escape safely.... A lorry full of soldiers stopped me and told me I should not be out in the street. No one should be out, they said. I told them I had to come out and take the risk; I had three hundred students who had nothing to eat. The soldiers had rice and they drove me back to the school and unloaded bags of rice. (Kolediejchuk 37)

Mother Teresa actively gave birth to a radical way of recognizing the poor and helping the oppressed. She urged others to cross political, ethnic, and cultural lines of conflict to find peace in action. In her Nobel Peace Prize speech delivered in Oslo, she challenged her listeners around the globe to see new avenues to achieve peace: "I think that we in our family don't need bombs and guns, to destroy to bring peace—just get together, love one another, to bring that peace, that joy, that strength of presence of each other in the home. And we will be able to overcome all the evil that is in the world." Her intentional use of the white sari and her establishment of the religious order it represented were outward signs of a new spiritual light being born into the world.

Mother Teresa delivered her message to the powerful as well as to the weak. Her concept was so revolutionary that she challenged all people to think of themselves as vehicles for God, even if they did not recognize any God or spiritual entity. She wanted all leaders, regardless of political or spiritual affiliation, to understand that they could also allow Jesus to work through them to serve the poor and oppressed. If they were Christian or not was irrelevant because they could all work to open doors for others. In 1985, she met with the Chinese Premier's son, Deng Pufang, who was confined to a wheelchair. He spoke with Mother Teresa about strategies to develop China's Welfare Fund for the Handicapped. Mother Teresa insisted on recasting him as an instrument of God. She said, "The same loving God has created you and me. What you do is your love for God in action. You put that desire into action and that is love" (Egan 488). Even though she contextualized her words in the language of Christianity, she focused less on organized religions and more on love. Her end purpose was not to evangelize or convert people to Christianity. She challenged Pufang to mother, nurture and sustain the oppressed, even in the face of animosity, contrary political views, and cultural barriers. In her view, because God created his children, all are capable of providing love, protection, and nourishment. In this way, Mother Teresa performed the physical, emotional, and spiritual work of mothering, thereby challenging existing cultural norms and giving birth to a new spiritual message. Even though they discussed the working conditions of the Chinese workers, her goal in the meeting was to receive a subsequent invitation so she could let the Missionaries of Charity work somewhere in the country (Egan 489).

Her message was filled with apparent paradoxes and contradictions. In her Nobel Prize speech, she leveled harsh criticism against those who support reproductive rights for women, especially abortion rights. She used her speech as a platform for an attack on abortion, labeling women as murderers with her message: "the greatest destroyer of peace today is the cry of the innocent unborn child. If a mother can murder her own child, in her own womb, what is left for you and for me to kill each other?" Her abrasive rhetoric sharply rebuked those who supported reproductive freedoms. To many, such rights seemed a responsible and reasonable route to avoid poverty and oppression for themselves and future generations. And yet, she was unwavering in her condemnation of abortion. As unreasonable as this sounded, the message should be understood in a context that is broader than this speech. The majority of her choices had been based on an unshakable commitment to those who have no voice. One would think this would certainly include impoverished, undereducated, and systemically disenfranchised men and women. Although she understood their misery, she was drawn to offer care to those who had no immediate assistance or care. Her lens narrowly sought people who had no power at all, such as a lame man lying in a ditch or a paralytic woman propped against a wall. She looked to serve the completely powerless. Although she influenced politicians and could solicit effective change, she usually did not seek out political leaders for her mission; she was often invited by them to speak. Usually, she left the details of policy and social change to others, while she focused on particular individuals, like the few families trying to survive in a war zone in Beirut (Egan 330). While political compromise and societal programs were not her primary areas of interest, she did not steer away from controversy. She left the social and economic questions of how to support children, to guarantee a living wage, and to produce reasonable housing, honest work, and health care policies to others to solve. Primarily, her desire was to seek out the completely voiceless, and to defend them. While this may seem rigidly narrow, it is characteristic of the way she saw her world through a sharply focused lens, and this gave her the concentrated effort to accomplish the work she did.

CONCLUSION

Each of the women in this essay worked within a patriarchal authority structure that was quick to limit and question them. Julian of Norwich, while describing the feminized body of Jesus, stood at the edge of orthodoxy and used careful language to create a space for a new vision of him. Mary Magdalen carved out a space within Jesus's inner circle and remained with him when his apostles did not, and recognized his risen body as a new way of understanding life after death. Mother Teresa, with her seemingly impossible and unsustainable model for a mission, overcame opposition by remaining in action, not only in India but around the world. None of them left the church or early versions of it, even though they struggled with and challenged existing authority. Rather, they appropriated a traditional structure to actively transform it and operate as agents of change. Although they did not change all areas of concern in their environments, they were not passive vessels. In the end their actions, writings, and words gave birth to revolutionary spiritual concepts.

In forging her own image of Jesus, Julian transcended patriarchal and matriarchal symbols and language. She forced Christians to employ a variety of images that offered a plurality of ways to envision "Jesus our Mother." Furthermore, her writings expressed reflections on her own mystical experience. She urged readers to continue to meditate on the illusive concepts that she introduced. In the Bible, Mary Magdalen selflessly cared for Jesus, but her brave actions, especially at his death and after his burial, could have been performed by men. Her place in the very centre of Jesus's most important moments of life and death secured her a privileged space in his life and those of his apostles. She not only transcended a gender barrier, but she broke through barriers of class and culture to bring forth a universally recognized message of salvation as well as a new understanding of life and death. She exemplified the way maternal work is accomplished by any person, female or male, who is willing to engage in maternal thinking and practice. In Calcutta, men and women both continue to work with the Sisters of Charity serving the poor and oppressed, and risk their own safety and comfort. Men and women both can see Jesus in the face of the impoverished. In founding her own order, Mother Teresa taught others to see Jesus in the face of every poor man, woman, and child, and, thus, transformed biases in serving the poor and oppressed, regardless of gender.

Although these women lived in different times throughout history, they still performed the "office of motherhood." They defied patriarchal expectations that women are passive vessels. In various ways they performed the physical, emotional, and spiritual labour of mothering within an active and self-aware spiritual life. They consistently challenged traditional church structures and carved out spaces and pathways for other women. These women lived boldly and remained steadfast in the knowledge and insights that they gleaned from their own actions and mediations. Individually, each still provides models for women who choose to embrace the spiritual life and nurture the spiritual gifts inside them. If their messages continue to move women to understand their own spiritual capacities as mothers, the world will continue to be reshaped and transformed.

NOTES

[1]For references to Julian's text, see Julian of Norwich, *A Book*

of Showings to the Anchoress Julian of Norwich: Part Two. Eds. Edmund Colledge and James Walsh. Toronto: Pontifical Institute of Medieval Studies, 1978. I will use this edition for direct quotes of Julian's text. Although Julian's text did not have titles, several manuscripts exist, and are often referred to with different labels. Colledge and Walsh refer to Part Two of her text as the long text (*LT*), but others subsequent editions refer to it as *Revelations of Love*. For this chapter, all subsequent quotes from Julian will be from the Colledge and Walsh edition and will be labelled as: (Julian of Norwich pp).

[2]Sara Ruddick's *Maternal Thinking* provides careful definitions of "caring labor." She notes that many more women engage in caring labor than in the mothering of small children. She also clarifies the notion that men and women can perform caring labor (46).

[3]In most cases, the Middle English of Julian's text can be understood without translation to Modern English, but in this instance, the translation is: "bear us," "feed us," and "sustain us."

[4]All scriptural quotes are from the *New Oxford Annotated Bible with Apocrypha*. New York: Oxford University Press, 1977.

WORKS CITED

Bell, David. *What Nuns Read*. Collegeville, MN: Cistercian, 1995. Print.

Bourgeault, Cynthia. *The Meaning of Mary Magdalen: Discovering the Woman at the Heart of Christianity*. Boston and London: Shambhala, 2010. Print.

Colledge, Edmund, and James Walsh, eds. *A Book of Showings to the Anchoress Julian of Norwich*. Vol. 2. Studies and Texts. 35. Toronto: Pontifical Institute of Mediaeval Studies, 1978. Print.

Daly, Mary. "After the Death of God the Father." *Woman Spirit Rising*. Eds. Carol P. Christ and Judith Plaskow. New York: Harper One, 1992. 53-62. Print.

Egan, Eileen. *Such a Vision of the Streets*. New York: Doubleday, 1986. Print.

Fiorenza, Elisbeth Schussler. "Women in the Early Christian Movement." *Woman Spirit Rising*. Eds. Carol P. Christ and Judith Plaskow. New York: Harper One, 1992. 84-92. Print.

Kolodiejchuk, Brian and Mother Teresa. *Mother Teresa: Come Be My Light: The Private Writings of the "Saint of Calcutta."* Garden City, NY: Doubleday, 2007. Print.

McAvoy, Liz Herbert. Ed. *Anchoritic Traditions of Medieval Europe.* Woodbridge: Boydell Press, 2010. Print.

Mother Teresa. "Acceptance Speech by Mother Teresa." YouTube, 10 Dec. 1997. Web. July 15, 2015.

Muggeridge, Malcolm. *Something Beautiful for God.* London: Collins, 1971. Print.

New Oxford Annotated Bible with Apocrypha. New York: Oxford University Press, 1977. Print.

Reames, Sherry L. "The Legend of Mary Magdalen, Penitent and Apostle: Introduction." *Middle English Legends of Women Saints.* Ed. Sherry L. Reames. Robbins Library Digital Project. Medieval Institute Publication, 2003. Web. 24 June 2015.

Ruddick, Sara. *Maternal Thinking.* Boston: Beacon Press, 1989. Print.

Saiving, Valerie. "The Human Situation: A Feminine View." In *Woman Spirit Rising.* Eds. Carol P. Christ and Judith Plaskow. New York: Harper One, 1992. 25-43. Print.

7.
Binding Ourselves to the Truth

Quakerism and the Paradox of Liberated Motherhood

ANN W. DUNCAN

WRITING IN HER JOURNAL soon after the birth of her first child, prison reformer Elizabeth Fry (1780-1845) evokes a quintessentially Quaker perspective on the universal maternal experience of self-doubt and worry in the face of a fussy newborn child. She writes, "Certainly I am ignorant about the management of such young infants, but I do not feel uneasy about the charge of her body, from my self-confidence I fear; but I believe if we endeavour to do our duty, even in such things, we shall find the way" (Fry 69). She continues one week later, "How anxiously do I hope this poor dear baby may be held in resignation by me to the Divine will. Oh! That I might feel dependence on that Almighty arm about her and about other things. Beyond everything else, I wish to do my duty, idle and relaxed as I am in performing it" (70).

This reliance on divine protection for the child and guidance for the new mother reflects a common Christian commitment to an all-powerful, providential divine. However, beneath that conviction also lies a Quaker perspective on the manifestation of that divine presence in each person as well as the power of individual strength and discernment in negotiating the difficulties of human life on earth. In breaking from other Protestant sects, Quakers insisted on a new view of spiritual authority and divine presence. As Quaker women's rights activist Lucretia Mott declared in an 1854 speech to the Woman's Rights Convention in Philadelphia, "We too often bind ourselves by authorities rather than by the truth" (Mott 101). According to Mott and the Quaker tradition more generally, each individual possesses within them an Inner Light that allows them to discern their own path and truth without mediation. As a result of this conviction and the myriad ways it transformed Quaker social relations, Quaker motherhood stands in stark contrast to other paradigms of Christian motherhood. Empowered by a sense of an inward dwelling divinity and relatively unconstrained by traditional gender roles, Quaker women have been able to encounter the joys, suffering, and challenges of motherhood while anticipating and adjusting to the challenges brought by the emergence of feminism in the mid-twentieth century. Accordingly, this chapter examines the theological and historical roots of this paradoxical mix of "binding" and liberation that shapes Quaker motherhood today.

More recent trends and conversations relating to feminism, womanhood, and motherhood in the twenty-first century have complicated Quaker motherhood, even as they affirm core Quaker principles. Narratives of intensive or attachment parenting and natural childbirth appeal to many Quaker women's desires to live simply and to honour the God within their children and themselves. At the same time, the freedom to live beyond the patriarchal gender norms that are still supported by many Christian traditions translates into careers and personal ambitions that sometimes compete for women's energy and time. The responsibility inherent in the Quaker conviction of the Inner Light, thus, serves as a force of liberation for contemporary Quaker mothers as well as a source of significant pressure to chart their own path in a way that is both true to themselves and beneficial for their children.

INNER LIGHT

The particularities of Quaker perspectives on motherhood, the family, and human sexuality directly follow from their Quaker unique understandings of human relationship with the divine, questions of vocation, and philosophies of living. In particular, the Quaker belief in the Inner Light, which guides each individual as well as its commitments to the spiritual equality of men and women and simplicity in lifestyle, lead to a philosophy of procreation and family planning that stands in dramatic contrast to other forms of Christianity. Though varying in their descriptions and experiences of it, Quakers share a conviction that there exists a divine presence within each person. As a result, personal communion with that Inner Light brings one closer to God and mandates certain actions in the world. For example, if God dwells within everyone, killing, even in warfare, becomes deeply objectionable. As Quaker theologian and activist Rufus Jones (1863-1948) explains, this theological concept has deep roots in the experience of the individual:

> Experience, then, is the Quaker's starting-point. This light must be my light, this truth must be my truth, this faith must be my very own faith. The key that unlocks the door to the spiritual life belongs not to Peter, or to some other person, as an official. It belongs to the individual soul, that finds the light, that discovers the truth, that sees the revelation of God and goes on living in the demonstration and power of it. For this there is no substitute. (47)

The idea of the divine presence not only within individual believers but also in the particularities of their experience necessarily leads to diverse understandings of what the Inner Light will lead one to do and what one's faith may look like. Since the divine resides within the individual rather than a particular doctrine, creed, or text, there is a lack of intermediaries in communion with God as well as a lack of distinctions among people based on their gender, social standing, religious training, or hierarchical status.

The Religious Society of Friends traditionally refrains from explicit doctrine, moral codes, or detailed theologies in conceptualizing the divine or navigating day-to-day life. Rather, the integrity of individual believers and their attentiveness to the Inner Light within themselves serve as the guiding force in their life and life decisions. For historical Quakers and the contemporary Hicksite branch, Meeting for Worship consists of silent worship without clergy and an allowance for anyone who feels led to speak out to the group. The use of monthly "Queries" also helps direct practitioners to examine their own lives and choices as well as to evaluate their alignment with Quaker Testimonies.

As a tradition that has long rejected formal doctrine in favour of the truths revealed through silent worship and personal discernment, Quakerism has no creed to standardize the expression of the faith. In place of a creed, Quaker communities often focus on the Quaker Testimonies, which outline several key paradigms for ethical and faithful living and responsible engagement with the broader world.[1] These testimonies find various articulations but often focus on integrity, peace, equality, and simplicity. This sense of personal responsibility as well as the larger goal of Quaker communities to support and guide individuals in their own decision making is further evident in the practice of using Clearness Committees to prepare couples for marriage, welcome new members, and assist members in negotiating difficult decisions and events in their lives.

This "diffuseness" of Quaker beliefs, along with the growing prevalence of "convinced Friends" who bring with them the history and ideologies of their past affiliations, remains a concern for some Quakers.[2] As Margaret Hope Bacon writes, "Since Quakerism has no set creed, and since the unprogrammed meeting is formless, it is easy for these newcomers to read into the Society those things they would like to hear and see" (224). The absence of dogma or doctrine and the format of Meeting for Worship require neither affirmation of particular beliefs nor any performance of religious rituals by individuals in attendance. For these reasons, one can find a remarkably wide spectrum of beliefs and additional religious affiliations in a typical Quaker meeting.

For many Quakers, such variety stands not as a threat to unity or a sign of weakness but represents a particular understanding of the root of religious sentiment and the common struggle for truth. As Rufus Jones writes:

> Religious truth must grow like all truth. It must spring out of living experience. It must fit the convictions and aspirations of the time. It must be current coin. Whatever is proved and verified is thereby orthodox. We owe immense debts to past centuries in which heroic souls fought their valiant fight for the truth and passed it on to us. But their loyal devotion and their glimpse of truth do not settle our issues or relieve us from personal decision and present-day action. (46)

Truth, then, depends upon human discernment, but it must also be responsive to the needs and realities of the present time. Such responsiveness does not indicate weakness but attests to the truth's vitality and rootedness in individual experience.

EQUALITY IN SPIRIT AND BEYOND

Spiritual equality in Quakerism means not only that clergy are not necessary as a conduit between the believer and the divine but also that both men and women have access to spiritual gifts and may be moved to the ministry. George Fox, the founder of the Religious Society of Friends, wrote in his journal of the experiences that led him to founding Quakerism in the seventeenth century. He expresses dissatisfaction with the particular position of women and the disparity between the genders in spiritual and organizational capacities. Referring to recent objections to the Friends' tendency to hold women's meetings and allow female ministry, he writes:

> Faithful women, who were called to the belief of the Truth, being made partakers of the same precious faith, and heirs of the same everlasting gospel of life and salvation with the men, might in like manner come into the possession and practice of the gospel order, and therein be helpmeets unto the men in the restoration, in the service of Truth, in the affairs of the Church, as they are outwardly in civil, or temporal things; that so all the family of God, women as well as men, might know, possess, perform, and discharge their offices and services in the house of God, whereby the poor might be better taken care of, the younger instructed, informed, and taught in the way of God; the loose and disorderly reproved and admonished in the fear of the Lord; the clearness of persons proposing marriage more closely and strictly inquired into in the wisdom of God; and all the members of the spiritual body, the Church, might watch over and be helpful to each other in love. (537)

Fox stops short of advocating for radical equality that would completely erase gender roles or traditional family structures.

For instance, he notes early on that women would often hesitate to speak their minds in the business meetings populated by both genders. Recognizing that women might feel more comfortable speaking their minds in separate women-only meetings, and in the interest of encouraging free and open participation, women held separate meetings until such gatherings were again united in the late nineteenth and early twentieth centuries (Bacon 22).

Fox also highlights how women's biological and social roles as wives and mothers presented particular challenges, limitations, and gifts. Views of procreation and family planning in Quakerism relate directly to ideas about social engagement and equality of the sexes. As members of a religious reform movement, early Quakers rejected the Catholic model of celibate nuns who are separated from society. In contrast, "a spiritually 'gifted' woman in the Society of Friends could pursue her ministerial 'calling' without renouncing marriage or motherhood" (Larson 134). To establish a Biblical basis for this conviction, early Quakers pointed to Adam and Eve as the model of a god-ordained marriage and balanced humanity. Indeed, "female, as well as male, Quaker preachers overcame their carnal selves, not by denying their gendered identities or procreative capacities, but by speaking from the Inward Light" (Larson 134). When women served such a spiritual role, family structures necessarily shifted to reflect this broader identity. Such a commitment to balance reflects both a hesitancy to create any spiritual differentiations between the faithful as well as a belief in the ability of each faithful person to choose their own correct path by overcoming sinful desires and balancing life responsibilities.

PERSONAL DISCERNMENT IN WORSHIP AND LIFE

Quakerism's commitment to personal discipline and restraint has also necessitated careful and constant self-examination, which has led to many strong and love-filled unions between travelling ministers and their partners. Implicit in this view is the possible co-existence of marriage, procreation, and spiritual calling. George Fox himself modelled this resolution in marrying fifty-five year old Margaret Fell. The value of their union had less to with potential procreation and more to do with the spiritual strength and resources that each brought to the relationship (Larson 138).

Such convictions underlie the marriage process as well as discussions about procreation and family planning within the Society of Friends. In assisting a couple considering marriage under the care of a Monthly Meeting, the chosen Clearness Committee is charged with, among other things, discussing whether the couple plans to have children and how they will manage the care of those children. With the Quaker commitment to simplicity in mind, Quaker couples often limit the size of their families or consider adoption. In a handbook published by the Philadelphia Yearly Meeting in 1993 and distributed to many couples seeking clearness for marriage, Elizabeth G. Watson writes:

> Overpopulation is now a grave threat to the human family and to the planet itself. We are surpassing the capacity of the earth to provide adequate food for everyone, and the quality of life is threatened by too many people. This is not just a problem for developing countries; we need to consider it seriously in North America. A concerned Quaker couple made the decision not to have children. Instead, they hope to make some creative contribution to the world that will call on the best talents of both and be symbolic of their shared lives. Other couples adopt children or care for foster children, some consciously choosing hard-to-place children with handicaps or problems. If a couple still decides, understandably, to have their own children, they should consider limiting the number. (11)

Commitment to simplicity arises for Quakers from a variety of concerns. On the one hand, it reflects a desire to reduce earthly attachments and commitments, similar to the justification for celibacy in Paul's writings or the decision to live an ascetic life as a Christian.[3] On the other hand, the presence and guidance of the Inner Light necessitates a sense of responsibility for the larger global community. This commitment has led Quakers to the forefront of activist groups to end slavery, racism, sexism, and war. Similarly, it has led to a concern with overpopulation and the resultant strain on the resources of the world and the health of the planet.

As with other denominations, the Quaker perspective on childbearing has often been conditioned by the relative precariousness of childbirth in each era as well as the prevalence of infant death. In her history of Quaker women in America, Margaret Hope Bacon notes that in the colonial era, "one estimate suggests that one out of every three children died before the age of five" (58). As Bacon shows, the Quaker response to this reality was different from their co-religionists. Whereas "Puritans dealt with the possibility of children's death by baptizing them and zealously supervising their moral development, lest any be consigned to hell.... Quakers, however, were quite sure that children of parents who had received the Light would not be punished" (58).

This confidence in the spiritual status of these lost children also translates into a confidence that divine providence leads to the creation and growth of families. Elizabeth Collins, a Quaker minister in Evesham, New Jersey, demonstrates this perspective in her 1793 journal during a yellow fever epidemic. As Bacon recounts, Collins wrote that she heard an inner voice saying "'[a] great sacrifice will be required of thee.' Shortly thereafter, she lost three children in a row. Sitting at the bedside of one dying child the day after burying another, she again heard a voice that said, 'Just entering the city whose walls are salvation and her gates praise.' This comforted her sufficiently to endure the loss" (qtd. in Bacon 58). Similarly, Quaker martyr Mary Dyer "found in herself and her relationship with the Holy Spirit the authority to find her own truth and proclaim it" (Westerkamp 64). Demonstrating her break from Puritan theology, Dyer refused to follow prominent Puritan minister John Cotton in believing the still birth of her severely deformed child was divine rebuke for her acceptance of Quakerism (64). Her theological perspective, thus, allowed her to maintain her faith in God and in herself through an emotionally devastating event.

DISCERNMENT IN MOTHERHOOD

Spiritual discernment plays a role beyond family planning and childbirth, including infant care, feeding, and the vocation of motherhood more broadly. One of the earliest Quaker converts, Mary Penington (1616-1682), wrote of her personal motherhood struggles as part of her memoir. In addition to providing an intimate and informative window into early Quaker life, this memoir provides an eloquent description of a deeply personal and transformational experience in deep prayer. It also uses Penington's mothering experience to affirm her often unpopular and unconventional faith. Soon after her beloved first husband died, Penington gave birth to a daughter and refused to have her baptized. Citing her own reading of Galatians in contrast to others' misreading of the text, she writes, "When I was delivered of her, I refused to have her sprinkled, which brought great approach upon me; so I became a by-word and a hissing among the people of my own rank in the world; and a strange thing it was thought to be, among my relations and acquaintance" (Penington 137-138).

The prevalence of female ministers and the openness to women's participation in the ministry of individual Meetings empowered women in their home life as well. Though biologically driven processes, such as pregnancy, childbirth, and breastfeeding, naturally fell to women in such families, the care and management of the family represented a shared responsibility of the father and mother. Feminist Biblical scholar Rosemary Radford Ruether points to the Quakers as one of the earliest Christian groups to embrace what she sees as the true message of the scripture—the view that Jesus was an advocate for equality and social justice. She explains how:

> During the Reformation, particularly left-wing Puritans in England rediscovered intimations of an egalitarian Christianity—that included women's right to preach and to act as lay governors of the Church. This egalitarianism was found, here and there, among Baptists and other left-wing dissenters in the mid-seventeenth century, the period of the English civil war. The Quakers, thanks in no small part to the role of Margaret Fell, developed such egalitarian intimations into a more coherent theology and Scriptural

> exegesis.... They wrote that the subjugation of women was not God's intent but represented the sinful distortion of human nature by sin. Israel and, still more, the messianic community of Christ restored woman to her original full personhood; but the seventeenth-century Quakers dared to assert the implications of this messianic sociology only for the Church, not for society at large. (35)

Reflected in their language, testimonies, and writings, Quakers have instilled this sense of equality into their children as well.

Quaker values also influence more practical concerns, such as infant feeding. Like many of their non-Quaker counterparts, colonial Quaker women not only breastfed but used breastmilk to treat a variety of ailments experienced by both infants and adults. Gulielma Penn, the first wife of William Penn, the Quaker founder of Pennsylvania, used breastmilk to treat the ear and eye ailments of adults (*Penn Family Papers* 103). Although most Quaker women continued to breastfeed and wet nurses remained a fixture of wealthy families, some explored other options as the numbers of Quakers continued to grow. As Margaret Hope Bacon writes:

> Mary Pemberton, the second wife of Israel Pemberton, wrote her brother-in-law that 'after much fatigue with nurses, have plac'd our Little boy abroad, with a honest Reputable woman, in an airey part of the town, much to our satisfaction, and he thrives well.' Young mothers, however, preferred to nurse because breastfeeding was considered a means of birth control. Also, Quaker women ministers preached against the practice of employing a wet nurse, claiming that it was motivated by selfishness and deprived the infant of tender care and "a close sympathy" between mother and child. (57)

In this way, Quaker women have been influenced by changing customs and mores regarding breastfeeding, but have generally supported the practice as the method most in line with convictions that support simplicity.

CONCLUDING THOUGHTS: QUAKERISM, MOTHERHOOD, AND THE PARADOX OF CONTEMPORARY FEMINISM

Whether making decisions regarding baptism, infant feeding, or instilling children with a sense of right, Quaker motherhood has long allowed for what might seem like a rather progressive understanding of gender and the family. Indeed, inherent within the theology of Quakerism are the seeds for a feminist view of motherhood. The concept of the Inner Light places divine wisdom squarely within the individual, to be accessed through silent prayer. The commitment to equality has long allowed Quaker women greater latitude in religious community as well as in family units. Imbued with freedom and wisdom from the Inner Light, Quaker women rely on the process of discernment in motherhood—and life more generally—to guide their decisions.

Unique in the Christian tradition for allowing such radical equality and reliance on personal discernment from its inception, Quakerism allows women the freedom to chart their own path in motherhood and beyond. However, with the emergence of second-wave feminism, many Quaker women have found themselves on the margins of an often secular feminist movement. As Lucretia Mott has insisted, Quaker women found authority in the scriptures and in themselves. Since they were less hindered by church authority and other patriarchal structures, they did not always share other women's experiences of sexist oppression (Bacon 222). By finding a balance between religious conviction and feminism, the theological challenges put forwards by second-wave feminism had already been somewhat resolved for Quaker women, even as they were far from resolved in the broader society.

To that end, it would seem that a new host of theological challenges arose during the second half of the twentieth century for Quaker women, and they have stretched into the present. For instance, many women have found natural mothering paradigms that promote personal choice, simplicity, and female empowerment to be paradoxical to the radical freedom and equality that defines Quaker motherhood. As their belief in gender equality propels them to pursue educational and vocational opportunities, women's desires to exclusively breastfeed and intensively mother their children prove more difficult. For those who desire natural childbirth without interventions, complicated birth experiences can be seen as personal failures rather than empowering rites of passage.

As Chris Bodel describes in *The Paradox of Natural Mothering,* the complexity of contemporary lives and the competing demands of family, career, and personal health make "natural" choices logistically challenging and existentially frustrating. In the case of Quaker mothers, the belief that personal discernment is the source for truth presents an incredible pressure to make the "right" decisions, not only for oneself but also for one's children. Contemporary socio-economic realities make the desired outcomes all the more elusive. Accordingly, the challenge for Quaker women in the present day is to drown out the competing paradigms of motherhood in contemporary society that continue to inform women's internal dialogues, personal choices, and experiences of motherhood, and listen all the more intently to that voice within, not only for direction in the myriad of choices facing contemporary women, but also for grace to realize one's own needs, strengths, and limitations. It is in this meeting of discernment and grace that women can achieve the inner quiet and peace, so elusive in this day and age, which best allows that Inner Light to shine.

NOTES

[1]The exact articulation of the Testimonies has varied over time and varies by group. To read current articulations, the most reliable sources are the publications created and adopted by monthly meetings and larger organizations throughout the world. These publications detail the history and core values of the community as well as guidelines for organization and conducting business and worship. Included are lists and descriptions of the Testimonies. A variety of such publications can be found online through Earlham School of Religion's Quaker Information Center.

[2]The term "convinced friend" contrasts with "Birth-right" Quaker to distinguish between those born into the tradition and those who convert into it. Quakers eschew the language of conversion as a

way of maintaining individual agency in this transition. Individuals discern their right path – they are not converted by another.
[3]Paul discusses celibacy most directly in his First Letter to the Corinthians. In Chapter 7 of this letter, Paul recognizes the fact that sexual immorality has been occurring in the Corinthian community. He begins the chapter by instructing married couples to "fulfill ... marital duty" to each other as a way to mediate otherwise unbridled passions. He then continues, "I say this as a concession, not as a command. I wish that all of you were as I am" (1 Corinthians 7:6-7, NRSV). Marriage is a concession to the weak who cannot control their bodies and passions and would otherwise engage in immoral behaviours.

WORKS CITED

Bacon, Margaret Hope. *The Quiet Rebels: The Story of the Quakers in America*. Wallingford, PA: Pendle Hill Publications, 1999. Print.

Bodel, Chris. *The Paradox of Natural Mothering*. Philadelphia: Temple University Press, 2002. Print.

Fox, George. *The Journal of George Fox*. Ed. Rufus M. Jones. Richmond, Indiana: Friends United Press, 1976. Print.

Fry, Elizabeth. *Elizabeth Fry: A Quaker Life. Selected Letters and Writings*. Ed. Gil Skidmore. Lanham, MD: AltaMira Press, 2005. Print.

Jones, Rufus M. *The Faith and Practice of the Quakers*. New York: Methuen & Co. Ltd., 1927. Print.

Larson, Rebecca. *Daughters of Light: Quaker Women Preaching and Prophesying in the Colonies and Abroad, 1700-1775*. Chapel Hill: The University of North Carolina Press, 1999. Print.

Mott, Lucretia. "Not Christianity, But Priestcraft." *Feminism: The Essential Historical Writings*. Ed. Miriam Schneir. New York: Random House, 1972. 99-102. Print.

Penington, Mary. "I Dust Not Mock Him with a Form." *The Quaker Reader*. Ed. Jessamyn West. Wallingford, PA: Pendle Hill Publications, 1992. Print.

Penn Family Papers, Vol. 6. Philadelphia: Historical Society of Pennsylvania Library. Print.

Ruether, Rosemary Radford. *Sexism and God-Talk: Toward a*

Feminist Theology. Boston: Beacon Press, 1993. Print.
Watson, Elizabeth G. *Marriage in the Light: Reflections on Commitment and the Clearness Process (A Revision and Expansion of Clearness for Marriage)*. Philadelphia: Family Relations Committee of Philadelphia Yearly Meeting, Religious Society of Friends, April 1993. Print.
Westerkamp, Marilyn J. "Puritan Women, Spiritual Power, and the Question of Sexuality." *The Religious History of American Women: Reimagining the Past*. Ed. Catherine A. Brekus. Chapel Hill: University of North Carolina Press, 2007. 51-72. Print

8.
Motherhood in Hindu Religion

Glorification without Emanicipation

ZAIRUNISHA

Yaa Devi Sarva Bhooteshu, Matru Rupena Sansitha |
Namastasyai, Namastasyai, Namastasyai Namo Namaha||
The goddess who is omnipresent as the personification of universal mother, I bow to her, I bow to her, I bow to her again and again.

—Devi Mahatmaya Purana

Jagdamba Vichitramatra Kim Paripoorna Karunaasti Chenmayi |
Aparadha Parampara Param Na Hi Mata Samapekshate Sutam||
O mother of the world Jagdamba, you are the one who looks after her children. Your love and kindness towards me is no surprise O mother goddess. Being a mother you forget all our sins and correct us without abandoning your children.[1]

—Devi Mahatmaya Purana

THERE ARE MANY Vedic[2] hymns and verses in which Hindu women are deified and venerated as mother goddesses. They are regarded as the universal feminine energy and latent power, or *Shakti*, through which God creates, preserves, and destroys the universe. Hindu communities worship malevolent and benevolent forms of *Shakti* or Divine Cosmic Mother Goddess, and call her by many names, such as Maa Kali, Durga, Jagdamba, Lakshmi, Sarswati, and so on. The ideal Hindu mother is seen as a manifestation of the divine mother *Shakti*, referred to as Maa, Mata, Devi, and Amma, among others, and is accorded a respectable status in society. However, like many other world religions, Hinduism is predominantly patriarchal (Jayaram). There are many other Vedic hymns that clearly illustrate women's subjugated position and construct the procreation of male offspring as women's primary life purpose. To that end, during India's freedom struggle, national identity was reimagined in the form of "Mother India" to reaffirm the importance of traditional motherhood and encourage Indian women to embrace this role. Moreover, in the contemporary social context of globalization, wherein women are becoming increasingly conscious of their rights and critical of patriarchal gender roles, the emerging forces of Hindutva[3] claim to rehabilitate Hindu women's traditional role as full time mothers. This reveals the deep disconnect between the symbolic reverence paid to mothers in Hinduism and the oppression that Hindu women experience in their daily lives. As such, women are lauded in most of the Hindu religious texts but primarily as creators of male progeny.

This chapter, accordingly, elucidates the ideological role ascribed to mothers in Hindu religious traditions. It analyzes social constructions of Hindu mothers and motherhood in the three fundamental and seminal texts—*Manusmirti*, *Ramayana,* and *Mahabharata*—which glorify the maternal role while subjugating women in a patriarchal gender hierarchy. In doing so, it addresses the gap between the symbolic adoration paid to motherhood and the oppressive conditions that shape women's lives. The chapter further considers how contemporary Hindutva forces are attempting to preserve "traditional" motherhood in response to cultural and economic globalization, which continues to challenge the Hindu ways of life.

SOCIAL CONSTRUCTIONS OF HINDU MOTHERS IN MYTHOLOGICAL TEXTS

In Hinduism, motherhood is a subject of apotheosis and great reverence (Bhattacharji). As stated in the Taitariya Upanishad, the expression "*Matru Devo Bhave,*" meaning "mother is a Goddess," reflects the deep respect afforded to mothers in Hindu religious consciousness. Mother goddesses are symbolically linked with fertility, maternal love, nurturance, and procreation. Likewise, Hindu mothers are envisaged as a divine mother goddess, as is illustrated in the three sacred texts, Manusmirti, Ramayana, and Mahabharata. These texts continue to play a key role in shaping beliefs about the ideal Hindu woman. Collectively, these texts glorify women's capacities as mothers but ultimately contend that the only way for women to gain social status and prestige is to bear male children and take care of their families.

Manusmirti

Manusmirti is generally accepted as the law book for Hindu life. Manu, the text's author, constructs a rigid gender hierarchy and gives the highest status to women as mothers but also imposes several restrictions on them. As one verse prescribes, "Where women are adored, there the Gods are delighted; but where they are not worshipped, all religious ceremonies become futile"(2.143).Other verses clarify that a mother is venerable to everything (2.133) and that she should not be treated with disrespect (2.225). At the same time, Manu establishes strict rules that deny women any freedom or autonomy. He portrays women who are of weak character and are, therefore, in constant need of protection. He states that "Her father protects [her] in childhood, her husband protects [her] in youth, and her sons protect [her] in old age; a woman is never fit for independence" (9.3).

Manu, likewise, emphasizes the importance of birthing sons rather than daughters. According to him, daughters should be raised in preparation for their future roles as mothers and hope to be blessed with many sons (Bhattacharji). A prayer in the sacred text of Atharva-Veda also indicates the common desire for a male child: "Grant the birth of a girl elsewhere, here grant a son" (5.4.23). In a similar manner, Manu mentions that the female was created by Brahma, the Supreme Creator God, as a part of the duality in creation. She was meant to be a companion to the male and facilitate the act of procreation to ensure his family lineage. A woman, therefore, has little value or status outside marriage. Similarly, a married woman without a male child has no respect in the family.

Ramayana

Many versions of the *Ramayana*[4] are available in different Indian languages, all of which depict King Rama, an incarnation of the god Vishnu, and his wife Sita, an incarnation of Vishnu's wife (i.e., goddess Lakshmi) as an ideal married couple. In this narrative, in order to fulfill his vow to his third wife, Keikeyi, King Dashratha banishes Rama, his son, from the kingdom of Ayodhya for fourteen years. Sita, daughter of King Janaka, is born from earth and is called the divine daughter of mother earth. Her identity and existence are defined by her dedication to Rama and her two sons. Sita, thus, accompanies Rama in his exile and remains an obedient and dutiful wife. After the killing of Ravana, her kidnapper, she is forced to prove her chastity by giving herself to fire ordeal. Rama banishes her from the kingdom to the forest to protect his own image as a righteous king. She ends her life by requesting mother earth to relieve her of further agony:

> If unstained in thought and action I have lived from the day of my birth, spare a daughter's shame and anguish and receive her, Mother Earth! If in duty and devotion, I have laboured undefiled, Mother Earth! Who bore this woman, once again receive thy child! If in truth unto my husband I have proved a faithful wife, Mother Earth! Relieve thy Sita from the burden of this life! (qtd. in Gokhale and Lal 21)

Such is the misfortune of an ideal wife who has to live at the mercy of her husband and be ready to sacrifice her life to prove fidelity to him. *Ramacharitmanas*, another popular version of *Ramayana*, devalues women by portraying them as illiterates and low caste *Shudras*[5] as well as by comparing them to drums and animals, which have to be beaten and scolded constantly (Tulsidas verse 58). These teachings illustrate the vulnerable condition of women in a society in which men are always viewed as virtuous and women are compelled to accept subordination as part of their destiny. Despite his unrighteous treatment of Sita, Rama is regarded as an ideal husband and king, also lauded as *Maryada Purushottama* (an ideal traditional man). In contrast, Sita is expected to assume full responsibility and blame for her misfortune, even though she remains devoted to Rama until death.

Hindu women are taught to emulate Sita in their own lives by remaining pure, chaste, and loyal towards their husbands, despite any rejection or mistreatment. They are encouraged to fast, pray, and sacrifice their own desires to ensure the well-being of their husbands and sons. As Sudhir Kakar indicates:

> [Sita's] unique standing in the minds of most Hindus, regardless of region, caste, social class, age, sex, education, or modernization, testifies to the power and pervasiveness of the traditional ideal of womanhood.... It is through the recitation, reading, listening to, or attending a dramatic performance of this revered text that a Hindu reasserts his or her cultural identity as a Hindu, and obtains religious merit. (*The Inner World* 74)

Like their mothers, Hindu daughters are also expected to follow Sita and prepare for their future roles as wives and mothers. It can, thus, be argued that the feminine ideal embodied by Sita permeates Hindu cultures and psyches. Kakar aptly states it:

> From earliest childhood, a Hindu has heard Sita's legend recounted on any number of sacral and secular occasions; heard her qualities extolled in devotional songs; and absorbed the ideas of feminine identity she incorporates through the many everyday metaphors and similes that are associated with her name. (*The Inner World* 74)

Mahabharata

Mahabharata, meaning the great story of India, presents a similar view of women. It was initially narrated by seer Krishna Dvaipayana Vedavyasa, with additions compiled later on by other authors. It is a story of struggle between two groups of cousins: the Kauravas and Pandavas. Princess Draupadi is forced to marry the five Pandava brothers simply because their mother, Kunti, says so. Kunti never gives Draupadi a choice in the matter.

Although a mother's status is considered higher than a father's, like *Ramayana*, this narrative depicts and legitimizes women's subjugated social position. Such a position is reflected in Pandava's grand uncle Bhishma's statement that "Either a husband or a father is the way of women ... since husbands, even weak ones, protect their wife" (3.13.60).

In this way, women are perceived as *Prakriti*, or "nature," and men are perceived as *Ksetrajna*, or "knower of the field," who should have control over women. In *Mahabharata*, it is claimed that "Women should be understood as causing the characteristics of the world. They are the nature, being the field; men are the form of the field. They are the eternal embodiment of the senses, hidden in passion" (12.206.7-8). Similarly, this text ascribes an inferior status to daughters in comparison to sons, since the birth of a daughter is seen as a source of misery, whereas a son is seen as the saviour of the family (1.173.10).

Many other accounts and narratives of ideal Hindu womanhood are stories of suffering, cruelty, oppression, discrimination, and injustice. Hindu texts claim that a woman who is dedicated to following her *pativratadharma*, the duties that are ascribed to a wife, is not an ordinary human but a divine goddess. Describing the status of mother goddess in Hinduism, Kamala Ganesh contends that

> The mother-goddess can be interpreted as expressing ideas of power, autonomy and primacy in the widest sense of the terms. She conveys not so much the idea of physical motherhood but a worldview in which the creative power of femininity is central; the goddess mediates between life and death and contains in herself the possibility of regeneration. (73)

No religious, social, or domestic ceremony of prayers for divine blessings can be considered complete in the absence of a wife. However, contrary to this divinization of women, they are often depicted as property owned by males and regarded similarly to *Shudras* in many sacred texts. This commodification and objectification of women contribute to their degradation and marginalization in social life. In this sense, a disconnect exists between the glorification of motherhood in the Hindu sacred texts and Hindu women's lived experiences of motherhood.

HINDU NATIONALISM AND IDEOLOGY OF MOTHERHOOD

During the period of freedom struggle against British colonial rule, India was viewed as the motherland under a foreign yoke. The British rulers were the aggressors who had invaded the *Matribhoomi* or motherland, and India sought to gain *Svaraja*—self-rule and independence. In constructing the identity of India as a nation, a recourse was taken to revive and reappropriate the ancient Indian religious heritage. Articulation of Indian nationalism revolved around the image of "mother India" as *Bharatmata* or "motherland Bharat." "*VandeMataram*," meaning veneration for the mother India, a song written by Bankim Chandra, became a powerful political anthem for the nationalists during this time (Bagchi60-70). The worship of mother goddesses Kali and Durga was invoked to overcome the slavery of mother India, who had to be saved from British oppression.

Indian women of all communities were encouraged to participate in the movement to free mother India from the clutches of the alien rulers. Mahatma Gandhi was the first Congress leader to use the potential strength and emotional power of such mythological icons for mobilizing modern women to participate in the freedom straggle. Gandhi lauded traditional Hindu values and promoted the iconic Sita as a national role model for Indian women by glorifying her chastity, devotion, and domestic virtues. As he states it, "if you want *Swaraja*, or *Ramaraja* you have to become as pure as Sita...only a woman who keeps her body and mind pure is worthy of our reverence, therefore, sisters wear *Khadhi* ply *Charkha*[6] and become pure" (538). To that end, despite their active participation in the freedom movement, women were expected to place their primary value in their traditional roles as wives and mothers.

During the colonial rule, British rulers legally prohibited widow burning, early child marriage, female foeticides, and they permitted widow remarriage. There was a strong reaction to the Christian missionaries and the spread of Western values, and Hindutva, accordingly, emerged as a nationalist response against the Westernization or modernization of Indian society. Kakar indicates, "In searching for alternative modes of life as a response to the disruptions of modernity, the reformulation of Hinduism was being strongly influenced by a nationalist, religious activism" (*The Indians* 135). As such, the Hindutva response to reforms introduced by the British was regressive and reactionary. As Jyotsana A. Gupta argues:

> By extolling an ideology that apparently rested on a show of the empowering women, it was reinforcing a social philosophy of deprivation for women; it was a signal to women to sacrifice everything for their men folk. The internalisation of this so-called ideal that nationalism put up for women simply reinforced the traditional notion that the fruition of women's lives lay in producing heroic sons. The nationalist ideology, therefore, simply appropriated this orthodox bind on women's lives by glorifying it. This renewed ideological legitimacy made it even more difficult for women to exercise their choice or autonomy in the matter. (98-99)

After independence, the new Indian republic was invested with a sense of purpose and a moral vision with exciting possibilities for the people of free India. The preamble to the Indian constitution assures "equality of status, opportunity and dignity, freedom of belief and expression, social justice to all its citizens without any discrimination on the basis of caste, creed or gender" (Gautam 54).The directive principles of state policies include the provision of universal education, adequate means of livelihood for men and women, equal pay for equal work, and protection from abuse. A radical transformation is, thus, required for Indian society to break the hold of caste and gender hierarchies. Protecting the rights of women, children, *Shudras*, and minorities remains a serious challenge for the democratic governance of India as Hindutva forces strive to preserve traditional Hindu culture in the country (Gautam 55).

GLOBALIZATION AND HINDUTVA FORCES: CHANGING HINDU MOTHERS

Since the spread of globalization in the mid-1980s, rampant reforms have influenced the Indian economy and social life in significant ways. With the introduction of new technologies for sharing information, goods and services can now be quickly exchanged, which has provided India's middle classes with unprecedented access to goods, ideas, services, and values at a global level (Gautam 56). Indian women have become aware of women's movements from all over the world and are now questioning patriarchal ideologies and reinterpreting the ancient texts from feminist and *Shudra* (Dalit) perspectives. They are also challenging the atrocities and abuses inflicted on them.

Many critics of consumerism and corporate culture suspect that traditional Indian values are in grave danger and require a proactive approach to preserve them. *Hindutava* activists, also called *Sangh Parivar*, claim to be self-appointed guardians of the Hindu tradition. They profess their commitment to protect the superiority of India's traditional spiritual culture and its symbolic representation through the rehabilitation of traditional gender roles. They further regard it as necessary to safeguard Indian women and mothers from corrupt and laxWestern morality and its influences. The women's wing of *Sangh Pariwar,* named *Rashriya Sevika Samiti,* is dedicated to the protection of women's chastity and the traditional Hindu ideology of motherhood (Gangopadhyay 71-73).

Despite their success in moving beyond traditional domestic roles, Hindu women are expected to remain subservient to patriarchal domination. Although the *Hindutva* activists cannot afford to openly oppose the constitutional rights of women, they actively question and condemn women's struggles for securing better working and living conditions. Furthermore, these self-appointed protectors of traditional Hindu culture do not hesitate to use Western technologies for female foeticide or similar efforts to ensure the birth of male children.

The traditional Hindu ideology of motherhood has strong physical, psychological, and social effects on girls and women. Now that many Hindu mothers have gained the advantage of education and employment in the new economy, they are expected to follow the norms and ideals prescribed for "divine" womanhood and motherhood in *Manusmirti, Ramayana,* and *Mahabharata.* This glorification and essentialism of motherhood marginalizes women in political, social, and economic realms. When such a hegemonic, patriarchal worldview is internalized, women have little space to move beyond traditional domestic roles. Furthermore, the traditional image of motherhood inculcates many other gendered family roles, such as the ideal daughter, sister, and so on. Women's sexual expression is expected to be confined only to marriage and motherhood, and acknowledging or embracing sexuality can be a cause for shame, social rejection, and condemnation.

It is more challenging for working mothers to negotiate their two roles, since they have to balance their priorities in accordance with traditional demands of being a "good" caring mother. They have to take care of their family as well as perform their public work, which creates immense mental and physical pressure. The inability to balance these two realms often affects their maternal and family relationships. Even women with privileged economic positions are not necessarily able to cope with these demands. For instance, Justice Leila Seth, the first woman justice in the Supreme Court of India, recalls the conflict she faced when her son expressed his anger about her being a working woman and not a traditional "caring" mother:

> I remember my own sense of guilt when a friend of mine told me what my young son Vikram had said when she chatted with him. She had stated, "It must be wonderful to have such an intelligent mother" and he retorted, "I do not care how intelligent she is, she is never here when I want her." It made me introspect, and I wondered whether I should give up my legal career. Was I failing my children? How was I to create that fine balance between my career, my obligations as a wife and my duties as a mother, so that none suffered? (13)

Women who are unable to give "proper" care to their families because of career aspirations are socially stigmatized and experience internalized guilt. They are called "bad" and "selfish" mothers, and are not accepted in traditional Hindu families. Celibate, childless, and sonless women are similarly viewed as a burden, who must be set aside through remarriage or abandonment. Meanwhile, Hindu tradition allows males to continue to remarry until they find a woman who produces a son for their family. Apprehension over such possibilities generates feelings of threat, dread, and insecurity among women, and makes their condition quite precarious.

In traditional Hindu wisdom, a woman's individuality is primarily celebrated in the realm of motherhood, which raises questions about whether a woman can be a dignified, autonomous person who is capable of making her own choices and decisions. Before marriage, her identity is attached to her father's name, and after marriage, she is known by her husband's name. This illustrates women's dependence and subordination during each stage of life, just as it reveals the complex relationship between discourses of women's rights and human rights. Even though the Indian constitution has a provision of equal rights for all, this is not true for women in reality. Inhibited by oppressive Hindu myths as well as their secondary positions in family and social life, women find it difficult to exercise their legal rights as equals. It is also pertinent to note that the ideological glorification of Hindu mothers as sacred beings does not end with the individual mother; rather, mothers are compelled to teach their daughters about the virtues of traditional gender roles. As religious texts prescribe, daughters should follow their mothers' ways of doing things, and girls are, thus, compelled to search for their emancipation within this patriarchal framework.

CONCLUSION: SEARCHING FOR MOTHERS' EMANCIPATION

This chapter has elucidated the unbridgeable gulf between the symbolic glorification of motherhood projected in *Manusmirti*, *Ramayana*, and *Mahabharata*, and the lived realities of Hindu mothers. In the process of deifying mothers, these texts stipulate specific norms and duties that restrict women to the maternal role and exclude them from the public domain. The glorification and veneration of Indian Hindu women is ascribed within the realms of marriage and motherhood, but there is little room for women to achieve honour and prestige beyond these traditional roles. Rather, they are oppressed and subjugated in the garb of divinity and are encouraged to embrace symbolic reverence in lieu of substantive emancipation.

Although globalization has played a significant role in improving the economic, cultural, and social position of middle-class mothers in India, women are still pressured to operate within this traditional patriarchal framework. With greater access to education, women are exploring new possibilities beyond their maternal work, just as they have begun questioning patriarchal ideologies and practices. However, the self-proclaimed guardians of Hindutva, influenced by the powerful texts and ideologies explored in this chapter, continue to police women. Indian women, thus, face a substantial struggle towards full dignity and autonomy. As Tanika Sarkar highlights, "women's bodies are still held to be pure and loyal to orthodox Hindu culture. The Hindu female body is not a free body, by any means, but one ruled by 'our' scriptures, 'our' customs" (202).To emancipate themselves from the imaginary glory of motherhood, women need proper healthcare, education, and full control over their bodies, including their procreative choices. An all-encompassing transformation is needed regarding cultural beliefs about what it means to be female and to embody femininity. In this way, a mere glorification can never be a substitute for substantive emancipation from oppression.

Acknowledgements: I would like to express my sincere thanks to my mentor and PhD supervisor, Professor Satya P. Gautam, for his continued encouragement and support. This work was possible because of the inspiration that I received from him. I also wish to thank Vanessa Reimer and Jesse O'Reilly-Conlin for their valuable comments, suggestions, and constant support.

NOTES

[1]English translation by Vinod Sood (www.speakingtree.in).
[2]The term "Vedic" refers to the views expressed in the four Vedas, the most ancient and sacred Hindu texts.

[3]"Hinduva" is a term coined by Veer Savarkar, a Hindu nationalist and understands Hindu traditions from a narrow, sectarian, fundamentalist, and dogmatic view.
[4]*Ramayana* means "the journey of Rama" also called "Adikavya" (first poem) it was first written by sage Valmiki in Sanskrit and later on many other versions in different languages by different authors are available. The most popular version is *Ramacharit-Manas* written by Tulsidas.
[5]In Hinduism, there is a hierarchical caste system consisting of four categories: *Brahmin*, *Kshtriya*, *Vaishya*, and *Shudra*. *Shudra* or Dalit caste is considered the lowest caste and its members are treated as "untouchable." They were forced to live apart from the other three castes.
[6]Mahatma Gandhi emphasizes the importance of wearing home-made cloths called Khadhi. Charkha is a hand-run spinning wheel for making Khadhi threads.

WORKS CITED

Bagchi, J. "Representing Nationalism: Ideology of Motherhood in Colonial Bengal." *Economic and Political Weekly* 25.42-43 (1990): WS65-WS71. Print.

Bhattacharji, Sukumari. "Motherhood in Ancient India." *Economic and Political Weekly* 25.42-43, (1990): WS50-WS57 Print.

Chand, Devi, ed. *The Atharvaveda: Sanskrit text with English Translation*. Trans. Devi Chand. New Delhi: Munshiram Manoharlal, 1982. Print.

Devi MahatmayaPuran, Trans. Ramnarayan Datta. Gorakhpur: Geeta Press, 1999. Print.

Seth, Leila. *A Working Woman*. Text of Dr. S. Radhakrishnan Memorial Lecture. Shimla, India: Indian Institute of Advanced Study, 2015. Print.

Gandhi, M. K. *Collected Works*. Ahmadabad: Navajivan Press, 1969. Print.

Ganesh, Kamala. "In Search of the Great Indian Goddess: Motherhood Unbound." *Motherhood in India*. Ed. Maithreyi Krishnaraj. New Delhi: Routledge, 2010. 73-105. Print.

Gangopadhyay, Monalisa. "Hindutva Meets Globalization: The

Impact on Hindu Urban Media Women." *FIU Electronic Thesesand Dissertations*. N.p., 2010. Web. 22 Feb.2016.

Gautam, Satya, P. "Globalization, Democracy and Social Justice." *Ethics, Values and Social Transformation*. Conference Proceedings of International Conference on Ethics, Values and Social Transformation. Ed. Ghazala Irfan. Karachi: Oxford University Press, 2006. 51-61. Print.

Gokhale, Namita, and Malashri Lal, eds. *In Search of Sita: Revisiting Mythology*. New Delhi: Penguin Books, 2014. Print.

Gupta, Jyotsana Agnihotri. *New Reproductive Technologies: Women's Health and Autonomy*. New Delhi: Sage, 2005. Print.

Jayaram, V. "Traditional Status of Women in Hinduism." *The Hindu*. N.p., n.d. Web. 12 Sept. 2015.

Kakar, Sudhir. *The Inner World: A Psychoanalytic Study of Childhood and Society in India*. New Delhi: Oxford University Press, 2015. Print.

Kakar, Sudhir. *The Indians: Portrait of a People*. New Delhi: Penguin Books, 2007. Print.

Sarkar, Tanika. *Hindu Wife, Hindu Nation: Community, Religion and Cultural Nationalism*. New Delhi: Permanent Black, 2001. Print.

Speaking Tree. Times Internet Limited, n.d. Web. 10 Dec. 2015.

The Manusmriti. Trans. Nene Gopalasastri. Varanasi: Chowkhamba Publication, 1935. Print.

Tulsidas. *Ramcharitmanas*. Trans. Puddar, Hanuman Prasad. Gorakhpur: Geeta Press, 1998. Print.

9.
Text Line, Blood Line

Familial Inheritance in Non-Biological Queer Jewish Mothering

EMILY MCAVAN

AFTER OVER A CENTURY of depictions in U.S. popular culture on radio, page, and screen, the image of the Jewish mother is a familiar one. There are two constants in much of this history of the Jewish mother: she is represented as heterosexual and as a biological mother. Similarly, Jewish mothers are represented as heterosexual and biological in Jewish religious and philosophical discussion of family and inheritance, in *responsum* to *halakha* (Jewish religious law), in normatively male theological discussions and, even at times, among Jewish feminists. Lesbian, bisexual, and transgender mothers have been, hitherto, largely invisible as Jewish mothers.

As Joyce Antler notes towards the end of her book about Jewish mothering, *You Never Write! You Never Call!*, "the new trends are changing how the Jewish mother is represented in our culture—gay Jewish mothers, Jewish mothers of gay daughters and sons, single Jewish mothers, Jewish mothers in mixed marriages, Jewish mothers by choice, Jewish mothers of colour, and working and professional mothers" (242). It is with this in mind that I write this chapter on queer Jewish mothering, with a particular view on non-biological parenting. I take from Sara Ruddick's influential paper "Maternal Thinking" the idea that "'maternal' is a social category" that arises out of "actual child caring practices," for which "biological parenting is neither necessary nor sufficient" (347). To that end, Jewish feminist theorist Judith Plaskow has poignantly written that "we learn to insert ourselves into silences" (1) as women, and this is doubly true for queer women—especially queer mothers. In this chapter, I discuss how queer mothering occurs in normatively heterosexual Jewish communities and texts by addressing the following questions: what does it mean to be a non-biological parent in a people wherein kinship is primarily defined matrilinealy? How might queer mothers rework Jewish ideas of kinship and inheritance? And finally, what kinds of inheritance occur when a queer non-biological parent is a Jewish parent?

BLOOD LINE

If there is one thing that Jews of all stripes—from Reform to ultra-Orthodox, Ashkenazim to Sephardim to Mizrahim—agree on, it is that Jewishness is matrilineal. The Babylonian Talmud states:

> How do we know that her [the mother's] child bears her religious identity? Rabbi Yochanan said in the name of Rabbi Shimon bar Yochai: Because the Torah says "your son." This means that your son from a Jewish woman is called your son, but your son from a non-Jewish woman is not called your son, but rather her son. (Talmud Kiddushin 68b)

The biological child born of a Jewish woman is, thus, incontrovertibly Jewish. When a child has only a Jewish father, that child by *halakha* is not considered Jewish by birth; only the socially liberal Reform and Reconstructionist movements recognize patrilineal descent, and then only if the child is raised Jewish.

In one sense, Jewish heredity for the Orthodox and Conservative movements is very simple—only the child born of a Jewish mother is a Jew. All others need to convert to Judaism, either as children with their parents or through study as adults. Nonbiological mothers, therefore, seemingly hold the same position as Jewish fathers and are not recognized in defining their children's Jewishness. Yet it would be a mistake to think that Jewish men are sidelined by the tradition's matrilineal descent. One key moment in Jewish tradition shows what I call the "biological imperative" in defining family—the covenant with Abraham at Mount Moriah. The covenant with Abraham, symbolized by the ritual circumcision of (assigned) male infants, establishes the Jewish people as a nation. Genesis 17 states that "such shall be the covenant between Me and you and your offspring to follow which you shall keep: every male among you shall be circumcised. You shall circumcise the flesh of your foreskin, and that shall be the sign of the covenant between Me and you" (17:11 *JPS Hebrew-English Tanakh*). In Genesis 22, Abraham almost sacrifices his son Isaac at God's behest—a problematic episode that has fascinated thinkers from Kierkegaard to Derrida—and is rewarded for his devotion with "descendants as numerous as the stars of heaven and the sands on the seashore" (22:17 *JPS*). Although there are some movements in Jewish communities towards replacing circumcision with a naming ceremony that enters the child into the Jewish people without the actual circumcision (sometimes called a *brit shalom*), circumcision as practice remains normative in all Jewish communities.

As a result, circumcision remains a powerful metaphor by which Jewishness is instantiated. For instance, theologian Michael Wyschogrod in his work *Body of Faith* notes that "Israel's symbol of the covenant is circumcision, a searing of the covenant into the flesh of Israel, and not only, or perhaps not even primarily, into its spirit.... The Law cuts into all the human modes of exercising life-force: eating, drinking, appropriating property, etc. All of these are circumcised in Judaism" (qtd. in Plaskow 83). The circumcision of men becomes the dominant metaphor of Jews' relation to the Law (*halakha*) and to Torah, in all their quotidian consequences. Abraham's near sacrifice of Isaac, therefore, becomes the key metaphor for Jewish reproductivity—it is Abraham's actions that have created the Jewish people, not Sarah's, his wife.

Understandably, this metaphor has been critiqued by feminists, such as Plaskow, for its insistence on the male body as normative. Women's relationship to circumcision—and hence to the Law—is that of spectator. This is one of the "shadowy forms" of female subjectivity that Plaskow discusses (1). The sign of the covenant—much like other signs of Jewishness, such as the *kippah* (skull cap, called a *yarmulke* in Yiddish), *tzitzit* (knotted fringes), and *tallit* (prayer shawls)—exclusively alights on the male body in traditional Judaism.

Furthermore, this covenant establishes Jewishness as what queer theorist Lee Edelman calls "reproductive futurism" (2)—the culturally compulsory promise of future production of children. Abraham's covenant with God, which is inscribed on his body and those of his male descendants, is rewarded with heterosexual fecundity, therein tying together religious practice with a normatively male body. Not only does this covenant exclude women, but it instantiates a norm in which queers of all kinds, including queer parents, can only partially inhabit. Queer reproductivity is many things, but it is not *easy*. Unlike the famously large families of the Hareidim (ultra-Orthodox) today, queer families are rarely as numerous as the stars, and they often feature either a technologizing of reproduction (via IVF) or a prior heterosexual union (adoption and step-parenting). Non-biological parents may still enter their (male) children into the covenant through circumcision, but they do not share a portion in Abraham's reward. In other words, neither the patrilineal tradition symbolized by the *brit* (the covenant between the Jewish people and God) nor the matrilineal tradition of descent in the Talmud adequately accounts for the important investments that non-biological parents make in their children's Jewishness.

THE END OF MONOMATERNALISM

Yet if one thing is also apparent in the present day, it is that the question of who is a Jew and what that means is decidedly *not* simple. Contemporary forms of step, adoptive, and queer family are proliferating, not to mention the ballooning intermarriage rate—up to 70 percent of Reform Jews are now marrying Gentiles ("A Portrait of Jewish Americans"). The modern Jewish family, then, is undergoing a profound transformation. To simply define Jewish families by *halakha* is to leave a large number of Jewish families out in the cold. It is my contention that Jewishness, and indeed Judaism, needs to be seen as a more capacious category that responds ethically to the challenges of LGBT Jews. Moreover, Jewish mothering must be seen as an in-process activity that may be performed by more than one woman rather than as a solely biological inheritance. Mothers, whether or not they have given birth, engage in maternal thought, thereby "acting in the interests of preservation and growth" (Ruddick 354). To see mothering as such challenges what Shelley Park calls "monomaternalism" (3), the ideology that there is one *and only one* type of mother. The twentieth-century Jewish mother studied by Antler must now be recognized as irrevocably plural—and perhaps she always was so.

To that end, Park discusses how non-biological mothers are sidelined by the ideology of monomaternalism:

> Within blended families ... the nonbiological or "step" mother is frequently reduced to a secondary status due to a lack of blood ties (combined, perhaps, with a lack of seniority). Lesbian co-mothers often encounter a similar phenomenon, wherein the status of their relationship borne of their partner is queried and they find themselves named (sometimes by their own partners or ex-partners) as something other than mother. (5)

Monomaternalism, thus, posits a "real" sole mother, primarily founded on a biological link between one mother and her child. To be sure, there may be rare cases when two mothers both share a biological relationship to their child, as when a transgender woman impregnates her cisgender female partner. These relationships may struggle to be recognized *as* queer. But, otherwise, most queer relationships, where there are two (or more) mothers, involve non-biological parenting, which problematizes the ideology of monomaternalism and the heterosexual nuclear family. Stepmothers may find themselves trapped in a double bind of needing to be simultaneously close (because they are women) and distant (because their relationship to their child is not biological), a "combination of the myths of motherhood and womanhood ... and the focus on the biological nuclear family that makes it impossible for stepmothers to be seen as other than pathological parents" (Sonowska-Buxton 462). Whether step or otherwise, queer non-biological co-mothers may struggle for symbolic and legal recognition of their familial ties with their children—monomaternalism demands that there only be one "real" mother.

As queer theorist Sara Ahmed puts it, "to define a family as queer is already to interrupt one ideal image of the family, based on the heterosexual union, procreation and the biological ties" (153). Heterosexual families align gendered, sexual, and racial norms into a straight line of heterosexual inheritance that collapses biology with culture. In contrast, queer families interrupt the easy equation of ethno-religious lineage in Jewish communities—families with two mothers are easily visually identifiable as not being bound by a biological bond. This disjunction is even more apparent with intercultural adoption (and intercultural marriage, for that matter).

TEXT LINE

Yet there are emancipatory parts of Jewish tradition that can be highlighted to construct a more queer-friendly approach to family. In contrast to the biological story of Abraham, I propose that the giving of Torah at Sinai offers a more capacious understanding of familial inheritance. Tradition teaches that all the souls of the Jewish people from the past, present, and future were present at Sinai, including converts and others who do not come to Judaism biologically. Inheritance is, thus, imagined to be something other than biological, a relationship to Torah rather than parental lineage. By extending the covenant to the entire Jewish people, not just the individual patriarchs, Sinai introduces the mediation of text to the Jewish relationship with God, for tradition teaches not merely that the Written Torah (the Pentateuch, the first five books of the Bible) was given to Moses, but the Oral Torah was as well (the oral tradition recorded in the Mishnah and Gemara, which together make up the Talmud). The Exodus Mechilta midrash teaches that God recited all Ten Commandments together in one instant, a kind of divine cacophony that required Moses to then recite the commandments again. (This is medieval rabbinical commentator Rashi's[1] interpretation.)

I suggest that this cacophony can represent a queer relationship to Torah, wherein the voice of God overwhelms in dissonance and in multiple and contradictory demands from the divine. Queer Jews know too well the pain imbued by some aspects of the Law, and although the commandment in Leviticus 18:22 ("thou shalt not lie with a male as one lies with a woman: it is an abhorrence") is directed only to men, the prohibition against homosexuality has hurt all queer Jews. We queer and transgender Jews *cannot* follow the Law in its entirety, even if we were so inclined. And for queer mothers especially, this model of dissonant Law mirrors not only the noises of our houses (or every house with a child!) but a noisy relation to Torah that takes in chaos. In other words, although we may not be able to hear all of the Law, or be able to bear it, it remains our inheritance.

It should be noted, however, that the giving of Torah on Sinai in Exodus 19 does assume that Jews are all men, as Moses says to "the people, 'be ready for the third day: do not go near a woman,'" a statement that Rashi interprets to mean that the men should refrain from sexual intercourse with women. Understandably, Plaskow critiques this: "Moses does not say 'men and women do not go near each other.' At the central moment of Jewish history, women are invisible" (25). It is for this reason that Plaskow decides, as the title of her landmark book states, that women must stand again at Sinai to hear the Law again (and for the first time as equals)—and this is especially so for queer women, including queer mothers, who are doubly marginalized.

In their wonderful book *Jews and Words*, Israeli novelist Amos Oz and historian Fania Oz-Salzberger argue that Jewish inheritance is a textual inheritance, one that entails a necessary relationship to the Hebrew language as well as to the Tanakh (the Hebrew Bible) and the Talmud. "Ours is not a bloodline but a textline" (1), they argue eloquently, and it is an argument with important implications for non-biological queer mothering. Queer non-biological parents may not pass on any biological material, but they do, nevertheless, pass on a Jewish textual inheritance to their children. Oz and Oz-Salzberger argue that it is the reproduction of text in Jewish tradition that has kept the Jewish people alive through persecution and diaspora. As they state:

> [I]n order to remain a Jewish family, a Jewish family perforce relied on words. Not any words, but words that came from books. Jewish parents did not merely *recite* the stories, the laws, and the fundaments of faith in the family circle, they *read* them. For even if they did not own any books, the ritual texts they recounted were in books. (27)

The central role of text in Jewish life—Jews are, after all, called the People of the Book—has resounded through generations in the transmission of Jewish religion and culture. The Hebrew word *dor*, meaning generation, is repeated numerous times through the Bible and the Talmud, and it is this concern for the coming generations that has animated Jewish discussion and debate from the Talmud to the pages of the *Jewish Daily Forward* in the present.

CONCLUSION

Indeed, inheritance may be the most quotidian and profound form of textual transmission. From the rituals of Shabbat (the Sabbath) to celebrating the many Jewish holidays throughout the year, non-biological parents can instruct their children in the practices and traditions of Judaism as much as biological parents. Inheritance may be in the form of a family challah recipe, the reading of the Haggadah at Pesach, or in the gestures or melody of lighting the Shabbat candles, as it is in eye colour or skin tone. Familial inheritance may also be in the forms of objects, from Torah and Tanakh, to a seder plate for Passover, or *chanukiah* (menorah) for Chanukah. Non-biological parents teach their children to read Hebrew, to pray, and to interpret texts, just as they drive them to Jewish day schools, Hebrew school, and Shabbat services. In short, they teach them how to live Jewishly, just as they affirm the Jewish inheritance that is found in the *lived experience* of the Jewish religion. Eating, drinking, and appropriating property, as Wyschogrod describes, need not be solely inscribed in the bodies of men and transmitted in a straight line of inheritance. Inheritance should no longer be limited to the biological narrative of the heterosexual nuclear family or to the normatively male covenant.

Instead, we might queer the lines of inheritance to see Jewishness and Judaism as a cluster of possible qualities, practices, and relations that are bequeathed to the child from their loved ones, whoever they may be. Mothering as a cultural practice is far more than a biological relationship to a child—all mothers are "real," not just those who birth their children, and all provide their children with some kind of birthright. Just as the giving of Torah on Sinai was a noisy, dissonant affair, so too are the relationships to heteronormative culture and the ideologies that construct dominant understandings of family in the present day. Non-biological mothering, represented as partial and incomplete when it is represented at all, must be recognized in its full importance in the Jewish imaginary. In queering inheritance, we can refigure Jewish images of family, most especially those of motherhood, and queer Jewish relationships to the texts that have guided us as a people. In doing so, we can work to create a Judaism that is reliant on knowledge of Jewish tradition, transmitted by text, and fully encompasses the great diversity of Jewish mothers living and mothering today.

NOTE

[1]Rashi—real name Shlomo Yitchaki—was a medieval French rabbi, whose commentaries on Torah, Tanakh (the entire Hebrew Bible, known as the Old Testament to Christians) and Talmud are among the most important of the rabbinical commentaries to Jewish tradition.

WORKS CITED

"A Portrait of Jewish Americans." *Pew Research Center: Religion and Public Life*. Pew Research Center, 1 Oct. 2013. Web. 10 Jan. 2016.

Ahmed, Sara. *The Cultural Politics of Emotion*. New York and London: Routledge, 2004. Print.

Antler, Joyce. *You Never Write! You Never Call! A History of the Jewish Mother*. Oxford and New York: Oxford University Press, 2007. Print.

Edelman, Lee. *No Future: Queer Theory and the Death Drive*. Raleigh: Duke University Press, 2004. Print.

JPS Hebrew-English Tanakh. Philadelphia: Jewish Publication Society, 2003. Print.

Oz Amos, and Fania Oz-Salzberger. *Jews and Words*. New Haven and London: Yale University Press, 2012. Print.

Park, Shelley M. *Mothering Queerly, Queering Motherhood: Resisting Monomaternalism in Adoptive, Lesbian, Blended and*

Polygamous Families. Albany: State University of New York Press, 2013. Print.

Plaskow, Judith. *Standing Again At Sinai: Judaism From a Feminist Perspective*. San Francisco: Harper San Francisco, 1990. Print.

Ruddick, Sara. "Maternal Thinking." *Feminist Studies* 6.2 (1980): 242-367. Print.

Sonowska-Buxton, Patrycja. "Step Mothers." *Mothers, Mothering and Motherhood Across Cultural Differences*. Ed. Andrea O'Reilly. Toronto: Demeter Press, 2014. 451-467. Print.

10.
Reading Hindu Devotional Poetry through Maternal Theory

Maternal Thinking and Maternal Figures in *Bhakti* Poetry of Sūrdās

FLORENCE PASCHE GUIGNARD

IN *MATERNAL THINKING: Towards a Politics of Peace,* initially published in 1989, Sara Ruddick outlines three demands of maternal thinking and their corresponding maternal practices. These demands have generally been understood to be universal, even though their specific contents and implementation are culturally variable. In this chapter, I ask which elements of maternal thinking are present in the Hindu devotional poetry attributed to Sūrdās, a prominent literary and religious figure of early-modern northern India. I read a selection of his poetry through the lenses of motherhood studies, with the intent to shift the focus from the Kṛṣṇa, the god as a baby and a child, to the maternal and feminine figures that surround him. My analysis primarily addresses historians of religions and motherhood scholars interested in the complex intersection of religion, motherhood, and mothering, but specialists of South Asia may also find it valuable. My main purpose is to show the relevance of some of the key tenets of maternal theory for the study of literary representations of motherhood that do not stem from the same cultural context as those in which theories about maternal thinking first emerged.

Ruddick explains that maternal thinking is rooted in and shaped by the activities in which mothers engage. She identifies three demands of maternal thinking, defined as "those requirements that are imposed on anyone doing maternal work" (*Maternal Thinking* 17). Ruddick adds:

> In this sense of demand, children "demand" that their lives

> be preserved and their growth fostered. In addition, the primary social groups with which a mother is identified, whether by force, kinship, or choice, demand that she raise her children in a manner acceptable to them. These three demands—for preservation, growth, and social acceptability—constitute maternal work; to be a mother is to be committed to meeting these demands by works of preservative love, nurturance, and training. (17)

This constitutes "maternal practice." In her more recent "Conversation about Maternal Thinking" with Andrea O'Reilly, Ruddick further specifies: "[s]ome practices are recognizable in some but not all or even most cultures.... Some practices are virtually ubiquitous; there is something suspicious about their apparent absence. Mothering is such a practice" (O'Reilly and Ruddick 17). Ruddick is aware that "this demand to foster children's growth appears to be historically and culturally specific to a degree that the demand for preservation is not" (19). When analyzing literary material from a religious context that is distant both in time and in space from Ruddick's feminist philosophy, it is important to acknowledge that the third demand, that of shaping social acceptability, is even more culturally determined than the other two. What is socially acceptable varies across and even within cultures, and if all mothers are expected to teach their children social acceptability, they obviously do so differently.[1]

Many South Asian works of art and literature represent motherhood as an institution as well as mothering as a woman's experience. This distinction between motherhood and mothering, initially made by Adrienne Rich in *Of Woman Born* (13) and another key component of maternal theory, also applies here. Even if "gender" has become a widely used critical category of analysis for studying South Asian material from anthropological, sociological, historical, and literary perspectives, there still is little scholarship that attempts a systematic reading of literary material on South Asian mothers.[2] It is beyond the scope of this chapter to determine to what extent the literary descriptions of mothers who are mythological figures (but not necessarily mother goddesses) in Hindu devotional poetry correspond to, stem from, or give shape to social realities in their contexts of production, transmission and performance. Rather, my purpose is to show how reading devotional poetry, such as that attributed to Sūrdās on the theme of Kṛṣṇa growing up, through the lenses of maternal theory can highlight the relevance of Ruddick's distinction between the demands of maternal thinking and their corresponding maternal work. I start with a brief contextualization of the poetry of Sūrdās and the mythology of Kṛṣṇa.

1. SŪRDĀS AND HIS POETRY

1.1 Building Up on the Mythology of Kṛṣṇa

One of the most famous and prolific poets of his time, Sūrdās composed in *brajbhāṣā* (the language of Braj), a common vernacular language of the area of northern India in which he lived. Braj is also the mythological site where most of the religious themes that he sings about are located. Scholars lack certified sources to retrace an exact biography of Sūrdās. As John Stratton Hawley writes, "all we can know is that this great poet lived somewhere in north India in the course of the sixteenth century" (*Sur's Ocean* xii). Tradition retains that he was blind,[3] and the authorship of many poems attributed to Sūrdās is questionable (*Sur's Ocean* xiii-xv).[4] What is important to consider is that at least some part of his poetry may be the product of collective and mostly oral authorship. Sūrdās probably did not "write" all of his poems, but these were circulated, collected, and transcribed during his lifetime and long after his death, until they were compiled into manuscripts of various lengths. The devotional and mostly oral poetry of that time in vernacular languages was widely accessible, even to women and uneducated people (as opposed to Sanskrit texts of the literate religious male elite, to use broad categories). In the nineteenth century, one manuscript of the *Ocean of Sūr* (*Sūrsāgar*) contained almost ten thousand poems (*Sur's Ocean* xii). Most editions, however, feature only several hundreds of poems. Kenneth E. Bryant and John Stratton Hawley's newest edition and translation, which I quote in this chapter,[5] consists of 433 poems.

Sūrdās adds colourful and sensual details to the already rich mythological layout present in earlier Vaiṣṇava Sanskrit texts, such as the *Bhāgavata Purāṇa* or the *Harivaṃśa*. Generally keeping with the original mythological narrative, he expands on details and elaborates on descriptions that are less developed in earlier texts while also drawing from oral, iconic, and popular traditions. Feminine and, at times, maternal figures that surround the god Kṛṣṇa during his infancy and childhood are well represented in Sūrdās's poetry. The selected poems quoted in the following section feature Devakī, who gives birth to Kṛṣṇa in her jail cell, and Yaśodā, his foster mother and wife of Nanda, the chief of a village in the Gokul rural area. There, Yaśodā and Nanda raise the child-god as their son. Another figure of interest is Pūtanā, a female demon who, under the guise of a beautiful wet-nurse, attempts to kill the infant by suckling him at her poisonous breast. Some poems focus on the relationship that Kṛṣṇa shares with one or several of these distinctive figures, whereas other compositions feature women and men in groups such as the *gopīs*, cowherd girls or milkmaids, who are the wives and daughters of the Braj villagers (*gopās*) among whom Kṛṣṇa grows up. When he comes of age, Kṛṣṇa departs to Mathura to fulfill his destiny by killing the king who usurped the throne and by reestablishing *dharma*, the right order. That he does not immediately return to Gokul causes sorrow to the *gopīs* and the villagers. Other texts, in particular the *Mahābhārata*, feature a grown-up Kṛṣṇa, who becomes a charioteer for his cousin Arjuna during a war and, eventually, a king.

Although the mythology of Kṛṣṇa is much broader, my focus here is on poems that relate to his birth, infancy, and childhood, or memories thereof. Yaśodā and Nanda often are labelled the "foster parents" of Kṛṣṇa, but it would be inaccurate to say that they "adopted" him as in the legal or administrative contemporary definition. In fact, Kṛṣṇa was born to Devakī and Vasudeva in the city of Mathura, which is ruled by the evil king Kaṃsa, Devakī's brother, who has usurped the throne. According to a prophecy, Devakī's eighth child will kill the usurper. Kaṃsa attempts to eliminate his sister on the day that she marries, but Devakī's husband, Vasudeva, convinces him otherwise. Kaṃsa then keeps his sister and her husband in jail. He kills the first six children born to them. The fetus of Devakī's seventh child is exchanged *in utero* and is born directly in Gokul as Kṛṣṇa's elder brother, Balarāma. Later, Kṛṣṇa is born as their eighth child. Through a series of miraculous interventions, his father Vasudeva brings him to safety at Yaśodā and Nanda's house in Gokul. The girl child whom Yaśodā has just given birth to is exchanged with Kṛṣṇa and brought back to Mathura. As Kaṃsa kills her human baby form, she reveals herself as a goddess and reiterates the prophecy. Although Kṛṣṇa's birth parents are aware that their child is safe in Gokul, it seems that Yaśodā and Nanda as well are not fully aware of all the intricacies of the situation. There are different versions of the myth, but all show that a divine power of illusion (*yogamāyā*) is at work in many episodes preceding and following the birth of Kṛṣṇa.

*1.2 Love and Devotion on the Parental Mode (*Vātsalya Bhāva*)*

Sūrdās's poetry participates in a movement known as *bhakti*, a term frequently translated as "devotion," which comprises varied traditions. In *bhakti*, the devotee (*bhakta*) engages in a "loving participation in divine life" (another translation for *bhakti* suggested by Carl-A. Keller) through imagining and reliving the scenes of Kṛṣṇa's life. In the context of *bhakti*, an "emotional-devotional-relational mode" to relate to the divine is known as *bhāva*. There are several prominent *bhāvas* that consist in relating to God as a servant, as a friend, as a parent (*vātsalya bhāva*), or as a lover, the latter being the most significant in most devotional traditions and poetry. In some instances, *bhakti* operates a "gendering" of the *bhakta* by positioning the devotee, whether a man or a woman, as feminine in relation to God who, in the form of Kṛṣṇa, is masculine. This is an unsurprisingly heteronormative relational model. All these *bhāva*s are present in Sūrdās's poetry, and he is not the only one to celebrate *vātsalya bhāva*.

When relating to God through the *vātsalya bhāva* or parental mode, devotees do not become God's beloved child (as with "God the Father" in Christianity); rather, they become the loving and affectionate parent of an "adorable, beautiful babe" (Kinsley 18). Kṛṣṇa as a child prompts an "intimate, parental response" (18). As David Kinsley puts it, "God, revealing himself as an infant, invites man to dispense with formality and undue respect and come to him openly, delighting in him intimately" (18). In his poetry, Sūrdās insists on such intimacy and expresses a full range of emotions felt by mothers towards their children, including love, concern, anxiety, awe, sorrow, guilt, irritation, and wrath. Because these maternal (and sometimes paternal) emotions have great spiritual potentials, they are turned into a model of devotion that women and men still emulate today.[6] In the following discussion, however, rather than address actual or contemporary practices of *bhakti*, I examine a selection of poems attributed to Sūrdās that reflect *vātsalya bhāva* as a significant or even dominant mode.

2. RUDDICK'S THREE DEMANDS OF MATERNAL THINKING AND PRACTICES OF MATERNAL WORK IN SŪRDĀS'S POETRY

I now set out to identify the three demands of maternal thinking and how maternal practice is shaped in poems by Sūrdās. that reiterate and reinterpret mythological narratives. For the first demand, protection, I contrast mother Yaśodā with Pūtanā, a negative feminine figure who imitates a maternal position through breastfeeding. I then compare Yaśodā with Devakī, Kṛṣṇa's birth-giver, as I consider the maternal practice of nurturance and contrast the positions of the two women who can claim to be the god's mother. Finally, in order to discuss the shaping of social acceptability, I examine the theme of the confrontation of other *gopīs* with Yaśodā, a mother who faces criticism because of her son's pranks.

2.1 Protection and Preservative Love: Yaśodā and Pūtanā

Providing "protection" through "preservative love" is the first of the maternal practices that constitute "maternal thinking" (Ruddick 65-81). This demand for protection poses a challenge in the case of mothering a child-god. Pūtanā is the first of a series of demons sent to Gokul by king Kaṃsa to kill newborn Kṛṣṇa. Through her powers, Pūtanā takes the guise of a beautiful wet-nurse. As there are many and occasionally contradictory versions of the myth, some more precise than others, it is difficult to determine if the episode of Pūtanā's fatal breastfeeding happens in the presence of Yaśodā and other women in her household or if Pūtanā approaches the child while he is momentarily left alone. The fake wet-nurse starts suckling the newborn at her poisonous breast in order to kill him, but Kṛṣṇa is immune to any harm. In fact, the divine child goes on suckling "the life breath from [Pūtanā] by clinging, clinging to her breast" (Sūrdās, *Sur's Ocean* 35, line 3). As she dies, she reveals her real horrendous appearance to the inhabitants of Braj. As is the case for other demons or enemies defeated by Kṛṣṇa, an intimate contact with him—be it through a poisoned nipple—also brings salvation: the female demon, and any danger, is eliminated, but Pūtanā also is granted his grace.

In the following poem, past, present, and future intersect in just a few lines. Sūrdās captures a recollection of the Pūtanā episode in which Yaśodā could be seen, at first view, as unable to provide protection: her now grown-up son is facing a risky situation, just as he had as a baby. A *gopī* friend tries to reassure a worried Yaśodā that Kṛṣṇa will be safe even as he has headed to confront and kill Kaṃsa:

> In Kānh I have full faith.
> Listen, Yaśodā, don't worry yourself
> at the fear of what Kaṃsa might do:
> long ago, cunning Pūtanā arrived
> with poison spread across her breasts,
> and that two-day-old child had strength enough
> to kill her before your very eyes (179, lines 1-4)

This and other episodes featuring Kṛṣṇa as a baby or a child portray a mother who is worried but prevented from exercising one of her maternal practices: actively protecting her child from harm. This is the case, for instance, when Kṛṣṇa dances on the snake Kaliyā to subdue him. To ensure that the life of her child is preserved, Yaśodā engages in religious practice, more precisely prayer. This religious strategy can be seen as part of her "preservative love" (Ruddick 17). Furthermore, she is shown as willing to take upon herself any harm, as expressed in the following poem, which starts with her teaching Kṛṣṇa how to walk:

> Mother Yaśodā is teaching him to walk.
> He wobbles a little, so she gives him her hand;
> he sways and puts his foot back on the ground.
> Sometimes she sharply summons Balarām:

"Play here in the courtyard, you two!"
Sometimes she prays to the household gods:
"Let little Kāhn, my son, live long!"
Sometimes she stands there just staring at his face,
so that any harm to her heart's beguiler
would rest on her instead.
The Lord of Sūrdās is the giver or all happiness,
and King Nanda reaps the utmost joy. (9)

For the readers or listeners of Sūrdās, a theological irony lies in this poem: Yaśodā prays to other gods to protect her son when, in fact, he himself is not only *a* god but also the supreme divinity. As part of his playful divine game (*līlā*), he takes the guise of a fragile infant so that his mother (and the devotees who will imitate her attitude) can express love for him through their wish to protect him, even if this is impossible. Far from needing maternal protection, Kṛṣṇa will later reveal himself as a divine protector for the people of Braj (for instance, when he swallows up a forest fire and when he protects the people of Braj from the pouring rain by lifting up Mount Govardhan) and, later, for the devotees and the poets themselves.

2.2 Fostering Growth and Nurturance: Yaśodā and Devakī

The importance of the second demand of maternal thinking (fostering growth) and of its corresponding practice (nurturance) can be identified in the devotional poetry of Sūrdās even more poignantly than in the original Sanskrit mythology. Sūrdās gives voice to two mothers: the birth-giver, Devakī and the nurturer, Yaśodā. On the one hand, Yaśodā is unable to provide protection to her child who does not need it anyway because he is God. On the other hand, Devakī is deprived of the opportunity to provide nurturance. She does, however, provide protection by sending her son away to Gokul.

Devakī's feelings as a mother who is deprived of her newborn son are expressed in the following excerpt of this poem that Bryant and Hawley chose to place first in their edition of the *Sūrsāgār*. Here is how Sūrdās phrases Devakī's lament:

...this dark night—

> soldiers have closed the streets, dear, shut the doors,
> and the fear of Kaṃsa is heavy everywhere.
> ...
> "Husband, why did I heed your words that day?
> Better I'd been slaughtered there and then,
> for look at this child, and tell me how a mother
> could live if torn from such a son."
> Devakī's wail was heard by the One
> who pities the poor and removes his servant's pain.
> The chains were loosed, says Sūr, the gates undone.
> He gave her his wisdom and banished her distress. (1, lines 1-2 and 5-8)

Devakī states that it would have been better for her to be killed by Kaṃsa on her wedding day rather than be forced to experience separation from this very special newborn son. The painful feeling of separation (*viraha*) is an important theme in *bhakti* poetry (Hardy), but most of the time, this *viraha* is experienced by the beloved *gopī* waiting for her lover Kṛṣṇa (and the *bhakta* amorously longing for God). In this and other poems, the separation between mother and son (and, sometimes, father and son, as in poem 187) is as intense and painful as that between lovers.

Other poems reflect the attachment felt by the two mothers of Kṛṣṇa, the potential tensions or rivalry between them, as well as their difference in status (queen versus wife of the village's chief), in location (city versus rural area), and in lifestyles (taste for elaborate delights versus simple pleasures). In the following poem, Yaśodā addresses Devakī after Kṛṣṇa, now a young man, has left Gokul, killed Kaṃsa, and freed his birth parents but has not returned from Mathura:

> You are the wife of Vasudeva, a queen,
> and I'm just a boor from Braj [*gavāri brajbāsī*],
> but it's time to send me my darling boy
> and put this joke to an end.
> It was fine for him to kill Kaṃsa and the rest,
> doing the work of all the gods,
> but the worry that weights so heavy on my heart is:

who's to herd these cows?
You can ply him with thousands of royal delights—
handsome clothes and the finest food and drink—
but there's nothing better than a bowl of butter, says Sūr,
to delight my little cowherd Kānh. (191, lines 3-8)

In another poem, Sūrdās puts the following plea, also addressed to Devakī, in Yaśodā's mouth:

How might I see your son [*tumhāre sut*]
just one more time?
You are the mother [*jananī*] who showed the world
this sun, says Sūr; I was only a sort of nurse [*dhāī*],
but because of that tie, perhaps he could come
just a day or two and let me see
his face. (190, lines 6-8)

Two maternal functions are outlined in these (and other) poems: giving birth to children and nurturing them, in particular through breastfeeding, which Devakī could not do. This distinction is also made in Devakī's voice in other poems, where her tears become another symbolic bodily fluid: the milk that her offspring, killed at birth, was denied. The poet positions Yaśodā as the mother who has raised Kṛṣṇa and knows his regular occupation (tending the cows) and his favourite food (butter). Now that the "little cowherd" has come of age and has left, Yaśodā and Devakī's positions are reversed: Yaśodā suffers from separation, whereas Devakī is finally reunited—though not for very long—with the son whom she had to give up at birth for his safety.

2.3 Social Acceptability and Training: Yaśodā and the Other Women of Braj

Training is the practice that corresponds to the third demand on mothers, consisting of shaping social acceptability in the child (Ruddick 103-123). Some of the tensions involved in this demand are reflected in Sūrdās's poetry. In the following poem, an adult *gopī* confronts Yaśodā and complains about the recurring pranks that Kṛṣṇa commits in her household. She urges the boy's mother to reprimand her son and take action so as to prevent further mischiefs:

> Why don't you reprimand that boy?
> What can I say? Every day it happens.
> I haven't the strength to endure:
> he swallows the butter, spills milk on the floor,
> smears his body with curd,
> then chases after any children in the house,
> spraying them with butter-whey.
> If ever I hide a thing, even in places
> far off and secret, he knows where.
> What do to? Defeated, undone,
> I'm driven to despair by your son.
> His thefts are so clever — that wish-fulfilling jewel! —
> that their tale cannot be told,
> And so, to get a hold on him, says Sūr,
> all of Braj is flowing, dashing here and there. (23)

The *gopī* reproaches Yaśodā for her lack of reaction and authority over her misbehaving son. Some occasional pranks may be tolerated from a mischievous boy, but this persistent behaviour drives the woman to despair. Here again lies some theological irony: is Kṛṣṇa ever *really* a child? How could mother Yaśodā have authority over God himself?

Through the lenses of maternal theory, it is tempting to read this as a literary representation of a (mythological) mother who fails at training her child to behave properly. However, at least to the devotee, the most evident interpretation is that of a spiritual metaphor: the *bhakta* relates to a divinity who is omniscient, even as a naughty little boy. The prankster child finds the dairy products even when the *gopī* (or, in other poems, his own mother) "hide[s] a thing, even in places far off and secret" (23, line 5). The retelling of his deeds by a *gopī* to mother Yaśodā is a way to further proclaim and celebrate them, to "tell the tale" again, including to the audience of the poems. This reminds devotees that, just as pots cannot be hidden in the *gopī*'s house, nothing can be hidden from God, not even secrets in one's heart. Commenting on another poet who composed on similar mythological motives, A. Withney Sanford observes that "Krishna's boyhood games and pranks intensify the passion Yaśodā and the other *gopās* feel toward him" and that the god's interventions are meant to "enhanc[e] the devotees' *bhāva*" (69).

Other possible readings of these poems through the lenses of maternal theory are not meant to invalidate or undermine the *bhakta*'s perspective. Nevertheless, a critical reading uncovers that some of the issues at stake in this poetry may not be just spiritual; they may also have material consequences for mothers. In poem 23, quoted above, Kṛṣṇa disrupts domestic labour and the product of the cowherd economy goes to waste (spilled milk, butter and curd used up by Kṛṣṇa). The poetry of Sūrdās grants its listeners access to an imaginary social universe. In such an idyllic pastoral community, it would be common to have children come and go between households during the day and not be constantly under their parents' surveillance. If the *gopīs* complain to Yaśodā, then the issue must be quite serious, and they cannot solve it by disciplining the child themselves. Furthermore, the direct consequences of his actions are to be remediated by the *gopī* herself, in addition to her other usual duties. The task of cleaning up and giving the other "children in the house" a bath and clean clothes will fall onto her and not onto the male *gopā* who is busy with other tasks (traditional gendered division of labour as reflected in this poetry).

The *gopās* sometimes also come to Yaśodā as a group, as victims of Kṛṣṇa's pranks. As the boy's mother, Yaśodā is urged to intervene and keep her son in check. The intended audience of this devotional poetry is aware that these pranks are manifestations of the child-god's divine character and that "the waywardness of childhood becomes an effective image for the divinity in one of its aspects.... In the story of Kṛṣṇa, childhood is associated with the sport or *līlā* of the transcendent form of the deity" (White 162). However, the audience may still be sensible to some of the specific economic issues in these idealized rural settings. This sort of disruptive interaction with the god can still be considered as positive when read on the spiritual (and not materialist) level: as in the case of Pūtanā's death through sucking out her life breath (see above), *any* contact with the god is to be regarded as desirable, even if this means suffering some inconvenience from his joyful pranks.

At first, mother Yaśodā simply does not believe the other *gopīs*: "But they: whatever has possessed these herder girls to come around pretending, complaining each dawn? How can they insist on blaming him ... when he never even touches his butter here at home?" (26, lines 5-6). She "sees their complaints solely as a pretext to see Krishna" (Sanford 70). However, when Kṛṣṇa disrupts her own domestic chores, the mother's reaction is far from mild and cheerful. In an episode narrated in detail in the ninth chapter of the tenth book of the *Bhāgavata Purāṇa*, Kṛṣṇa disturbs Yaśodā while she is busy churning butter. Her "two quivering breasts lactated due to affection for her son" (*Bhāgavata Purāṇa* 10,9,3) who demands to be breastfed. Yaśodā agrees, but she abruptly has to interrupt their breastfeeding, as she notices that some milk on the fire is about to boil over. She exits the room, leaving Kṛṣṇa unsatisfied and angry. The child then breaks the churning pot with a stone. Afterwards, he hides to eat the freshly churned butter that he has stolen. When his mother returns and notices what he has done, she sets out to find Kṛṣṇa, who is now distributing butter to a monkey. A stick in her hand, Yaśodā runs "after him, whom the minds of yogis, directed by the power of austerity, are not able to reach" (*Bhāgavata Purāṇa* 10,9,9; translations from Bryant's *Krishna* 124). The readers of the *Bhāgavata Purāṇa* and the audience of its poetic reprises appreciate the irony in her attempt to chase God with a stick. Finally, Yaśodā grasps her son and starts chastising him, but Kṛṣṇa begins to cry. The mother throws away the stick and, instead, attempts to bind Kṛṣṇa to a mortar as punishment. The rope is always too short by two fingers, even as Yaśodā joins one rope after another. In the end, out of pity for his mother, the child-god lets himself be tied to the mortar.

On the basis of this episode, Sūrdās imagines how other *gopīs* who witness Yaśodā's wrath plead with her to not discipline Kṛṣṇa too harshly, whereas they previously demanded that he be punished for similar pranks in their own houses:

> The eyes of the lad have filled, filled with tears.

> Look at your little boy's face, Yaśodā—
> Why are you so senselessly enraged?
> Loose from his belly that painful rope!
> Release from your hand that cruel stick!
> And tell me how you can feel such black emotions
> toward the one who is your very own son.
> The tears in his face and the little drops of butter
> on his breast bring joy to the eyes
> as if the moon had brought forth pearls of nectar
> to complement a necklace of stars.
> Sacrifice yourself in every way, every day,
> for that son, the Dark One of Sūr.
> Who knows whose merit has caused him to appear
> here in Braj and here in Nanda's house! (27)

In other poems on the same theme, the *gopīs* ask Yaśodā, "how could such a little bit of curd ... provoke in you such wrath?" and, though they see the rationale behind the reprimand, they wonder "how much cow's wealth could [Yaśodā] possibly have lost to justify berating him so" (28, lines 2 and 7). They berate Yaśodā for her extreme feelings of anger: "How could you have become so angry with Kāhn that you took a stick in that harsh hand of yours and let it touch his soft, tender frame?" (31, line 1). The *gopīs* are sensitive to the "tears [that] drip down from his eyes and glisten as they settle on his breast" (31, line 2).

Reading the poetry of Sūrdās reminds motherhood studies scholars that what is considered a socially acceptable mode of disciplining a child is culturally variable. Although some twenty-first century readers may be tempted to hastily label Yaśodā as harsh or even a "bad mother" for using a stick and a rope to tie her misbehaving child, we ought to remember that such reactions might not have been so unusual among the original intended listeners of Sūrdās'poetry, though not necessarily the educative norm. Even though they disagree with Yaśodā, the mythological *gopīs* are not surprised that she has grabbed a stick, as a form of threat, but that she intends (or even has started) to use it on her son. Would the *gopīs* have pleaded for a child other than the delightful Kṛṣṇa?

CONCLUDING REMARKS

When using maternal theory to read past or contemporary sources from South Asia—or, in fact, from anywhere else—motherhood studies scholars ought to carefully contextualize these literary productions, their intended audience, and their primary purpose. Kṛṣṇa growing up and not Yaśodā's mothering is the central focus of poems on *vātsalya bhāva* by Sūrdās. However, motherhood studies scholars can still identify in this poetry the three demands of maternal thinking and their corresponding practices as defined by Sara Ruddick. The primary purpose of this poetry, not composed by a mother but attributed to a male saint poet, is to draw the *bhakta* closer to God and to celebrate Kṛṣṇa's feats. The range of emotions that are expressed, nevertheless, tell listeners or readers a lot about Yaśodā's feelings—not towards a god or God but towards the child that she regards as her very own son. Sūrdās's poetry very well captures ambivalent maternal feelings, such as irritation and pity, and it shows how a mother is supposed to train her child towards the goal of social acceptability. His behaviour should not disrupt her own household tasks or her relationship with other women of the community. Are these emotions predominantly religious or maternal? *Vātsalya bhāva* blends them together and validates maternal feelings as appropriate for a *bhakti* path. Even irritation and anger felt by a mother—or other women dealing with the naughty child—are channels for *bhakti* in the *vātsalya bhāva* "emotional-relational-devotional" mode.

Addressing one example does not prove Ruddick's claim that maternal thinking and its demands are universal. However, this analysis of a selection of poems shows that diverse expressions of mothering are reflected in Hindu devotional poetry of early-modern India. As the other chapters in this volume illustrate, investigations on mothering (and not motherhood or mother goddesses)[7] and religion are still largely focused on English-speaking and Euro-American Christian contexts of the late twentieth and early twenty-first centuries. With this chapter, I hope to have shown how looking at South Asian literary materials can help validate the relevance of maternal theory. In addition, looking at mothers, mothering, and motherhood in non-Christian and non-Western contexts can uncover maternal figures that are not always portrayed as perfect, resilient, and cheerful mothers but that can still be looked at as models for devotional practices. Some feelings or positions experienced in mothering, such as irritation towards the child or strong sadness in separation, are frequently categorized as ambivalent, negative, or excessive. Outside of the religious and cultural frameworks that influenced the contexts in which most maternal theorists live and write, we might find that such maternal emotions can also be channelled positively as part of coherent religious systems, as is the case for the maternal feelings of Yaśodā and Devakī in the devotional poetry attributed to Sūrdās.

NOTES

[1]For examples in a contemporary context, see Andrea O'Reilly's edited reader *Mothers, Mothering and Motherhood Across Cultural Differences.*

[2]See Sangha (413-427) for a few examples of literary analysis included in her review of the state of research, focusing on contemporary South Asian motherhood. Recent references include volumes by Sangha and Gonsalves, by Krishnaraj, and by Kumar Pramanick and Manna.

[3]See Hawley, Vaudeville, and Rousseva-Sokolova for more details and discussions of the tensions between hagiography, biography, and history.

[4]Hawley and Bryant's works on Sūrdās provide a wealth of philological information.

[5]I always give the number of the poem (and not the page) in Bryant and Hawley's edition and translation, which I quote from in this chapter. For consistency's sake, I have modified back to their Sanskrit form the transliteration of names (e.g., Yaśodā instead of Yashoda).

[6]Haberman provides a concrete fieldwork example of a woman engaged in tending the image of Kṛṣṇa and relating to him as a child (136).

[7]Mother goddesses are a classical topic of investigation for scholars of religions. Although there is an increase in the number of historical studies on motherhood and religion as institutions, the

study of mothering as experience often remains difficult due to a lack of available sources (such as first-hand accounts by women who focused their writing on the maternal component of their multiple identities). For more on the intersection between the academic study of religion and motherhood, see Pasche Guignard.

WORKS CITED

Bryant, Kenneth E. *Poems to the Child-God: Structures and Strategies in the Poetry of Sūrdās*. Berkeley: University of California Press, 1978. Print.

Bryant, Kenneth E., "Krishna in the Tenth Book of the Bhagavata Purana." *Krishna: A Sourcebook*. Ed. Kenneth E. Bryant. Oxford: Oxford University Press, 2007. 111-136. Print.

Haberman, David L. *Acting as a Way of Salvation: A Study of Rāgānugā Bhakti Sādhana*. New York: Oxford University Press, 1988. Print.

Hardy, Friedhelm. *Viraha Bhakti. The Early History of Krishna Devotion in South India*. Delhi: Oxford University Press, 1983. Print.

Hawley, John Stratton. *The Memory of Love: Sūrdās sings to Krishna. Translated with an Introduction and Notes by John Stratton Hawley*. New York: Oxford University Press, 2009. Print.

Keller, Carl-A. *Ramakrishna et la voie de l'amour*. Paris: Bayard, 1997. Print.

Kinsley, David R. *The Sword and the Flute: Kālī and Kṛṣṇa, Dark Visions of the Terrible and the Sublime in Hindu Mythology*. Berkeley: University of California Press, 1975. Print.

Krishnaraj, Maithreyi, ed. *Motherhood in India: Glorification without Empowerment?* New Delhi-Abingdon: Routledge, 2010. Print.

Kumar Pramanick, Swapan, and Samita Manna, eds. *Women in India: Motherhood and Multiple Identities*. New Delhi: Serials Publications, 2010. Print.

O'Reilly Andrea. Ed. *Mothers, Mothering and Motherhood Across Cultural Differences: A Reader*. Toronto: Demeter Press, 2014. Print.

O'Reilly, Andrea and Sara Ruddick. "A Conversation About

Maternal Thinking." *Maternal Thinking. Philosophy, Politics, Practice*. Ed. Andrea O'Reilly. Toronto: Demeter Press, 2009. 14-38. Print.

Pasche Guignard, Florence. "The Academic Study of Religions and Mothering, Motherhood/s and Mothers." *Maternità e Politeismi / Motherhood and Polytheisms / Maternités et polythéismes*. Ed. Florence Pasche Guignard, Giulia Pedrucci, and Marianna Scapini. Forthcoming.

Rich, Adrienne. *Of Woman Born: Motherhood as Experience and Institution* New York: Norton, 1976. Print.

Rousseva-Sokolova, Galina. *Jeu et dévotion: aspects ludiques de la bhakti kṛṣṇaïte au Braj*. Paris: Champion, 2005. Print.

Ruddick, Sara. *Maternal Thinking: Towards a Politics of Peace*. New York: Ballantine Books, 1989. Print.

Sanford, A. Withney. *Singing Krishna: Sound Becomes Sight in Paramānand's Poetry*. Albany: State University of New York Press, 2008. Print.

Sangha, Jasjit K. "Contextualizing South Asian Motherhood." *Mothers, Mothering and Motherhood Across Cultural Differences: A Reader*. Ed. Andrea O'Reilly. Bradford: Demeter Press, 2014. 413-427. Print.

Sangha, Jasjit K. and Tahira Gonsalves, eds. *South Asian Mothering: Negotiating Culture, Family and Selfhood*. Bradford: Demeter Press, 2013. Print.

Sūrdās. *Sur's Ocean. Poems from the Early Tradition*. Ed. Kenneth E. Bryant. Trans. John Stratton Hawley. Cambridge: Harvard University Press, 2015. Print.

Vaudeville, Charlotte. *Pastorales par Soûr-Dâs*. Paris: Gallimard, 1971. Print.

White, Charles S. J. "Kṛṣṇa as Divine Child." *History of Religions* 10.2 (1970): 156-177. Print.

11.
Charlotte Brontë's *Villette* as Spiritual Quest for the Mother

ELVIRA CASAL

THROUGHOUT CHARLOTTE BRONTË'S 1853 novel *Villette,* Lucy Snowe, the heroine-narrator, identifies the Roman Catholic Church as a system based on hypocrisy and moral weakness. Yet the Catholic Church also holds a powerful fascination for Lucy, to the point that during a crisis in her life she turns to the confessional. Later, she acknowledges that had she gone back to a priest who showed her kindness, she might have ended up "counting [rosary] beads in a certain Carmelite convent."[1] Literary critics have examined Lucy's attitudes towards Catholicism within a variety of contexts, ranging from analyses of Brontë's use and subversion of Gothic narrative conventions to studies that situate the novel within the genre of Victorian anti-Catholic literature. However, I have not yet found a discussion that links Lucy's fearful fascination with Catholicism to the lack of maternal presence and love in her life.[2] As I read it, *Villette* is largely driven by Lucy's unconscious hunger for a mother figure, and her experiences both in England and in Labassecour (Brontë's name for Belgium in this novel) represent a spiritual quest—not only for the "missing mother" in her own lifebut also the "missing feminine" in Christian patriarchy.

LUCY SNOWE AND THE MISSING MOTHER

Villette is the story of an Englishwoman who, after losing everyone who matters to her in England, somewhat impulsively emigrates to French-speaking and predominately Catholic Villette (Brussels) in Labassecour (Belgium). Lucy Snowe begins her first-person narrative with an account of her last visit to her godmother, Mrs. Bretton. A younger child, Polly Home, also visits Mrs. Bretton and becomes devoted to Graham, the son of the house, who treats her as a plaything and mascot. All three of these characters reappear in the story after Lucy has moved to Villette, but the text gives no hint of this. Lucy describes this period of her life as the last period during which she felt safe and cared for by the adults around her.

Although she is never clear about what happens, a few years after her last stay with her godmother, Lucy is alone in the world and forced to earn a living. A kindly neighbour, Miss Marchmont, offers her a position as a companion, and Lucy stays with her until Miss Marchmont dies. At this point, Lucy is once again bereft and penniless. Thinking that she may find work in a French-speaking country, she decides to leave for Labassecour. Upon her arrival, Lucy is hired by Madame Beck, the head of a *pensionat* or girls' boarding school in Villette. She meets M. Paul Emmanuel, Madame Beck's kinsman, who gradually becomes very important in Lucy's life. The rest of the novel addresses Lucy's experiences as a woman alone in a foreign country.

The novel is in part inspired by Charlotte Brontë's own feelings and experiences during her time in a Brussel's *pensionat,* yet it is far from an autobiographical novel. Lucy Snowe is not Charlotte, and her story is very different from the author's own life. In this chapter, I avoid focusing on the biographical connection—although the resonance of Brontë's own motherless state is impossible to overlook completely[3]—because what I wish to explore is not the relationship of Brontë's art to her life or the way in which personal experience led Brontë to make certain artistic choices but the way in which Lucy Snowe's search for a missing mother dramatizes a central problem of religion for English women in the Victorian period.

Lucy's particular case as a motherless single woman who is also without beauty, influence, social skills, or wealth is representative not only of Brontë's own experience but also of a problem with patriarchy more broadly. Lucy's emotional and spiritual intensity—for Brontë, emotion and spirituality are inextricably linked—as well as her capacity for and commitment to "reason" represent qualities that her own culture does not value.[4] In the first scenes in the novel when she is only fourteen, Lucy is already expected to suppress emotion and even curiosity to put the comfort and well-being of others ahead of her own. This expectation is linked to the Victorian ideology that, as Elaine Showalter puts it, "prescribe[s] that a woman should be a Perfect Lady, an Angel in the House, submissive to men but stronger in her inner purity and religiosity" (14). Middle-class women in the Victorian period were, thus, taught that if they were to submit to patriarchy, accept masculine primacy and dominance gracefully, and not inconvenience others with their wants or needs, they would be rewarded with love, protection, security, and even the veneration of those around them.[5] However, as the novel unfolds, it is clear that one important aspect of this ideology is missing from Lucy's experience. What Showalter calls the "subordination and repression inherent in the female ideal" (22) does not bring Lucy the rewards of love and security. The best that plain, motherless Lucy can expect is acceptance, mild affection, and the eventual opportunity to make her own way in life. The novel, thus, emphasizes the deprivation of women by centring on a protagonist who has experienced the most fundamental of deprivations: the absence of a loving mother.

FLAWED MOTHER SUBSTITUTES

It is striking that the first sentence in *Villette* speaks of a mother figure: "My godmother lived in a handsome house," begins the narrator (I.5). This godmother had "come in person to claim" Lucy from the household in which the fourteen-year-old lived "at that time" (I.5). It is one of the few instances that someone takes care of Lucy. It is a noticeably incomplete account of Lucy's childhood, as it covers only a brief period during her early adolescence. Yet the first three chapters of the novel provide the most detailed information that the reader has about Lucy's past, and her relationship with Mrs. Bretton is the closest thing Lucy has to a mother-child relationship.

Throughout the novel, Lucy never mentions her parents. In her brief outline of her past, she talks about uncles, a school, and a former schoolmate but never mentions her family of origin. She briefly introduces a kindly former nurse, but she never mentions her mother, not even in connection with her feelings of loss and aloneness. Indeed, it is not clear when, or if, her mother died. Lucy speaks of losing her family without particularizing whom she has lost. The reader assumes that she is an orphan, but Lucy never *says* that her mother has died. Although she describes several mothers with their daughters, she never says anything about her own. In short, the most significant fact about this missing mother is her *absence*. The narrative that begins with the words "my godmother" is the story of someone who never says "my mother."[6]

What is known about this godmother? She is "a middle-class, English gentlewoman ... habitually independent of pretence, constitutionally composed and cheerful" (XX.219). The child Lucy finds comfort in her company: "My visits to her resembled the sojourn of Christian and Hopeful beside a certain pleasant stream" (I.6), the narrator says, alluding to the River of God, which is also the River of the Water of Life in *Pilgrim's Progress*. Even as an adult, she finds her "godmother's lively black eye and clear brunette cheek, her warm, prompt hand, her self-reliant mood [and] her decided bearing ... all beneficial ... as the atmosphere of some salubrious climate" (XVII.180).

Yet for all her good qualities, Mrs. Bretton is "not generally a caressing woman: even with her cherished son" (I.8). Furthermore, although she is "motherly," she is not "overly-sympathetic" (III.19), and she deserts Lucy on more than one occasion. At the beginning of the novel, she has "come in person to claim" Lucy from the household in which the fourteen year old lived (I.5) because she had some hint of "events coming" that may change Lucy's life. Yet when these events occur during some unspecified time after Lucy's last visit to her, Mrs. Bretton is not around to help: "Impediments, raised by others, had, years ago, come in the way of our intercourse, and cut it off. Besides, time had brought changes for her too," Lucy explains (IV.35). Later, after the two have been reunited in Villette, Mrs. Bretton becomes so occupied with other friends that she forgets to visit or even contact Lucy, even though she knows the latter is recovering from a nervous illness brought about by isolation.

This readiness to shift her attention away from Lucy is apparent from the first chapter of the novel. Although it records that Mrs.

Bretton went "in person" to fetch Lucy to stay with her, it also shows how when another child visits the household, Lucy is forced to shift from the role of "child" to that of "care giver" in relation to this younger child. She is expected to share her room, and she even takes the child into her own bed when the latter is too upset to sleep alone (III.34). During earlier visits Lucy was the only "child in a household of grown people," and consequently, as she puts it, "much made of ... in a quiet way" (I.5). But during Lucy's final stay at her godmother's house, it is Polly—younger, prettier, and, therefore, more likely to be "much made of"—who receives special attention. The same passage that describes Mrs. Bretton as "not generally a caressing woman" goes on to say that she made an exception for Polly; this temporary visitor receives caresses that Lucy, the godchild and frequent visitor, has never received.

Noting the cool distance that young Lucy displays towards Polly in most of these scenes, some critics argue that adult Lucy's account of these memories is coloured by the resentment that she feels towards adult Polly.[7] It is true that when Polly reappears as the beautiful Paulina de Bassompierre, Lucy, who craves the affection of "Dr. John," as the now adult Graham Bretton is known, has to admit that she has no chance of attracting him as Polly does. However, although adult Lucy surely feels some jealousy towards the adult Polly, she also expresses an affectionate contempt. She may affirm that she "likes" Paulina (XXXII.371), but she cannot help comparing the younger woman to a spaniel who was "very tiny, and had the prettiest little innocent face ... the finest dark eyes in the world" (XXXVI.415). Whatever jealousy the adult Lucy feels towards the adult Polly is balanced by an adult sense of independence and dignity. As a child, however, Lucy sees little Polly as a rival for Mrs. Bretton's limited affection.

By the time Lucy and Paulina meet in Labassecour, Lucy has to some extent accepted that her role in Dr. John's life is, at best, a sisterly one. She may hope for more, but she never fools herself that he has any romantic interest in her. In the Bretton scenes, however, Polly displaces Lucy as the "visiting child" and enjoys more attention (caresses) than Lucy received in the past. The ambivalence of Lucy's description of Polly as a child does not have its roots in thwarted romantic love but in maternal deprivation.

Although Mrs. Bretton feels genuine affection towards Lucy, she has no strong ongoing concern for her goddaughter's well-being. As stated above, she is perfectly willing to lose contact with Lucy for years, even though she must have suspected that Lucy was alone in the world. Similarly, her neglect following Lucy's return to the *pensionat* after her illness raises questions about how truly "motherly" her relationship with Lucy ever was. In fact, Mrs. Bretton is only consistently maternal in her relationship her son, John Graham—her "own comfort and nonpareil" (II.15). Lucy finds out early that her godmother's love, though sincere, is limited.[8]

The two other possible mother figures in Lucy's life, her former nurse—Mrs. Barrett, and her first employer, Miss Marchmont—offer her little more than temporary and unsatisfactory support. Mrs. Barrett "comforted, but knew not how to advise" (V.44). The problems of an impoverished gentlewoman are beyond Mrs. Barrett's understanding and not at all her responsibility. For a time, Miss Marchmont seems like a viable substitute mother. She calls Lucy "my child" (IV.42) and makes her feel wanted: "I could wait on her and sit beside her with that calm which always blesses us when we are sensible that our manners, presence, contact, please and soothe the persons we serve," Lucy says. Even her occasional scoldings are "rather like an irascible mother rating her daughter" (IV.37). However, Miss Marchmont needs to be cared for; she is not a caregiver, and she dies before she can carry out her intention of providing financially for Lucy.[9] Symbolically, Miss Marchmont's death repeats the pattern of maternal desertion that, perhaps, begins with the death of Lucy's never mentioned mother and continues with Mrs. Bretton's failure to stay in touch. Capable of forming intense emotional attachments herself, at no point does Lucy have a mother figure who reciprocates her attachment or provides the nurturing protection that she craves.

EMOTIONAL ISOLATION AND THE APPEAL OF CATHOLICISM

This emotional deprivation is experienced by Lucy as a *spiritual* deprivation. As allusions to *Pilgrim's Progress,* Old Testament moral trails, and the New Testament apocalypse make clear, the novel is largely concerned with Lucy's spiritual development. Various critics have remarked that one of the models for *Villette* is "the Protestant spiritual autobiography" (Dolin xix). However, whereas most readings of *Villette* as a spiritual quest emphasize the heroine's movement away from the temptation of Catholicism to a reaffirmed faith in Protestantism, I am more interested in what this temptation says about the roots of Lucy's emotional hunger and how it is connected to the spiritual quest.[10]

For Lucy, the internal battle between "reason" and "feeling" (or, in some cases, "imagination") is a battle for her soul. Denied the emotional nurture that she craves, Lucy struggles to maintain the role of calm, undemanding usefulness that her culture demands she embrace. In this, Mrs. Bretton's treatment of Lucy is important because as her title of *God*mother suggests, she is a mother figure whose role is to support the child's spiritual well-being.[11] Although her relationship with Lucy is always presented in secular terms, the original relationship is connected to the baptismal promise that parents and godparents make together on behalf of the infant being baptized in the Church of England. Thus, Mrs. Bretton's very secular (and, in many ways, superficial) relationship with Lucy marks one of the failures of the Protestant religion to supply Lucy with satisfactory spiritual *and* emotional support. Perhaps, the key to Mrs. Bretton's failure as an adequate mother substitute is that the "God" of Lucy's experience is a distant masculine figure; he is a "father" who, instead of protecting Lucy, seems to have deserted her to life's "storms." Mrs. Bretton, though a woman and a mother, represents a patriarchal system that has no place to offer a woman like Lucy. Much as Lucy is attached to English Protestantism, it has been a rather cold "father" to her.

After Miss Marchmont's death, Lucy is suddenly without employment, in addition to being emotionally and spiritually untethered. Her decision to leave England to find a job abroad reflects both her isolation and her sense of disenfranchisement. She links these sentiments to the absence of love in her life, but they clearly connote a spiritual emptiness that stems from her awareness that there is nothing for her in the land of her birth: "I had nothing to lose," she says. "Unutterable loathing of a desolate existence past forbade return. If I failed in what I now desired to undertake, who, save myself, would suffer? If I died away from–home, I was going to say, but I had no home–from England then, who would weep?" (VI.50). Prior to leaving England, Lucy asks herself, "What friends had I on earth? Whence did I come? Whither should I go? What should I do?" (V.47). Although Lucy is experiencing a practical crisis, the language in this passage emphasizes that it is the emotional and spiritual loneliness that threatens to overwhelm her. The questions of "Whence did I come?" and "Whither should I go?" mark a moment of doubt about her relations, not only with other people "on earth," but with a higher power, which, it seems, is not protecting her. Her emotional isolation, here and elsewhere, is also a spiritual isolation. Significantly, it is the tolling of the church bell which finally brings her comfort: "I lie in the shadow of St. Paul," (V.47) she reassures herself. That is, she is the hand of God.[12]

Still, the God of her Protestant religion is male, and Lucy's hunger is for a nurturing mother. It is for this reason that the Catholic Church—referred to throughout the novel with feminine pronouns—appeals to Lucy. Yet there is a problem; as noted above, Lucy regards Catholicism with profound suspicion, as she identifies it with the denial of individuality and autonomy. "Each mind was being reared in slavery," she claims in one of her earliest diatribes against "Romanism" (XIV.127). Later, she concludes that the Protestant faith is superior because it "kept fewer forms" between the individual and God (XXXVI.421). These, however, are fairly standard anti-Catholic criticisms. The very vehemence with which Lucy utters them testifies to the strength of the appeal that she is trying to resist.[13] For example, after stating that "Each mind was being reared in slavery," she goes on to say:

> [T]o prevent reflection from dwelling on this fact, every pretext for physical recreation was seized and made the most of. There as elsewhere, the CHURCH strove to bring up her children robust in body, feeble in soul, fat, ruddy, hale, joyous, ignorant, unthinking, unquestioning. "Eat, drink, and live!" she says. "Look after your bodies; leave your souls to me. I hold their cure–guide their course: I guarantee their final fate." (XV.127)

In case the reader should find the exhortation of "eat, drink, and live" and "leave your souls to me" too appealing, she hastens to add: "Lucifer just offers the same terms." She also goes on to quote the devil's promise to Jesus during the temptation in the Wilderness (Luke 4:6-7). Since this particular diatribe occurs in the context of describing life in a girl's school in Villette, the demonization of the encouragement to "eat, drink and live" seems disproportionate—unless the temptation to do so should be great. Lucy's fear of the power of Catholicism and her echoing of cultural anxieties characteristic of the novels of the period suggests the allure of a spiritual doctrine that is presented in the guise of the feminine nurturer rather than the cold father-God Lucy has experienced in Protestantism.

In her excellent essay, "Fables of Rebellion: Anti-Catholicism and the Structure of *Villette*," Rosemary Clark-Beattie argues that one of the problems that Lucy faces is that Protestant society—and by implication, the Protestant God that she worships—is largely indifferent to her needs: "The misery she suffers at the hands of Protestant society is not attributable to human tyranny. The authority of a community that visibly espouses the cause of liberty is the authority of God. God is the original cause of [Lucy's] isolation" (830). In other words, the Protestant God offers independence but at the price of isolation.

Lucy's sense of the Protestant God as indifferent to her needs is the key to her voluntary exile from England. Although she never admits that the God she worships has left her spiritually, materially, and emotionally bereft, leaving England for her is a way of disconnecting from an experience of emotional and spiritual bereavement too painful to articulate. Linking Lucy's emigration to the "colonialist impulse" of her times is the impulse to escape "her insignificance within English society by fleeing to a setting where her adherence to the mores of the very culture she has fled sets her apart, in her own mind, as superior" (825). Clark-Beattie further connects Lucy's anti-Catholic rhetoric with the "need for a theater of action where her deprivation may appear exceptional" (828). Because Protestant society does not allow her to identify her sacrifice of self *as* a sacrifice—because the world, represented by Mrs. Bretton and Protestant Englishness, regards the suppression of self by the unmarried woman as natural and appropriate—Lucy's critique of Catholicism provides an opportunity to present her emotional and spiritual struggle in terms that may appear heroic by embracing "the fiction of the Protestant preserving her virtue in the face of Papist corruption" (Clark-Beattie 828).

Yet I argue that Lucy's journey is not just the search for a place where her Englishness will make her superior but for a place where she will be welcome and useful. Defining her worth (as many Victorians did) in terms of the services that she could provide for others, Lucy's spiritual impulse here is closer to the Catholic emphasis on works than the Protestant emphasis on faith. Being useful and needed is the next best thing to being loved. Being loved, for Lucy, is the equivalent of being "saved."

Interestingly, although she has no idea where or how to find a job in England, all Lucy has to do is set foot in Villette and she is almost supernaturally guided to a school where she is welcome—first as a nursery governess and, eventually, as a respected teacher. Her rise in Madame Beck's establishment indicates the readiness of the Catholic community to accept and embrace the foreigner, even when her own people back in England will not do so.[14] To be sure, Lucy also experiences isolation in Madame Beck's school. For example, after speaking too frankly about her belief that telling the truth is more important than church attendance, she is subtly separated from regular intercourse with impressionable pupils (IX.84). Yet the very fact that someone takes the trouble to separate her from the students indicates that she is being noticed and listened to, neither of which happens when she is with Protestant English society.

One of Lucy's main criticisms of Catholic society is its reliance on surveillance rather than individual conscience. Yet one important point about surveillance is that, aside from intrusiveness, it may indicate concern and caring. For instance, after Lucy's visit to the confessional, she loses her way home, faints, and wakes again in the home of her godmother and Dr. John. The wonder of recovering these old friends and, in a sense, "coming home" to her lost childhood, tends to obscure the fact that this reunion was made possible by the confessor, Père Silas, who, concerned about her well-being, follows her and seeks help after she faints. In other words, it is a representative of the Holy Church of Rome who is the initial agent in her rescue and recovery. His humane intent, however, is minimized both by Lucy and Dr. John, the latter of whom speculates that, "with the subtlity [sic] of his class," the priest may have followed her in order to discover her address and so he may visit and convert her (XVII.185-86).

This negative construction of everything that priests or the Catholic establishment may do to meet her needs is characteristic of Lucy's response to the religion that she finds so frightening. It is significant that, despite her complaints about surveillance, Lucy shows an interesting tolerance for being spied on—even in her early days at the *pensionat*, during which she observes her employer examining her belongings. She reports almost admiringly that

> I divined [Madame Beck's] motive ... the wish to form from the garments a judgment respecting the wearer, her station, means, neatness. The end was not bad, but the means were hardly fair or justifiable.... All being thus done decently and in order, my property was returned to its place, my clothes were carefully refolded. (VIII.69)

Indeed, Madame Beck earns Lucy's respect as a "great and very capable woman" (VIII.74), and her surveillance is seen as part of her (mistaken) notion of "duty." As a mother image, Madame Beck is interesting because descriptions of her seem to parallel descriptions of the Catholic Church as Lucy chooses to see it. Like the Church, Madame Beck is good at providing for the physical needs of her charges: "[T]here was a liberty of amusement, and a provision for exercise which kept the girls healthy; the food was abundant and good.... She never grudged a holiday; she allowed plenty of time for sleeping, dressing, washing, eating" (VIII.73). Nevertheless, she is presented as cold, "forbearing with all the world and tender to no part of it. Her own children drew her into no deviation from the even tenor of her stoic calm" (X.93). Madame Beck, according to Lucy, "seemed to know that keeping girls in distrustful restraint, in blind ignorance, and under a surveillance that left them no moment and no corner for retirement was not the best way to make them grow up honest and modest women," (VIII.73) yet does it anyways because "blindness and ignorance" coupled with "surveillance" are characteristic of her Catholic culture. Interestingly, Lucy accepts Madame Beck's tactics towards her students as motivated by her employer's concern for the well-being of her school. Indeed, Lucy does not seem to mind the headmistress's surveillance of her as much as her often stated "independence" would suggest. In a later scene when she catches Madame Beck going through her things again, she retreats rather than protests. If she were to confront her employer, Lucy's own pride might force her to resign, which she does not wish to do: "I was not angry, and had no wish in the world to leave her," she tells the reader. "I could hardly get another employer whose yoke would be so light and so easy of carriage; and truly, I liked madame for her capital sense, whatever I might think of her principles: as to her system, it did me no harm" (XIII.119).

Lucy's tolerance for this "Romanish" surveillance is even greater when the guilty spy is M. Paul Emmanuel. Although she tells him that his spying on people is wrong and accuses him of "banquet[ing] secretly and sacrilegiously on Eve's Apples" (XXXI.366), it is clear that when M. Paul's surveillance turns to *her*, Lucy finds it as much flattering as annoying. Similarly, she tolerates his illogical and unfair accusations that she is frivolous or even a coquette because she sees all these acts as reflecting his interest in her.[15]

Insofar as Lucy is starved for attention, being watched is preferable to being ignored. It is because she is so haunted by the "insufferable thought of being no more loved, no more owned" (XV.160) that she goes to the Catholic church where she kneels "down with others on the stone pavement" before entering the confessional with the thought that "to take this step could not make [her] more wretched than [she] already was" and might "soothe" her (XV.161). What she confesses to the priest is no sin—only her loneliness.

Explaining to the startled priest that she "ha[s] been perishing for a word of advice or an accent of comfort" (XV.161), Lucy pours out her story of lonely illness and isolation. She does not expect advice, much less absolution, since she is not Catholic. She only wants the "relief of communication in an ear that was human and sentient, yet consecrated." Although the priest states that "I am hardly furnished with counsel fitting the circumstances," he listens to her and acknowledges her feelings (XV.161). He validates the seriousness of her feelings and recognizes their spiritual import in a way that no one in her Protestant world has done. "[A] mind so tossed can find repose but in the bosom of retreat," he states. "The further I look into this matter, the more plainly I see it is entirely out of the common order of things. On no account would I lose sight of you" (XV.162-63). Even though he sees conversion to Catholicism as the solution to her isolation, he recognizes that she is not an ordinary person with an ordinary problem. He does not tell her that she needs to "cultivate happiness," as her Protestant friends do but validates her spiritual anguish by responding to it with caring words.[16] Moreover, he proceeds to follow her and to watch over her body as well as the soul that he longs to save. In short, the Catholic Church *wants* her. In contrast, Protestantism barely gives her a framework in which to exist in isolation.

Why then does Lucy not convert? Incident after incident in the novel emphasizes how her Protestant Englishness distances her from others as well as how she is marginalized among Protestants while becoming increasingly central among the Catholics in her world. Her desire to confess to a "consecrated" ear further suggests that she sees some aspect of the confessional as framing a connection with God. Yet Lucy tenaciously resists the urge to turn to the seemingly more caring "Holy Church," as she insists not only on the superiority of her creed but also the corruption of Romanism. Beyond showing that Lucy—like the Catholics whom she criticizes—has accepted the indoctrination and prejudices of her religion, this resistance to conversion is linked to her ambivalent relationship to mothers and mother images, which is further connected to her anxieties about women's roles in both Catholic and Protestant society.

PATRIARCHAL RELIGION AND THE MISSING MOTHER

At the centre of these anxieties is Lucy's strong need for acceptance and approval, which circles back to the absence of maternal love in her life. Ironically, Lucy knows the role of "mother" only from a perspective of loss. All the mother figures in her life have failed her. Her efforts to define herself as a woman, therefore, do not include maternal identification as one of the means by which she might reconcile herself to the role of women in her society. Yet this also makes it impossible for her to define herself, as many daughters seeking self-definition do, in opposition to the mother.

Because she has no real mother, Lucy is both fascinated and repelled by the Catholic Church's use of mother imagery. In this connection, the relative absence of references to the Virgin Mary throughout *Villette* may be significant. Living in a Catholic country, Lucy would have encountered frequent references to the Mother of God. The nineteenth century, after all, is a period of great attention to the Virgin Mary by Catholics, and Protestant anxieties about Catholics generally included concern about the Catholic "worship" of Mary.[17] Lucy, therefore, might have been expected to include criticisms of "Mariolatry" among the failings of the Catholic faith, yet she does not. This relative silence about the Catholic worship of Mary may be connected to Lucy's other silences. Just as she never mentions her mother or explains what crisis deprived her of family and security, and just as she delays telling the reader how she has discovered that Dr. John is the same Graham Bretton from her childhood, Lucy may be suppressing her response to the Virgin Mary. Leaving this powerful feminine figure out of her personal account of Catholicism is another way to avoid examining the longing for a positive maternal figure—especially since, as a Protestant, she has been conditioned to reject the appeal of Mary as a universal mother figure. For Victorian Protestants, venerating the Virgin Mary is linked to the worship of false gods—or worse, goddesses—and is therefore highly suspect.

In *Victorians and the Virgin Mary: Religion and Gender in England 1830-1865,* Carol Englehardt Herringer notes that during the nineteenth century, many "Protestants denounced the Virgin Mary as an interfering mother and a pagan goddess who testified to the links between ancient and modern Rome" (2). The accusation that Mary is an "interfering mother" is very similar to Lucy's complaint about the intrusiveness of the Catholic Church in the lives of those "she" touches. The link with paganism makes explicit a connection between the Christian "Mother of God" and the divine feminine. Ironically, the Virgin Mary seems to have all the attributes that Victorian patriarchy wanted to see as quintessentially female. For this reason, many scholars have assumed that "nineteenth century Marian representations ... ratified the ... status quo of the docile domestic woman" (Herringer 2) and would, therefore, have found favour with mainstream Victorian culture. However, Herringer argues the opposite and notes that Protestant patriarchy was made "uneasy with envisioning women as powerful by virtue of their motherhood and moral superiority" (21-23). If Mary's maternal power makes it possible for her to influence her son, who is also God, then what kinds of power could the "Angel" of the Victorian hearth not claim? The Protestant condemnation of "Mariolatry" and anxieties over the Catholic Church's "worship" of the Virgin Mary is a reaffirmation of a patriarchal rejection of what is "feminine" in religion.

As a good Victorian Protestant, Lucy knows that to look for the "feminine" in religion is not only mistaken but potentially sinful. Her God is a Patriarchal God who does not grant power to any woman, not even His mother. Yet as a Victorian woman, she yearns for comfort and understanding that this Patriarchal God cannot give. Although she seems to have no problem resisting Catholicism, the hint of a feminine sympathy in the Church attracts her and repels her in equal measure. Ironically, the absence of a mother in her life makes her long for the maternal aspects of the Catholic Church, yet it also makes her distrustful of them.

Lucy's own experiences have not taught her to trust in maternal nurture or to find security in turning her problems over to others. It is, therefore, not surprising that she is particularly skeptical of M. Paul's attempt to convert her by presenting the Church in its maternal role. When he leaves the book of Catholic propaganda among her things, she expresses how "This meek volume was not addressed to the hardened and worldly; it was not even strong meat for the strong; it was milk for babes; the mild effluence of a mother's love towards her tenderest and her youngest; intended wholly and solely for those whose head is to be reached through the heart" (XXXVI.518). Yet the reason that M. Paul has chosen this particular book as the first step in the attempt to convert her to Catholicism is precisely that he has recognized in her an emotional hunger that is indistinguishable from a spiritual hunger. For him, it seems natural that the Catholic Church will appeal most to her when it manifests as "mother church."

He is not entirely mistaken—Lucy is, indeed, attracted to the motherly care and nurture that the Church promises. The problem is that she does not trust these promises, not only because of her Protestant upbringing but because of her experiences with mother figures who have not met her needs. Why should she trust "Rome" to be any different? "I smiled then, over this dose of maternal tenderness, coming from the ruddy old lady of the Seven Hills" (XXXVI.419) she states skeptically after first reading the little pamphlet.

Craving love above all, Lucy has become accustomed to settling for less than what she needs; she buys a little affection and acceptance by denying and disguising her strongest desires. To earn Mrs. Bretton's motherly approval, Lucy knows that she must suppress expressions of her inner self and deny her need for more love than is offered to her. To earn Miss Marchmont's motherly approval, Lucy has to isolate herself from the world and nurture her mother figure. To earn the respect of Madame Beck and the others in the *Pensionat*, she must present a front of calm and control that is at odds with the emotional and spiritual hunger that drives her. The women in her world—her students, Paulina, and even her fellow teachers—value her only insofar as she nurtures and supports *them* without demanding the same in return. Thus, when the Catholic Church offers its protection and comfort in the form of a motherly message, Lucy focuses on what she must give up in exchange and concludes that the price is too great. As Lucy sees it, the spiritual comfort offered by the Church would have to be bought by the loss of self.

THE ROMANTIC PLOT AND THE MISSING MOTHER

The novel has no answer for Lucy's longings to connect with her lost mother, in part because the text—like all Victorian novels—is constructed within a patriarchal set of assumptions, in which the search for the mother is confused and obscured by what was seen as a more appropriate search for a romantic partner. Since *Villette* shows the heroine's hunger for the love of two different men, and since it ends with her waiting for the man who has promised to marry her when he returns, it is easy to see the novel as a quest for romantic love. Yet the quest for love in *Villette* is not really focused on the search for a romantic partner. Although it could be argued that Lucy conceals from the reader the extent to which she is looking for a man to love, her readiness to submit to Miss Marchmont's limited life suggests that she is interested in a love that is maternal rather than romantic. Possibly echoing her author's feelings at the time of writing, Lucy is determined not to indulge in romantic dreaming. The love that she hungers for is presented as greater than the love of a man.[18] Women who seek masculine attention are often presented as shallow, frivolous, and even mercenary in the novel. Madame Beck's interest in "Dr. John" is shown to be a weakness. Paulina finds John Graham Bretton's love without seeking it—slipping easily from a relationship where her father is the centre of her life to a relationship that includes a lover. Hers is the only story of conventional romantic love in the novel and, perhaps, the least believable. It represents an ideal that Brontë recognized was unlikely to be realized; Paulina is less a real person than a representation of what Lucy cannot be.

Although Paulina, too, is motherless, she has no difficulty finding love because she possesses qualities that make her intensely appealing to men (fathers and potential husbands). In addition to her prettiness, Paulina's strongest allure is her capacity for projecting adoration of the male subject.[19] In this, she is linked to the "angel of the house," the Victorian ideal that demanded self-sacrifice and immolation from women, but allegedly offered them protection and status as wives and mothers in return. Since Lucy seems to have been denied the options of becoming a wife and mother—her hopeless attraction to Dr. John emphasizes that she is no match for a pretty heroine like Paulina—the protection and status appear to be beyond her reach.

Yet in the end, the novel *does* offer Lucy what may be termed a "romantic" relationship with M. Paul—a man who seems to love, accept, and want to protect her. Interestingly, that man is a devout Catholic who describes himself as a sort of "lay Jesuit" (XXI.460), and whose history includes a ruined romance with a woman who was forced to become a nun. His connection with

Lucy, thus, offers the elements of emotional and spiritual love that she seeks yet fears to find in the Catholic Church.

This is not to suggest that Lucy, through her relationship with M. Paul, comes to admit that the Catholic Church may give her the spiritual comfort she craves. On the contrary, the novel shows M. Paul developing greater acceptance for Lucy's Protestantism than she ever develops for his Catholicism. Lucy remains critical of Roman Catholicism and its rituals and doctrines. As she sees it, the Church wants to convert her and turn her into a nun, and it wants M. Paul to become a priest or monk or, at least, marry a Catholic woman of the community. Lucy's hostile perception of Catholicism is connected to her view of the Church as repressive.

Although some of the repressiveness is associated with female figures—for example, Madame Walravens, the elderly grandmother of M. Paul's first love—the efforts of Père Silas to convert her become identified in Lucy's mind with the patriarchal power and hierarchy of the Church. The Church may be referred to in feminine terms, but it is run by men. The mythology of Catholicism sees the priest, a man, as the representative of God and the Church as the female who submits to God and His vicars. Furthermore, as Madame Walravens's case illustrates, women who seek power by allying themselves with the repressive elements of the Church become monsters.[20] The offer of maternal support from the Church—like the image of the Virgin Mary as a maternal figure that will speak for the sinner to her Son—disguises how Catholicism disempowers women. The deception of "mother church" is that, in Lucy's mind, it is really no more maternal than the cold father of her Protestant religion.

Returning to the crucial confessional scene, what Lucy seeks in the confessional is not advice or absolution, but acknowledgment. She needs a listener, someone outside herself who can be entrusted with her thoughts and whose response to her will represent that she can be valued for herself. The Catholic Church appeals to her insofar that it acknowledges her existence. However, insofar as that same Church (as represented primarily by Père Silas) wants to bring her into the fold, she is distrustful, even terrified, because on some level she recognizes that despite its somewhat more feminized message, Catholicism is as much a patriarchal institution as

Protestantism. Indeed, Gilbert and Gubar suggest that "Brontë's virulent anti-Catholicism is informed by her strong attack on the masculine domination that pervades all forms of Christianity" (415). Whether or not the reader sees Brontë as anti-Catholic—to confuse the author and the narrator is not always wise—Lucy's unsuccessful search for a spiritual mother is an indictment of the limitations of patriarchy.

The best the novel can offer Lucy is not a "mother" but a man who is nurturing and devoted to her well-being. M. Paul, the little man with the explosive temper who leaves the odor of cigar smoke wherever he goes, is in some ways less a lover than a mother substitute. Like the "angel of the hearth," he is identified with making sacrifices, but unlike the idealized feminine "angel," he makes these sacrifices with energy and without docility. Because he is a man, he has the freedom to show anger. Because he is not English, he has the freedom to show emotion. He is the only person in Lucy's world who recognizes, and to some extent validates, her emotional passion. Similarly, his history—tragic as it is in some ways—serves as a model for balancing "reason" and "emotion" without succumbing to spiritual anguish.

It is not a coincidence that M. Paul is repeatedly associated with providing treats, small pleasures, and comforts. He leaves books and bonbons in Lucy's desk (XXIX. 435), and when he takes the students and teachers to "breakfast in the country" (XXXIII.474), he has to be restrained from giving a "large order for 'jambon' and 'confitures'" in addition to the hot coffee, chocolate, cream, new laid eggs, fresh rolls, and butter already provided (XXXIII.478-479). When he finds Lucy asleep at her desk, he provides a shawl to pillow her arms and a second shawl to keep her warm (XXI.451). His final act before leaving Labassecour is to find a house where Lucy may start her own school; he offers her the opportunity of an independent livelihood, which may be seen symbolically as a new life.[21] Although the novel does not clarify if this new life includes M. Paul as a husband, I am among those readers who feel that it does not. For Lucy to marry at the end of the novel not only would go against its general theme of loneliness and isolation, but it would undermine the narrative of spiritual quest that is far more important than the romantic story that disguises it.

CONCLUSION

Insofar as this novel is read as a Protestant spiritual journey, Lucy succeeds in resisting the temptation of the Popish "Harlot" which by presenting herself in maternal form, tries to take over her autonomy and immure her in a convent for the greater glory of the Church. However, if the reader looks at Lucy's spiritual journey as the quest for a spiritual mother who will make up for the absence of an earthly mother, Lucy's quest fails. Her experiences only offer weak substitutes for the feminine connections that she unknowingly craves. In patriarchy, as the novel illustrates, women's relationships are ultimately shadowed by their relationships with men. And in her religious quest, Lucy's unrecognized longing for a feminine spiritual connection is never satisfied. Neither the Protestant nor the Catholic Church offers her a spiritual mother because as male-dominated institutions, both recognize only a masculine God.

NOTES

[1]All references are to the Oxford World's Classics edition (1984, reissued 2000). Because there are so many editions, the roman numerals indicate chapter numbers.

[2]For *Villette* and the Gothic see Wein, "Gothic Desire in Charlotte Brontë's *Villette*" and Crosby, "Charlotte Brontë's Haunted Text." The classic essay examining Brontë and the Gothic tradition is Heilman's "Charlotte Brontë's 'New Gothic.'" For discussion of anti-Catholicism in *Villette*, see Armitage, "Melting Miss Snowe"; Clark-Beattie, "Fables of Rebellion"; Clarke, "Charlotte Brontë's *Villette*, Mid-Victorian Anti-Catholicism"; and Schiefelbein's "A Catholic Baptism for *Villette*'s Lucy Snowe." See also Thormählen, *The Brontës and Religion* for biographical and historical insights. The chapter on Brontë in Gilbert and Gubar's *The Madwoman in the Attic* includes not only an influential feminist reading of the Gothic but psychoanalytic insights. Most critical attention to the "missing mother" in *Villette* (and other Brontë novels) tends to be psychoanalytic in approach, which emphasizes the author's own maternal deprivation; see Keefe, *Charlotte Brontë's World of Death*, for example.

[3]Brontë, who was five when her mother died, claimed to have only one shadowy memory of her own mother, but most biographers agree that her relationship with her siblings filled much of the emotional gap left, and she had mother substitutes in an aunt and a dedicated family servant, "Tabby." See Guerin, *Charlotte Brontë*.

[4]It is beyond the scope of this chapter to analyze all the ways in which Brontë's use of "reason" and "feeling" or "imagination" to suggest psychological and spiritual anxiety may be understood. Among other things, the words are not used consistently throughout the novel, inviting often contradictory interpretations. Gilbert and Gubar argue that "'Reason' and 'imagination' are the terms [Lucy] uses to describe the conflicts between her conscious self-repression and the libidinal desires she fears"(411). Schiefelbein, on the other hand, suggests that Lucy presents "reason and imagination" as "destructive external forces" (320). As I read it, Lucy generally associates "reason" with her Protestant culture and "imagination" and "feeling with what is forbidden in that culture and therefore—insofar as they endorse sentimentality and superstition—with the Catholic Church. However, insofar as she associates the Catholic Church with repression, Lucy sees it as abusing the power of the imagination and the appeal to the senses through its glorifying of sentimentality. Furthermore, although she frames the dialogues between "reason" and "imagination" as binary oppositions, they do not, in fact, always function as opposites in the novel, nor can they be pinned down to mean the same thing at all times. For the purposes of this chapter, I am focusing on the appeal of the Catholic Church as allowing more range of emotion and, therefore, of spiritual expression.

[5]The ideal of feminine submission and self-denial, though not yet linked with the term "angel in the house" (which first appears in Coventry Patmore's 1854 poem idealizing his wife as the perfect woman), had been evolving since the eighteenth century and continued to evolve throughout the Victorian period. At the time that Brontë wrote *Villette*, living up to the ideal required a "single woman of limited means [to] control her feelings of loneliness, make no [economical or emotional] demands ... and fend for herself" without burdening her community (Clark-Beattie 826). For a useful (classic) summary of the evolution of ideas about women in

the Victorian period, see Houghton, *The Victorian Frame of Mind* (348-53). For a discussion of the appeal of the "angel" ideology to women as well as men and a discussion of the development of ideals of self-restraint for men as well as women, see Adams, "Victorian Sexualities."

[6]The "absent mother" is sometimes more powerful in women's novels than more present figures. As Greenfield puts it in *Mothering Daughters*, "[w]hether she is dead, missing, emotionally detached, or present without the daughter realizing it, the mother is conspicuous in her absence"(18). McKnight speaks of the absence of the mother as "creating a vacuum that destabilizes the protagonist" and forces the heroine to negotiate experience without the option of protection and guidance (*Suffering Mothers* 18). Lucy's mother is an extreme example of the absent mother because she is not even mentioned.

[7]Carlisle, for example, while granting that young Lucy may have resented the visiting child, argues that "there are at work here forces ... that ... cannot be explained of even the most jealous of fourteen year old girls" (271). I disagree.

[8]Clark-Beattie suggests that the "bland affection" shown to Lucy by her godmother is worse than "actual cruelty" (826).

[9]The relationship with Miss Marchmont is interesting in that it places Lucy in the role of adult daughter who must care for her parent without first giving her the experience of being a child who is cared for by the mother figure. Furthermore, Miss Marchmont's reclusiveness isolates and limits Lucy's ability to find other sources of love and support. She represents a type of maternal love that meets only her own needs and ultimately leaves Lucy no better off than she was before she went to work for this "kindly" woman.

[10]For an analysis of *Villette* as autobiography, see Carlisle. Clark-Beattie suggests that Villette may be read as a "subverted confession" (824). Insofar as it has been argued that one of the tasks of female autobiography is "killing the mother off" (Johnson, "My Monster/Myself" 4), the "absent mother" may represent Lucy's metaphorical killing (by erasing from her history) the mother who she has experienced as deserting her. This does not mean that Lucy does not mind the absence of her mother, but quite the contrary. The mother becomes unmentionable because the process of separating

from her—either in the lived experience or the imagination—is too painful to articulate.

[11]It may be significant that in the Church of England, a girl child is supposed to have two godmothers and one godfather. Although not all families observed this, Brontë, a clergyman's daughter, may have been making another point of maternal absence when only *one* godmother is mentioned. It is also possible to see Mrs. Bretton as a failed fairy tale godmother. Where the fairy tale godmother helps Cinderella get her prince, Mrs. Bretton cannot imagine Lucy with a prince, much less help her get him. In a different reading, Gilbert and Gubar call attention to the "fairy-tale elements" of chapter XXXIV (titled "Malevola") where Lucy enacts the "typical fairy-tale little girl who must carry a basket of fruit" to an old woman" (431). For another discussion of fairy tale elements in *Villette*, see Katherine Kim, "Corpse Hoarding," which links M. Paul and Lucy herself with Bluebeard.

[12]In naming her hero Paul Emmanuel, Brontë is not only alluding to the apostle Paul but connecting him to the English church as represented by St. Paul's Cathedral. For a discussion of the significance of Paul Emmanuel's name, see Wilks "*Villette* and the Biblical/Theological Impulse" (271).

[13]Various critics have contextualized the novel within the increased anxiety about Roman Catholicism in England at this time. Schiefelbein argues that "if any novel has earned the epithet 'quintessentially anti-Catholic,'" it is *Villette* (319). Armitage suggests that Brontë uses Lucy's anti-Catholicism to point to the flaws not of Catholicism but of fanaticism. See also Jędrzejewski, "Charlotte Brontë and Roman Catholicism" as well as Clark-Beattie and Clark. For a concise account of anti-Catholicism in England during this period, see Ingram "Protestant Patriarchy and the Catholic Priesthood in the Nineteenth Century."

[14]To be sure, another way of reading Lucy's success in Labassacour is that it represents the superiority of hardworking, Protestant Englishness in contrast to the mediocrity of ordinary Catholics. Yet the novel shows that there is hard work and dedication among the Catholics and that they are less impressed than puzzled by what is foreign about her. Just as she does not really understand her new community, they do not understand her. But because she

is not one of them, they grant her a place as "the foreigner"—and a freedom to be herself, that she does not experience among her own countrymen.

[15]It is irrelevant to this chapter that M. Paul Emmanuel is based on M. Heger, Charlotte and Emily Brontë's professor in Brussels, and that Madame Beck is a portrait of Madame Heger. Although it is true that Brontë derived these characters and, among others, the character of Dr. John Graham Bretton from her the personality of her publisher George Smith, this is not Brontë's autobiography but Lucy's. For a discussion of the inspiration for the different characters in *Villette*, see Guerin, 490-501.

[16]In a typical scene, Dr. John who knows that Lucy is in anguish at losing one of his letters, hides the letter, which he picks off the floor before she sees it, until she is almost hysterical. She recognizes that he is just teasing and is so happy to have the letter back that she does not "reprove" him for teasing her. In the same scene, he urges her to "cultivate happiness" as a cure for her "long-continued mental conflict." Lucy does not find this a useful suggestion. "No mockery in this world ever sounds to me so hollow as that of being told to *cultivate* happiness," she says to the reader. "Happiness is not a potato, to be planted in mould, and tilled with manure" (XXII, 249-50). Dr. John's idea that Lucy's unhappiness represents not a natural response to her circumstances but some form of mental weakness is in sharp contrast to M. Paul. Although both are authoritarian males, Dr. John has scant interest in her mind and even less in her soul, whereas M. Paul is acutely sensitive to both.

[17]For a full discussion of Victorian attitudes towards Mariolatry, see Herringer.

[18]Without denying that suppressed sexual passion is an element in her response to both Dr. John and M. Paul, I see this novel as ultimately suggesting that Lucy does not want a lover as much as she wants a spiritual connection. Her repressed sexuality yearns less for the bedroom than for a communion of souls, which I believe is linked to a yearning for the infantile stage in which the child does not distinguish between mother and self. At the same time, Lucy fears nothing as much as she fears losing her *self*. The submission of the "angel in the house" ideal is not for her, and it is for this reason that the novel shows that her attraction to John

Bretton, unlike her attraction to M. Paul, is misplaced.

[19]Although in many readings—including Gilbert and Gubar's—Paulina is seen as an alter ego to Lucy, I am more interested in how they represent different types of women. Lucy's distancing of herself from Paulina reflects a recognition of the vulnerability of women who depend on men.

[20]Lucy links Madame Walravens not only with the repressive elements of the Catholic Church but with its manipulation and power. Yet as Gilbert and Gubar point out, Madame Walravens is both "the terrible mother who seeks to take revenge" and an "image of Lucy's repressed anger at the injustice of men and male culture" (431).

[21]I am not suggesting that M. Paul is presented as a mother figure, only that the kind of love that he offers is the closest that Lucy experiences to true maternal caring. And I believe it is significant that although his leaving replicates the absent mother who (whether or not she died before the start of the novel) may be perceived by the child (Lucy) as having abandoned her, M. Paul leaves Lucy equipped to deal with the world.

WORKS CITED

Adams, James Eli. "Victorian Sexualities." *A Companion to Victorian Literature and Culture*. Ed. Herbert F. Tucker. Melden, MA: Broadview, 1999. 125-38. Print.

Armitage, Nicholas. "Melting Miss Snowe: Charlotte's Message to the English Church." *Brontë Studies* 34.3 (2009): 209-19. Print.

Brontë, Charlotte. *Villette*. Eds. Margaret Smith and Herbert Rosengarth. New York: Oxford Worlds Classics, 2000. Print.

Carlisle, Janice. "The Faces in the Mirror: *Villette* and the Conventions of Autobiography." *ELH* 46.2 (1979): 262-89. JSTOR. Web. 27 May 2003.

Clark-Beattie, Rosemary "Fables of Rebellion: Anti-Catholicism and the Structure of *Villette*." *ELH* 53.4 (1986): 821-47. JSTOR. 25 June 2003.

Clarke, Micael, M. "Charlotte Brontë's *Villette*, Mid-Victorian Anti-Catholicism and the Turn to Secularism." *ELH* 78.4 (2011): 967-89. *Project Muse*. Web. 9 Apr. 2015

Crosby, Christina. "Charlotte Brontë's Haunted Text." *Studies in English Literature* 24.4 (1984): 701-715. Print.

Dolin, Tim. Introduction. "Introduction." *Villette*." By Charlotte Brontë." Eds. Margaret Smith and Herbert Rosengarth. New York: Oxford Worlds Classics, 2000. x-xxxv. Print.

Gérin, Winifred. *Charlotte Brontë: The Evolution of Genius*. Oxford: Clarendon Press, 1967. Print.

Herringer, Carol Englehardt. *Gender in History: Victorians and the Virgin Mary: Religion and Gender in England 1830-1865*. Manchester: Manchester University Press, 2008. Print.

Heilman, Robert. "Charlotte Brontë's New Gothic" [1958 reprint]. *The Victorian Novel: Modern Essays in Criticism*. Ed. Ian Watt. New York: Oxford University Press, 1971. 165-88. Print.

Houghton, Walter E. *The Victorian Frame of Mind: 1830-1870*. New Haven: Yale University Press, 1957. Print.

Ingram, Phillip. "Protestant Patriarchy and the Catholic Priesthood in the Nineteenth Century." *Journal of Social History* 24.4 (1991): 783-789. Print.

Jędrzejewski, Jan. "Charlotte Brontë and Roman Catholicism." *Brontë Studies* 38.4 (2013): 269-80. Print.

Johnson, Barbara. "My Monster/Myself." *Diacritics* 12.2 (1982): 2-10. Print.

Kim, Katherine J. "Corpse Hoarding: Control and the Female Body in 'Bluebeard,' 'Schalken The Painter,' and '*Villette*.'" *Studies in the Novel* 43.4 (2011): 406-27. Print.

McKnight, Natalie. *Suffering Mothers in Mid-Victorian Novels*. New York: St. Martin's Press, 1997. Print.

Schielfelbein, Michael. "A Catholic Baptism for *Villette's* Lucy Snowe." *Christianity and Literature* 45.3-4 (1996): 319-29. Print.

Thormählen, Marianne. *The Brontës and Religion*. Cambridge: Cambridge University Press. 1999. Print.

Wein, Toni. "Gothic Desire in Charlotte Brontë's *Villette*." SEL *Studies in English Literature 1500-1900* 39.4 (1999): 733-46. Print.

Wilkes, Brian. "*Villette* and the Biblical/Theological Impulse." *Bronte Studies* 37.4 (2012): 332-38. Print.

III.
SHARING RELIGIOUS AND SPIRITUAL MATERNAL NARRATIVES

12.
Storytelling as a Way to Reconnect and Co-create Spiritual Contexts

Conversations with Five Muslim Mothers

RANNVEIG HAGA

> *Compared to other women, Somali mothers are in my mind the strongest women on earth whether they are in a Western country or in Somalia.... They always aim to survive and swim through parenthood with ease. There is a saying that if there is more water than your size, if other people [outnumber] you, then it will swipe you away.... Somali mothers are facing something bigger than themselves. And everything that is more powerful than you comes with problems.* (Personal interview with Sahra)

SAHRA, A FINNISH-SOMALI mother, compares the situation of Somali mothers living in Western countries with a person "swiped away" by insurmountable waters. Sahra was interviewed as part of my qualitative research project *Parenting and Islam: Somali Mothers in Sweden and Finland*, carried out between 2011 and 2016. This research project began after I observed increasing numbers of Somali mothers leaving Europe and North America for the Middle East and Africa together with their children. The aim of the project is to start conversations concerning how Muslim mothers can become more comfortable with raising their children in Nordic countries. In performing this research, I have found that these mothers experience epistemic injustice. This is a form of injustice that is done to someone in their capacity as *knowers*, where their narratives are not given due credibility.[1]

A great obstacle that these mothers encounter in conversations with school teachers and social workers is the preconceived notion that many Westerners have of Muslim women. I address this issue in previous research with Somali women traders in Dubai and Hargeisa (Haga, *Tradition as Resource*). However, the problem remains that external voices largely continue to speak *for* Somalis. They are not given the space to tell their own narratives. As a young Finnish-Somali mother and activist whom I interviewed states: "The power to define yourself, to write your own narrative, is something that's ... removed from [Somalis]. That's something that also should be challenged, like who tells the narratives, how they tell it, and most importantly, why?"

Moreover, as this mother also emphasizes, researchers should focus more on the structural injustices that Somali mothers face in Nordic countries instead of focusing on cultural explanations. For too long, researchers and media in the Nordic countries have ignored this larger context, and my focus on epistemic injustice is, thus, an attempt to see the "water" that surrounds these women and attempts to "swipe them away." At the same time, I wish to be a "space maker" (Haig-Brown 415) so to create space for Somali mothers to "swim through parenthood with ease." Of course, as one of many white researchers who has sought to draw attention to racialized Muslim women's lived experiences, the question arises as to whether I am in a position to share Somali women's narratives, let alone "create space" for them.

To that end, Safia Aidid has initiated an important discussion about the production of knowledge within academia on Twitter with the hashtag #*cadaan*studies, which translates to "whiteness studies." Contributors to this conversation question how whiteness gives access to the power that is needed to define the injustice done to Somalis who are systematically marginalized and denied the space to tell their own narratives. Can space be made by others, or must it be taken by the subjects themselves? Although the privileged have a responsibility to make room for others to swim, I have come to the conclusion that I cannot create this critical space if I claim to be the narrator of these women's stories. Rather, I can attempt to generate such space by speaking from my own experience.

As such, my standpoint is shaped by my status as a white Muslim convert who is married to a Somali man and is mother to two children. The powerful image of being overwhelmed by "waters bigger than your size" resonates with my own feeling of being a Muslim woman and mother in Sweden and Norway. My experience is that the waters continue to expand, and the words I use to express my own narrative are taken away from me one wave at a time. However, I also realize that I have been standing at the shore for too long as a distant and detached researcher; I have not been able to create space for myself or for others. Through my conversations with other Muslim mothers, I have learned that spirituality cannot be easily or concretely defined. In order to create space for growth, researchers' narratives must include spaces for spirituality that are not controlled by others' definitions. In this way, although I have particular privileges as a white researcher, I share the feeling of being "swiped away" by cultural and academic discourses that do not make space for spiritual beliefs and experiences.

As researchers, we often give the false impression that the reality of the people we study can be defined and thus translated into sameness. As Audre Lorde observed many years ago, it is not the differences among people that separate us "but rather our refusal to recognize those differences, and to examine the distortions which result from our misnaming them and their effects upon human behavior and expectations" ("Our Difference is our Strength" 315). Quite contrary to such dominant ideals of objectivity, my goal is to create space by using my subjectivity as a resource for research. I can only leave space for others to express their truth if I express my own truth. Only through telling my own story can I truly engage with Somali mothers in an attempt to understand their concerns. It is a story of how such conversations with other mothers have allowed me to foster a sense of belonging as a Muslim woman in Sweden. I have entered the water by allowing our talks to lead me to the existential question of how to belong. These mothers face greater obstacles than me in this respect, but many of them have found a way to swim through parenthood with relative ease. Through listening to and engaging with their narratives, I ask how we as Muslim mothers can move forwards in creating necessary spaces for our own spiritualities as well as those of our children to be nurtured and to bloom.

In this chapter, I do not attempt to "translate" the words of my research participants into sameness. Instead, I aim to learn from them by asking questions in accordance with the principles of "existential anthropology" as developed by the award-winning poet and anthropologist Michael Jackson. I use fieldwork as well as existential theories to explore ways of being and relations between people as they appear in various cultural settings. This is an attempt to understand more of the human condition by examining the various manners in which this condition manifests itself cross-culturally. At the same time, I acknowledge the limits of such understanding because, as Jackson phrases it, "while human existence is seldom a matter solely of ourselves, but of our relations with others, it is *grasped only within ourselves*" (xxviii).

SPIRITUALITY AND EPISTEMIC JUSTICE

Marginalized people are given less space to grow and thrive because of epistemic injustice (Fricker). Certain types of epistemologies are heard, supported, and accepted as rational. Statements that are viewed as rational do not require explanations to reveal their "actual" meaning, whereas epistemologies that are viewed as irrational require a secondary explanation to understand what is "really" meant. Lila Abu-Lughod argues that "culture" operates in anthropological discourse to enforce separation. Such separation, she claims, inevitably carries a sense of hierarchy. In my opinion, "religion" has the same function within religious studies. According to popular usage, the terms "religious" and "secular" construct a dichotomy in which "the secular" is understood as rational, individualistic, egalitarian, and free. "The religious," in contrast, is understood as collectivistic, hierarchical, and traditional. Even if the religious is accepted as privatized rationality that can carry positive connotations, such as compassion and love, it is still commonly seen as less free and less critical by European secular discourse (Talal et. al).

Commonly, views that are understood as irrational are explained by a third "objective" person, and this person is often a researcher. Therefore, my position becomes paradoxical because if I explain the views of Somali parents and attempt to make space for their epistemologies, I am at the same time supporting the assumption that their views must be explained. Instead, I will try to create space by making visible different stories and exploring ways in which I can "affirm and interrogate the histories, memories and stories of the devalued others who have been marginalised from the official discourse of the canon" (Giroux 101).

I do not claim to access "truth" in this research, and much less the truths about my participants' experiences and struggles, which could delegitimize their right to define their own claims. Instead, I strive to reclaim my subject position as author as well as agent. I agree with the sociologist Kitty Calvati that this does not imply agonizing endlessly about my own subjectivity, "but that we must be willing to let our humanity show" (14). Calvati further suggests that claiming our agency and authority as researchers need not disempower other agents. This is because researchers can simultaneously make clear that we are constructing an argument rather than imparting truth. Calvati, accordingly, suggests that we can learn from black feminists in claiming our agency as public intellectuals. This is important, as white people are taught to see their perspective as objective and representative of all humanity. In claiming my agency, I understand that my actions have consequences, and I accept my limitations without trying to overcome or escape them.

The poet David Whyte writes that honesty ultimately begins by accepting powerlessness as part of the human condition. Perhaps in order to become empowered collectively, we must first understand our limitations as individuals who are influenced by sexism, racism, and ableism, among other prejudices. However, it is not possible for me as an individual to situate myself outside the social world, which is defined by structural discrimination that privileges certain epistemologies above others. I want to create space that will nurture and support marginalized epistemologies, but I really do not know how. Perhaps the most important thing each of us can do is strive to be honest about our privileges and our powerlessness as well as the impossibility of stepping outside embedded power structures. David Whyte contextualizes honesty as

> grounded in humility and indeed in humiliation, and in admitting exactly where we are powerless. Honesty is not

> found in revealing the truth, but in understanding how deeply afraid of it we are. To become honest is in effect to become fully and robustly incarnated into powerlessness. Honesty allows us to live with not knowing. We do not know the full story, we do not know where we are in the story; we do not know who is at fault or who will carry the blame in the end. Honesty is not a weapon to keep loss and heartbreak at bay, honesty is the outer diagnostic of our ability to come to ground in reality, the hardest attainable ground of all, the place where we actually dwell, the living, breathing frontier where there is no realistic choice between gain or loss.

There is no power, and no good or bad, outside human relationships. Even if my intentions are honest, the question of whether my actions uphold or counteract racism is only possible to evaluate in accordance with the consequences that my actions have, and they cannot be judged beforehand. One could say that the more privileges one has, the more one has to lose. Therefore, it becomes more difficult to be honest. The very language I use is the master's tools, which I, according to Lorde, cannot use to dismantle the master's house. I struggle to let go of the language that I have learned. I am also encouraged by Lorde's words that poetry is not a luxury ("Poetry Is Not a Luxury" 249), and so I have written a poem of my own:

I have the
gift and the curse
of speech

A word can be a
Window
Or a screen

Whatever you say
Whatever I say

I am

What I grow
to be

Part of the struggle against epistemic injustice is to understand how people's experiences and opinions can never be captured by our research. A closed language is ultimately a violent language since it impedes growth.

All people belong to particular communities that shape their aspirations and understandings of the world. We as human beings may, therefore, not have a voice that is entirely our own. Nonetheless, it is only by attempting to speak with the voice we have that we can take full responsibility for what we convey. As we consciously reflect upon the types of language we use and make moral decisions in the process of writing, we should "scrutinize not only the truth of that we speak, but the truth of that language by which we speak it" (Lorde, "The Transformation of Silence into Language and Action." 83).[2] Compassion and empathy are our only tools for understanding human beings. To scrutinize the truth of what we say and the truth of that language by which we speak is to scrutinize whether our language is able to invite compassion into the bloodstream of our writing. In the words of Toni Morrison, this invitation is "more than civilizing, more than ethical, more than humane, it is humanizing."

There have been times when I was tempted to leave academe because I felt there was no space for me to express myself in a language that is true. The academic language that I had adopted was ultimately a closed language. I am trying to let go of this language that tells the lie that others' realities can be defined in words that do not point beyond their meaning. But rather than leave, I learned to let go of the academic need to be "scientific" and leave a part of me outside my research and writing. I consider this a method for testing the space that is available to me as well as a way to make space. As Thrinh T. Minh-Ah contends in regard to Lorde's words about the master's tools, "The more one depends on the master's house for support, the less one hears what he doesn't want us to hear" (246). I now recognize how I have become dependent on "the master's house," and I am trying to let go of this attachment. When we start to listen, we can co-create new stories and make space for spirituality and growth. In this respect, this chapter explores how to find belonging as a spiritual being in spaces where secular rationality and functionalist materialism have become the norm.

METHODOLOGY

My methodology consists of the process of continued testimonial practice, together with (self-) critical reflections on such practice, in an attempt to grow and mature as a responsible listener. I have been challenged as to whether this methodology is simply an attempt to avoid criticism, and whether what I am suggesting is a multiculturalist stance or a cultural relativist one. On the contrary, I suggest that if communication is blocked, growth is also impeded. As such, to strive for the possibility of communication is to work towards the possibility of mutual criticism and to enter a process of change. I see potential in communication as a tool for researchers, social workers, teachers, and parents to decolonize our minds; open communication is only possible if we strive to mature as responsible listeners (Haga, "Freedom Has Destroyed the Somali Family").

This chapter[3] primarily draws from in-depth interviews with five mothers who are given pseudonyms to guarantee their anonymity: Sahra, a nurse; Noora, a teacher; Ayaan, an assistant nurse and interpreter; Amaal, a stay-at-home mother; and Leyla, a retiree. Sahra is forty years old and has five children between the ages of five and fifteen, and twenty-six-year-old Amaal has four children under the age of five. Noora, Ayaan, and Leyla are between the ages of forty-five and sixty, each of whom has between four and six children, who range from teenagers to mature adults.

LIFE IS A CIRCLE

Luce Irigaray speaks of the importance of learning the story of our mothers through generations in order to connect to, understand, and appreciate their work (30-39). If we accept that our mothers are complex human beings, we can understand and appreciate their struggles and gains in conjunction with our own. Consequently, the past becomes a resource that can help us learn and grow. To that end, the mothers I interviewed pass on what Andrea O'Reilly calls the "motherline." Their stories teach children both about their own experiences in life and about the values of the community. Somali mothers and fathers who are part of this study often speak of mothers as the children's first *madrassa*, or school. It is the mothers who have the main responsibility to teach the children about their ancestors, the values of Somali culture and Islam, and to keep memories alive. The mothers in my study express that "cultural bearing," or the task of raising their children in accordance with the values and beliefs of traditional Somali culture, as crucial. Whereas some emphasize Islam in this context, others emphasize culture; some speak of religion and culture as inseparable.

For instance, Noora spoke about the tradition of helping relatives in Somalia: "we are this chain which cannot be [broken]. We will not cut our chain!" She speaks of bonds made of love, and how cutting the chains would disempower individuals. She explains how her main task is to "raise, nurture and love" her children, and how faith is her guiding principle. Faith and social commitment are, for her, intrinsically linked: "The most important thing is faith.... That is what builds humanity. To respect and help those who need help. It is not just to believe in God; there is much else around too."

For the mothers whom I have met, an important part of their children's education is to teach them to stay close and committed to their parents when they grow old. As Amaal, a young mother in Stockholm, said: "we learn that life is a circle." She has heard stories about how hard it was for her mother to raise her, and she has great respect for the hard work that her mother performed. Her mother raised nine children in Somalia while they were poor. When I interviewed Amaal's mother, Leyla, she said she sometimes had to leave her small children alone at home in order to go out and sell sambosa or other foods that she had prepared. In order to illustrate how much easier it is for mothers to raise their children in Sweden, Leyla also narrated with a laugh how she in Somalia would go out to pick her children up from school and come home to find that their goat had eaten their lunch. She also commented on how she had to go to the hospital by herself when she was in labour, since her husband could not take a day off of work. It was very far; once, she walked half-way and took a cab the rest of the way, although she did not have money to pay for it. The cab driver got mad and ran after her, but he had to give up when they closed the door behind her to the delivery room. We all laughed at how she mimicked the cab driver waving his hands while the door locks behind her. Leyla also said it is easier today because we have wide access to contraception. She illustrated this by holding an imaginary small child with one arm and indicating a big stomach with the other.

The hard work that her mother did for her children is something Amaal thinks of often; consequently, she and her sisters are always caring for their mother. They cook food for her, clean the house, and keep her company. Amaal and her four small children live in an apartment on the floor above Leyla; the three other sisters live close by. They are a big family; they say that when all parents, children, and grandchildren are gathered together, they total fifty people. Amaal said that she thought that everyone had such a close bond with their family, but while growing up in Sweden, she discovered that this was not the case. I asked her when she first became aware of the difference, and she explained that it was when a friend of hers passed by her brother in the schoolyard without greeting him. She could argue with her siblings sometimes, but she would never pass by a sibling without acknowledging them.

The belief that life is a circle and that families are weaved together stands in opposition to the individualism that is at the centre of Western philosophy. We are not thrown into this world as many Western philosophers have stated; rather, we are carried into the world by a mother (Irigaray 30-39). Our survival is dependent on the care of others, often our mothers, after birth. Although this is obvious, I did not fully realize this before I became a mother myself and carried two children into the world. The sense of individuality and the control that I thought I had as a separate individual was replaced by a deep sense of vulnerability. My experience as a mother has enhanced my understanding of our interconnectivity and deepened my respect for and commitment to my parents. In an interview Toni Morrison warns about losing this connection: "[Grandparents and ancestors] were responsible for us, and we have to be responsible to them.... You can't just take. Our ancestors are part of that circle, an ever widening circle, one hopes. And if you ignore that, you put yourself in a spiritually dangerous position of being self-sufficient, having no group that you're dependent on" (qtd. in O'Reilly 16).

Somali-Swedish and Somali-Finnish mothers find it particularly challenging to teach their daughters the value of mothering and to be proud of the work they do in the house. A mother that public health researcher Barni Nor and I interviewed had recently come to Sweden. She said that she did all the housework, took care of the children alone, and worked outside the home. She said it is her job, and her husband was to do nothing in the house. She is proud of how hard she worked, and she said her daughter would learn from her example. She quoted a hadith where Prophet Muhammad according to her said "Do good to and serve your mother, then your mother, then your mother." Mothers who had lived longer in Sweden encouraged her to "take it easy." They said that if she continued that way she would burn out. According to them, her daughter would not look up to her for doing all the work; rather, she would see her as a doormat.

Noora said she was surprised at how her daughter reacted when she spoke about her childhood and the great things that she learned from her mother. She emphasized how it is important "that they know their story; it is important that we talk about how it is over there, and how we lived." She talked to her daughters continuously and proudly about how she could cook and wash clothes already at the age of seven. She told me that one of her daughters then asked her: "Did your mother love you?" Noora was shocked at this question and replied that her mother loved her very much. But her daughter doubted it: "Then she would not have given you jobs to do. You say you did the laundry; you cooked food." Her daughter continued: "Your mother did not love you; she was hard on you, poor you." Her daughter did not accept the message that she was proud of the important work she did.

FINDING A BALANCE—GOING INTO THE WATER

[Teaching our children to become Muslims in a non-Muslim country] is like taking the children into the water and

> *telling them not to get wet.... Our job as parents is to teach them to swim. I try to teach my kids, even though we live in an area with no Muslims. I try to teach them their own identity, but mostly I teach them good manners and that they are Muslims who need to be with other people also, but not too much which would make them drown in the ocean. For instance when my daughters become seven I usually give them small scarfs and after a while longer shirts with trousers. A bit by bit. But mostly I teach them the inside beauty and Muslim identity which are the good manners and so on.* (Personal interview with Sahra)

Here, Sahra speaks of how she tries to find a balance so her children will learn to be Muslims and "belong" at the same time. Letting children go and have their own experiences, good or bad, is hard for any mother. When the children are at risk of facing structural injustices, such as racism, sexism, or ableism, there is an even greater degree of worry. Letting go within a society that views Muslim parenting as problematic adds another dimension to this dilemma. Somali-Swedish and Somali-Finnish mothers ask how they can keep their children close in a society in which they are defined as a hindrance to the children's development. Commonly, freedom is defined in opposition to Somali culture and Islam. Furthermore, social workers and teachers do not try to understand these mothers and their views on childrearing, instead they are met with an assumption that Somali culture is inherently *not* free. This can be the consequence of growing anti-Muslim bigotry. Gender and religion are linked in this context, as the Nordic nation states are constructed as being inherently gender equal, whereas Muslim women and children are represented as victims who need help to become "liberated" from their particular family, culture, and religion (Karlsson Minganti 2; Eliassi; Haga). Freedom in this context becomes a code word for Swedish or Finnish culture.

Ayaan similarly spoke of how she tries to find a balance so that she will not become alienated from her children as she lets them become part of Swedish society. She reflects that if she does not let go, problems will arise:

> *It is really hard and if I emphasize my culture and my religion I will be lonely, and the children will be [also]. The children have more opportunities here than I have.... I have to balance, leave some of the tradition and some of the culture, you have to try to divide everything and try to keep in contact with the children.... You have to try to take half from here and half from there. It does not work for the children if you say: "No, you should only take this." It does not work because the children live here in Sweden. They live here in Sweden, and they have their friends here. You have to balance all the time. And if you do not balance then there will be a lot of problems in the family that has a background in another culture.*

Noora also emphasized the importance of balance. However, she felt it was easy to teach children about their culture and religion. This is perhaps because she does not see it as teaching them what they should not do, but focuses on what their culture and religion add. She explained:

> *When you raise your child in a different culture and you have a different religion, and then you end up here, it is very difficult.... The parents must know more and learn more.... This culture collusion has become a big problem between the children and the parents. But if the parents are open and know the way and can seek the knowledge and focus on what is the best interest of the child, then I think there will be no problems. So for me there was no problem. That my children are Somalis, Africans and Muslims is clear.... I have never forced them [when it comes to Islam]. The religion does not say that they must pray or fast ... they are children. Children are children. But if you have the possibility you should teach them the Quran, and you should tell them how it is to be a Muslim.... Some [of my children] have become practicing Muslims and some have not.... However, when they grow older they can seek knowledge [on Islam] themselves and go deeper.*

When the mothers speak of how they can let their children go into the metaphoric water and let them become a part of the Swedish or Finnish society, they speak of how the children can remain Muslim in a non-Muslim environment.

New generations of believers have engaged in feminist readings of the Quran by relying on their own intellect and knowledge to derive meaning. They emphasize that early scholars were influenced by their patriarchal culture, and that every reading is situational (Barlas 60). The mothers interviewed here are not scholars. However, they make choices in everyday life based on their experiences and their concerns for their children as well as their cultural knowledge and critical reflection. Although neither I nor the women I converse with here are experts on Islam, we are co-creating new spiritual contexts through the process of sharing our stories of how to integrate universal principles into our own lives.

BELONGING AS A MUSLIM

My method for making space is to speak from the centre of my own experience. Therefore, I ask: what does it mean for me to belong as a Muslim in Scandinavia? I started to believe in God twenty years ago, and ten years ago I converted to Islam. From the beginning, I understood that I had to speak metaphorically about my faith; I had to translate my beliefs into a "rational" language if I wanted to be understood and taken seriously. I had to avoid terms such as God, jinn, or destiny. In academe, words such as love, faith, and spirituality generally had to be avoided.

Within the social sciences, the desire for love is rarely stated as an explanation for the actions of a subject. The anthropologist Saba Mahmood has shown in her review of literature on women and Islam that the desire for freedom and liberation is assumed a priori to be the primary motivational force that governs the actions of women in Islam. An implicit liberal-progressive assumption is present in such studies because the researchers "understand agency as the capacity to realize one's own interests against the weight of custom, tradition, transcendent will or other obstacles" (8). The mothers in my study do not wish for separation from their families or tradition. Rather, they are focused on the growth and happiness of their children as well as on their hope that they would continue to be close to them. These women hope that their children will take care of them as they grew older. In other words, their main desire is to love and be loved.

I gradually came to understand that my attempt to translate into a secular rationality in order to be understood made it impossible for me to be whole. In this way, I did not initially feel there was space for me to be whole among my family and colleagues, nor with other Muslims. Often to become a Muslim will include breaking away from the religious tradition and culture that are held by one's parents. However, I have come to understand that "belonging" as Muslim is to acknowledge one's past and to integrate the universal principles of Islam into my life. Every Muslim is part of specific historical contexts and every Muslim, therefore, does the same, either consciously or unconsciously. As bell hooks claims, it is necessary to pay "tribute to the past as a resource that can serve as a foundation for us to revision and renew our commitment to the present, to making a world where all people can live fully and well, where everyone can belong" (*Belonging* 5).

Right before I converted to Islam, Ayaan, one of the participants in my study, asked me if I would begin wearing the hijab. She and two other Somali-Swedish women patiently listened as I explained how I would not wear the hijab immediately because I believed that my mother would feel alienated from me if I converted and changed my way of dressing at the same time. This was not because she held prejudices against Islam in particular, as she would probably feel the same if I had become a Christian. As a secular feminist, my mother had certain presumptions about what it means to be religious. She feared that my choice would lead me far away from her and her values. I told them that if I do start to wear the hijab it would be part of a gradual process, along with praying and fasting. It is a process wherein I am learning to integrate the Islamic principles of compassion and love into my own story. Otherwise, I would feel as if I were losing myself while appropriating another culture. These women's concentrated attention made me feel accepted and gave me hope that I could find authentic belonging as a Muslim.

The hijab has become such a strong symbol of righteous femininity in Islam that for some, it may be more important than honouring my relationship with my mother. However, during this initial conversation, Ayaan related to and respected my wish to be close to my mother. Many years later when I formally interviewed Ayaan for this research project, she expressed her belief that the main difference between Somali and Swedish cultures is the distance within Swedish families. In contrast, she shared how she was raised to be close to her family and to take care of her parents as they grow old:

> *I was raised to love my parents. I love my whole family, my siblings, and we are a group and a family.... Because we do not have insurance—here in Sweden we have insurance and we also have a pension—we don't have that in our country. So when we have children, the children are like our insurance, the children are our pension. Like when my mother got old, it is me who pays her rent, and I give her food and make sure she has a place to sleep. It is I who should take care of her. So I feel this responsibility.... So it is a great difference between the children who are raised here in Sweden, and the children who were raised in my country.... I saw how my mother took care of her mother and I was raised that way, and my religion also says that when my mother grows old, it is I who must take care of her, not someone else. So that is part of our upbringing.*

Ayaan further discussed how different it seems to be in Sweden: "When I studied to become an assistant nurse I had an apprenticeship in a retirement home. The first week I was like, "Does [this woman resident] have children?" [Yes, she has three children] "Do they come and visit?" [Yes, perhaps once or twice a year] "Oh my God!" I just cried, so it was like: "how could you even leave your own mother?" Although this impression that Swedes do not care for their parents is exaggerated, I do miss a public debate on how it can become practically possible for us to best care for our parents and return their love, therein affirming that life is a circle and that there is a need to create social balance. There are many books on childrearing, and many "experts" who discuss how to balance children and a career. However, there is not much debate on how to balance our duties towards our parents with our work lives. One mother whom I interviewed spoke of how she accepts that her children will place her in a retirement home, as the conditions are so different in Sweden compared to Somalia.

Although it is important for me to be close to my parents and assist them in every way I can, and even if this enriches me, I feel that I come short. Being a woman, there are high expectations and ideals to live up to as a mother and daughter. In the Quran, there are many verses that cherish parenthood, especially motherhood, and many verses that speak about our duties to return our parents' love. However, as most of the commentaries on the Quran and Sunnah have been written by men, and since care work has traditionally been the task of women, there are few ethical guidelines on how to fulfill these duties in everyday life (Wadud). Instead, these duties have been expected to be carried out without an appreciation of the skills and resources needed.

Just like so many women who have been raised to be caretakers, I have invested heavily in an attempt to improve and maintain loving relationships within my private life. I have always thought of such attempts as separate from my professional life as well as separate from my politics. At times, I have even thought of this work as a waste of time and energy when I could be doing "real" work. However, as hooks teaches, the work to maintain healthy relationships is revolutionary (*Rock my Soul* 7). I use subjectivity as a resource in order to make space for myself because only a self can be part of a relationship in which interaction and an exchange of ideas are central. My writing is an exploration into the possibility of loving relationships. Central to building such relationships is to let my humanity show and to recognize that my writing need not impart truth or decisive conclusions; rather, it is an act of listening and expressing what I have heard and learned. Similarly, to teach my children to swim in the waters of their culture and their relationships rather than be swiped away by them—or, in other words, to integrate Islamic values into our specific historic and cultural location—is to build a relationship in which love has a central value. Thus, I conclude with the words of bell hooks as she describes how we can make space for love:

> Love in action is always about service, what we do to enhance spiritual growth.... Serving others is as fruitful a path to the heart as any other therapeutic practice. To truly serve, we must always empty the ego so that space can exist for us to recognise the needs of others and be capable for fulfilling them. The greater our compassion the more aware we are of ways to extend ourselves to others that make healing possible. (*All about Love* 216-217)

NOTES

[1]The philosopher Miranda Fricker finds there to be two particular kinds of injustice that can be done to people in their capacity as knowers, and she refers to these as testimonial and hermeneutical injustice. Testimonial injustice occurs when prejudices cause a hearer to give less credibility to a speaker's word because of for instance ethnicity, sex, physical ability, than he/she rationally deserves; hermeneutical injustice occurs at a prior stage, when a gap in collective interpretative resources puts someone at an unfair disadvantage when it comes to making sense of their social experience (Fricker 1).

[2]Truth in this sense refers to morality in the sense we speak of a "true friend" or of "being true to yourself."

[3]The data presented in this chapter are part of an ongoing ethnographic research project sponsored by the Swedish Research Council and the Baltic Sea Foundation. My project proposal has been approved by the Regional Ethical Review Board in Uppsala. The research in Sweden has been carried out in co-operation with the Public Health researcher Barni Nor. Moreover, I have been assisted by Amina Kasem Noor and Sahra Shukri Mohamoud who have performed translations and transcriptions, in addition to opening various doors for me. The data for this research project come from several sources. I have held seven focus-group discussions with fathers and mothers and individual in-depth interviews with nine mothers. I have also engaged in participant observations while attending the course "Better Parenting and Parenting Coach," taught by Ismail Miad. These classes took place in a mosque in Stockholm and were delivered in the Somali language. In Finland,

I have been assisted by Ramla Rafle and Hamdi Geddi, where I carried out three group interviews, several informal conversations, and in-depth interviews with seven mothers. The interviews in Sweden have been carried out in Swedish or in Somali, while the interviews in Finland were done in Somali. The interviews carried out in Swedish have been transcribed by a firm. The interviews carried out in Somali where done with an interpreter. The one who transcribed the interviews has translated the Somali interviews into English directly.

WORKS CITED

Abu-Lughod, Lila. "Writing Against Culture." Ed. Ellen, Lewin. *Feminist Anthropology. A Reader.* UK: Blackwell Publishing, 2006. 137-162. Print.

Talal, Asad, Wendy Brown, Judith Butler, and Saba Mahmood. *Is Critique Secular? Blasphemy Injury and Free Speech.* Berkeley: Townsend Center for the Humanities, 2009. Print.

Barlas, Asma. *"Believing Women" in Islam: Unreading Patriarchal Interpretations of the Qur'an.* Texas: University of Texas Press, 2002. Print.

Calavati, Kitty: "Engaged Research, 'Goose Bumps' and the Role of the Public Intellectual." *Law and Society Review* 36.1 (2002): 5-20. Print.

Eliassi, Barzoo. "Constructing Cultural Otherness within the Swedish Welfare State: The Cases of Social Workers in Sweden." *Qualitative Social Work* (2015): 554-571. Web. 15 July 2015.

Giroux, Henry. *Border Crossing: Cultural Workers and the Politics of Education.* New York: Routledge, 1993. Print.

Haga, Rannveig. "'Freedom Has Destroyed the Somali Family': Somali Parents' Experiences of Epistemic Injustice and its Influence of their Raising Swedish Muslims." *Making European Muslims. Religious Socialization among Young Muslims in Scandinavia and Western Europe.* Ed. Mark Segdwick. London and New York: Routedge, 2015. 39-56. Print.

Haga, Rannveig. *Tradition as Resource: Transnational Somali Women Traders Facing the Realities of Civil War.* Doctoral Dissertation. Uppsala University, 2009. Print.

Haig-Brown, Celia. "Creating Spaces. Testimonio, Impossible Knowledge, and Academe." *International Journal of Qualitative Studies in Education* 16,3 (2003): 415-433. Print.

hooks, bell. *All about Love: New Visions*. New York: HarperCollins, 2000. Print.

hooks, bell. *Belonging: A Culture of Place*. New York: Routledge, 2009. Print.

hooks, bell. *Rock my Soul: Black People and Self-Esteem*. New York: Washington Square Press, 2003. Print.

Irigaray, Luce. *To Be Two*. New York: The Athlone Press, 2001. Print.

Jackson, Michael. *Existential Anthropology: Events, Exigencies and Effects*. New York: Berghahn Press, 2005. Print.

Lorde, Audre. "Poetry is Not a Luxury." *Making Sense of Women's Lives. An Introduction to Women's Studies*. Eds. Michéle Plott and Lauri Umanski. San Diego: Collegiate Press, 2000. 248-250. Print.

Lorde, Audre. "Our Difference is Our Strengh." *Identity Politics in the Women's Movement*. Ed. Barbara Ryan. New York: New York University Press, 2001. 315-319. Print.

Lorde, Audre (2001): "The Transformation of Silence into Language and Action." *Identity Politics in the Women's Movement*. Ed. Barbara Ryan. New York: New York University Press, 2001. 81-86. Print.

Mahmood, Saba. *Politics of Piety: The Islamic Revival and the Feminist Subject*. Princeton: University Press, 2005. Print.

Minganti, Pia Karlsson. "Muslim Women Managing Women's Shelters: Somaya, the Muslimwoman and Religion as Resource." *Nora—Nordic Journal of Feminist and Gender Research* 23.2 (2015): 93-108. Print.

Minh-Ah, Thrinh T. *Woman, Native, Other: Writing Postcoloniality and Feminism*. Indiana: Indiana University Press. 2009.

Morrison, Toni. "Toni Morrison Nobel Lecture 1993." *YouTube*. 2011 Aug 4. Web. 23 May 2016.

O´Reilly, Andrea. *Toni Morrison and Motherhood. A Politics of the Heart*. New York: State University of New York Press, 2004. Print.

Wadud, Amina. *Inside the Gender Jihad. Women's Reform in*

Islam. Oxford: Oneworld Publication, 2006. Print.
Whyte, David. "Honesty by David Whyte." *Riverbank of Truth. The Inner Journey*. N.p., 18 Aug. 2013. Web. 11 March 2016.

13.
"What's a Nice Jewish Girl Like You Doing in a Place Like This?"

Reflections on My Unexpected and Evolving Journey Towards Jewish Feminist Mothering

SHARON LANG

THIS IS THE STORY of my life. It is a personal journey from the Jewish world in which I grew up to the non-Jewish suburb in which I now reside. It is also a reflection on internal border crossing, shifting identities, and becoming a Jewish feminist mother. My path of self-development entails a romanticized past, complex transformations, and bricolage—the seeking to piece together accessible fragments and craft a meaningful, integrated, and sensible whole. Ironically, perhaps, I found my Jewish maternal self only after leaving the world of Jews and moving to a place where Jewish life and progressive feminism are virtually non-existent.

After growing up in New York City and completing a doctoral program in the Boston area, I moved to a predominantly Christian town in Southern California for a university teaching position. Here, I am raising my three children and trying to create a home environment filled with love, support, and values of social justice. Here, I have tried to foster a meaningfully Jewish life. I have learned that one finds unique means to mother children whose multicultural identities and life circumstances stand in stark contrast to one's own. And the maternal journey unfolds still in its ambiguous, contradictory, and convoluted ways; it continues to be informed and challenged by ongoing questions and the disturbing realities of anti-Semitism, racism, and terrorism. I hope this personal reflection will speak to those who find themselves searching for a place to call home; to those who feel alone without a likeminded community; and to those who are determined to raise and educate children with personal and moral authenticity.

BECOMING A JEWISH DAUGHTER: GROWING UP IN THE BRONX

Growing up in Riverdale and the Amalgamated, a co-operative housing community in the Bronx, New York, it would be my destiny to make matzoh ball soup and latkes for my children. I did not know or think about it back then of course, but I was embedded and raised in a thoroughly Jewish world. Sundays meant loud family get-togethers amid bagels, lox, chopped liver, and pickled herring. Loesher's, with its round and square knishes, Hebrew National hot dogs, corned beef on rye, half-sour pickles, and Dr. Brown's cream soda, was a favourite and indulgent place for take-out. December meant eight nights of lighting the menorah, dreidel spinning, chocolate gelt, and Chanukah presents. Mondays, Wednesdays, and Fridays meant walking to *shule* after "regular" school for five long years. I studied Jewish history, learned Yiddish, and performed in Purim plays at the Workman's Circle[1] on Hillman Avenue. Chana Krystal, a paratrooper who had rescued Jews during World War II, and Zalman Mlotek, the son of prominent Circle activists who became the executive director of the Folksbiene, the country's predominant Yiddish-language theatre company, were among my teachers. In the summertime, I went off to Hemshekh and later Boiberik with my brother and a group of children of my parents' friends. At these Jewish summer camps, we made up skits, fasted for Yom Kippur, sang songs around campfires, and made friends with other Jewish kids. One of my first crushes from summer camp would go on to become an award-winning composer, arranger, conductor, musical director, and performer of Yiddish music.

When I was young and would walk hand in hand with my grandmother, she would proudly show me off to neighbourhood ladies, who pinched my cheeks and fussed over her *bubbele*, deeming me a *shana meydele*. Walking across the overpass to Johnson Avenue, I would see dozens of elderly East European immigrants, men and women, carefully walking arm in arm, hobbling with canes, or slowly pushing walkers up and down the block. They would have a cup of coffee in the diner, wait in line at the bakery, or shop at the Judaica bookstore. Men with fedoras atop their bald heads and old ladies with kerchiefs pushing grocery carts would stop to rest on stone wall benches and chat, all speaking Yiddish or English with heavy accents. At the "train park" near our apartment building on Gale Place, my grandfather paraded me around to his Yiddish-speaking acquaintances, men who sat for hours reading *The Forward* and arguing spiritedly about how to fix the world. I never questioned why all elderly people sounded like this. In fact, I did not even notice or hear any accents; these were simply the voices of my grandparents and indeed of all elderly folk.

It was a Jewish world inside too, one that revolved around food, extended family, and cultural critique. Passover meant big get-togethers at my aunt's apartment, women cooking and preparing, and me helping set tables and polish the silver. There were silly plays performed by siblings and cousins, sweet wine, gefilte fish, and lots of loud conversation. There were great crescendos of noise until that moment when all would pause, and Grandpa Albert would begin his lecture on Jewish history, racism, and socialism. Religion and politics factored heavily in the ensuing conversation, and there was plenty of baiting and instigation. My brother, the budding scientist, would rise to the occasion when asked to make sense of the passage that describes Moses' miraculous parting of the Red Sea. "As always, humans have sought to explain the unexplainable," he would begin. "In this way, religion and science are similar. When people did not have a scientific understanding of the tides and the receding of waters, they attributed the temporary sand bar to divine intervention." Lots of laughter, conversation, and more Manischevitz would flow. Uncle Arthur would then lead the seder and calls on Uncle Jerry to read a poem, culminating in the final lines: "Next year in Jerusalem." The latter would refuse to utter these words, and instead delve into a speech critiquing policies of the Israeli state. Total breakdown of ritual order and an uproar of conversation would ensue, followed by more eating, drinking, and running around with siblings and cousins.

Engaging in political debate and cultural reflection, my elders were influential role models, and the women rivalled the men in terms of their strength and forceful leadership. My mother was always a powerful figure in the family, with her centrality emerging fully after her parents died. She is fiercely honest, principled, and an advocate for all that she believes in. Though certainly constrained by the patriarchal culture of her day, she was raised by educated political activists who met at a forum for Jewish socialists. Her mother, one of the four sisters remembered for their eclectic personalities and erudite dramatic flair, did not encourage her to pursue a career in physics but did raise an outspoken daughter who would later divorce my father and leave her teaching position to become an executive for a large insurance company. Women of my family and community both reinforced and challenged gender stereotypes, but despite contradictions, they embodied the matrilineal and often matriarchal nature typical of Jewish life. Certainly, they were indicative of the prominent position that women hold in the Jewish family.

My Jewish upbringing was a direct extension of my parents' own Jewish lives. As a second generation American, I grew up and lived in the same neighbourhoods and even the same apartment as my first-generation parents had with their parents. Despite the passing of several decades, my mother's childhood experiences were relatively similar to mine on Jewish and gendered fronts. These shared youthful experiences, however, stood in marked contrast to that of my grandparents, who were born in Russia and Poland and migrated to America prior to World War II because of extreme and widespread anti-Semitism and a general desire for a better life. Our Jewish upbringing also bears little resemblance to that of *my* children. Unlike the latter, my mother and I had formed a sense of "being Jewish" without thinking about it; it just happened by virtue of spending each day in a world where Jewish life enveloped our daily existence. Being Jewish seeped into my being as naturally as breathing air; it started before birth and remained a largely un-reflexive and innate kind of permeation for many years.

As such, despite living in the Bronx amid large African-American, Puerto Rican, Italian, Irish, and Asian populations, as a child I somehow thought that nearly all people in the world were Jewish until I was eleven or twelve years old. There was diversity in our Jewish community, however, with secular Jews as well as multiple Reform, Conservative, and Orthodox synagogues. My own family's beliefs diverted from those of many traditional Jewish

American families, as we never identified with any form of organized religion. There may have been conflict among some in the community, particularly between the secular and the orthodox, but still the Jewish spirit was everywhere. The Hasidim[2] were somewhat of a curiosity to me and my siblings back then, with their long dark suits, fur lined hats or *shtreimel*; *peyes* and *tzitzit* were regular sights, in addition to yarmulkes, which were typical for young religious boys. My family itself was an oddity, being descendants of the Hasidic leader Kotzker Rebbe (1787–1859). Known as "the rabbi who doubted God," his attributable quotes include, "People are accustomed to look at the heavens and to wonder what happens there. It would be better if they would look within themselves, to see what happens there" (Berk 73). Similarly, my grandparents were diasporic leaders in the Bund, a secular Jewish socialist party originally formed in the Russian Empire in 1897. They were against the formation of the State of Israel, believing that nation states embodied corrupt power and that the best course for the Jews was to abstain from the modern nation state system. To me, being Jewish had, therefore, always meant activism, empowerment, calling for social justice, asking questions, engaging in critical dialogue, and inhabiting a world of gender equity.

THE DIALECTIC TRANSFORMATION: BECOMING JEWISH IN A NON-JEWISH WORLD

I had my first child at Redlands Community Hospital in Southern California. Her father relinquished his parental rights when she was a toddler, so I raised her on my own. There was no doubt in my mind that she and my subsequent children born in the local Adventist hospital were Jewish from the start. *My* kind of being Jewish, that is. During pregnancy, I obsessed over who my children would be named after.[3] I embellished, as Jews are encouraged to do, and drew on the initials of both my paternal grandparents, but that was not enough. I arranged a baby naming ceremony in the local congregation in San Bernardino. Rabbi Hillel Cohn of Congregation Emanuel called us up to the *bima*, and my baby was welcomed into the Jewish community: Miriam Shoshanna bat

Soreh, certified through her matrilineal link according to Jewish law, and now publicly recognized as a "member of the tribe." This tradition felt right to me.

In alignment with Andrea O'Reilly's conception of feminist mothering, I understood my own maternal practices to be sites for empowerment and social change (1-22); this also seemed a natural extension of my Jewish outlook. From the start, I practised feminist mothering each day with all of my children. I challenged the norms of my patriarchal community by choosing to raise my children on my own, outside of traditional family structures, and by breastfeeding them regularly at work for years. I knew that public nursing was unacceptable to some around me, but at the purportedly "family-friendly" environment of my job, no one confronted me directly. I also knew that a local restaurant had barred patrons from their establishment for breastfeeding. I ignored sneers, disapproving looks, and mockery. Determined to give my children the best nutrition possible, I would not consider yielding to others' norms and values. Undeterred, and indeed empowered by my maternal role, I came to view my mothering as political, and in addition to my critics, I also had supporters who congratulated me for my "brave actions."

Similarly, when a colleague pointed out to me that I was the only faculty member (presumably in the history of the university) to have a child "out of wedlock," I renewed my determination to stare back at judgmental eyes, alter confining norms, and find new ways to integrate maternal and academic obligations. I developed a course on the anthropology of mothering, in which I brought diverse mothers to class to share real stories of parenting with students who were willing to contemplate the complexities and constructedness of motherhood and mothering. In doing so, I hope to have provided alternative models for at least a few women and men in the future generation.

Throughout the years, my children and I have celebrated Chanukah and other Jewish holidays in a low-key, small family way. My eldest daughter's father was a non-religious Christian, so we spent our first Christmas together with his mother in Maine, where there were lots of presents, a decorated tree, and a fancy red and green dress waiting for the baby. None of this was problematic to me. Although I had never celebrated Christmas at home, my family had celebrated it with friends in their homes, and people who enact Christmas rituals as a largely secular American gift exchange and a time for parties have long surrounded me. Secure in my Jewishness, I was comfortable participating in these festive events, and it seemed natural to allow my daughter to be a part of these engagements too.

Many of the summer activities for children in my current town are connected to churches, and as my daughter grew, she wanted to explore new realms. Not wanting her to be deprived, I signed her up for Vacation Bible School one summer when she was six years old. She went and played for a few hours with the other girls, and as I stood with the other parents waiting to pick her up, the group of children before us were singing Christian songs that they had learned during the week. Karen, a friend and the chaplain's wife at the university where I work, suddenly came up behind me and asked, "What's a nice Jewish girl like you doing in a place like this?" I laughed and told her that I was thinking the very same thing! It can be confusing to be a Jew in a Christian town. We did not go back to that particular church, but years later my daughter's friends were going to sewing, chocolate making, and dance classes at Christ the King Church, and the moms whom I had befriended asked me if I was signing my daughter up too. I hesitated, but one mom assured me quietly that the religious aspects were minimal, and so I did it. My child attended summer classes there and had a pretty good time, but one day she told me, "Mom, I don't know what to do. I really want the pieces of chocolate they're giving out, but I can only get them if I go up and recite verses about Jesus." We never went back to that summer camp either.

These incidents are indicative of my dilemmas while trying to mother appropriately and comfortably in a non-Jewish setting, but they are also more than that. They are moments of losing oneself, having no community, and having no way to connect one's children to their heritage. This town had little to offer in terms of Jewish living. This has not prevented me, however, from being labelled a "Jewish professor" at work from the start, when one of those who hired me announced, "it will be so great for our Jewish students to have someone on faculty to relate to." The epithet certainly meant something different to my colleague than it did to me. For years, I felt myself to be a foreigner whose reality was largely invisible. Even this year, no one in the administration noticed in planning graduation ceremonies that they were scheduled on a major Jewish holiday. The university holds "holiday luncheons" where Santa and his Elves collect and give out presents. In December, Christmas decor abounds, adorning the downtown shops. Crosses glow on top of the 120 or so churches in the town of eighty thousand people. Many find it uplifting, but these symbols cause me to wonder, "Am I welcome here?" Everyone wishes me a "Merry Christmas" and I am regularly invited to Bible study groups, once by a fast-food drive through clerk. There is a cross on the city seal, which effected an ACLU lawsuit; advocates argued that the cross should remain, since it is part of the town's history (and that it somehow stands for all religions!). My neighbours who know I am not Christian never say it aloud, but they seem to feel sorry for me and offer to take my children with them to Adventist services each Saturday. They are good and loving people; they just believe that I am some lost soul whom they should save. These are but a few moments when I feel marginalized and patronized.

Although I may not always feel at home, I have created my family and made my life here, and, thus, I confront the questions of how to raise my children so they, too, may identify as Jews and connect with their heritage. Attempting to forge a Jewish identity for my children, however, has been sporadic, challenging, and largely a creative reinvention. Far in time and space from the home I once knew, my kids and I celebrate the holidays year after year with non-Jewish friends, who now have come to know and anticipate our rituals. Children of all faiths search for the *afikomen* in our living room. To some extent, we have replicated the festivities of my childhood. We give out Chanukah presents, light the menorah, and sing songs in Hebrew and Yiddish; we even play dreidel and make up skits. My children live for matzoh ball soup. It has become part of the challenge and characteristic fussing each year to search for Jewish food products and ingredients here, where there is no Jewish or kosher market—only a sparsely stocked shelf in the local grocery store, down the "Ethnic Foods" aisle. To augment Jewish visibility and cultural literacy more widely, I go to my children's schools and teach classes on Chanukah, Passover, and Purim. Beyond that, I have created university courses that focus on Judaism, Jewish history, and practice.

And so a unique version of Jewish identity forms and takes hold in my children. A Jewish congregation moved to our area, and when my eldest turned twelve, she decided on her own that she wanted a bat mitzvah. I had seemingly succeeded in creating Jewish children, but the irony did not go unnoticed: my child was connecting to mainstream, traditional Reform Judaism and its practices. I was faced with Jewish cognitive dissonance. Since I never studied Hebrew as a child (only later in college and when I went to Israel) and I never had a bat mitzvah of my own, my daughter's path to Judaism was quite unexpected to me. We had never identified with organized religion or been a part of any congregation. None of us had ever attended Shabbat services. I was not sure at first if I wanted my daughter to memorize and chant prayers or to learn to read from the Torah. I was ambivalent. My mother, who had undergone somewhat of her own Jewish transformation since my sister moved to Israel in 2001, pushed for it. Institutionalized religion (namely in the form of Christian churches) surrounds us here, so in some ways it made perfect sense for this to be on my daughter's radar. With limited options, how could I question institutional practice as a meaningful path to her Jewish experience? Ultimately, I agreed to allow my daughter to pursue her endeavours and even encouraged them. This was *her* Jewish journey, after all, connected to but entirely distinct from my own.

And so after "regular" school, I drove her not to *shule* but to the temple for her lessons. She studied intensely with the rabbi, cantor, and tutors to prepare. We held her bat mitzvah in the rented halls of the congregation, and it was a big deal. Grandparents, aunts, uncles, and friends flew out to be a part of the celebration. We memorized the *aliyahs* and followed the rituals of passing the Torah from one relative to the next. We spent thousands of dollars, planned all year, and sent out formal invitations. We anguished over decor, table arrangements, and centrepieces; we even bought twelve large round pink tablecloths online. We hired a DJ and rented a canopy, tables, and chairs. We got a jumper and had a dance floor delivered, bought fancy dresses for my daughters and a suit for my son; the girls got their hair, make-up, and nails done. We got a chocolate fountain, had a feast, and gave my daughter the party of her life. For her part, my daughter studied hard and learned to chant verses of the sacred texts from the oldest Torah scrolls in Southern California. Despite her shyness, she stood in front of a crowd of family and friends for hours, draped in a *tallit*, leading services and delivering speeches she had written in Hebrew and English on the meaning of being a Jew. When the cantor finally sang the words, "May your life be a blessing," everyone was in tears. My daughter will always keep this experience; it is etched in her heart and memory as one of the most significant moments of her life. It might have meant even more to her in this community, surrounded by non-Jews. She accomplished something and became someone that her peers would not. By embracing her own Judaism in her own way, my daughter found her home.

MOTHERING JEWISH CHILDREN: DISCONNECTS, DILEMMAS, AND MORE SEARCHING FOR ANSWERS

After a brief marriage I had two more children for whom I currently share custody. They are of mixed ethnicity—Jewish and African-American, and as McKinney has written, I see no incompatibility whatsoever in these social identities, even if others do (95-97). Yet there are real obstacles: my ex-husband has placed them in a part-time Christian Sunday school at a local church. They do not like to go; they do not believe in Jesus, but they are given no choice about attending these activities. When they ask me about religion, I tell them that as far as I am concerned they are Jewish, but that it is entirely up to them to decide what they do or do not believe. I debate whether or not to enroll them in the School of Jewish Living at the local synagogue where my eldest had her bat mitzvah. Rabbi Cohn, the progressive activist and long-time leader who reminds me of the wise elders of my past, is no longer there. I do not want to confuse my children, but I do want them to know and feel their history. On the occasions where we participate in temple activities, there is an awkwardness. I sit with them through the short services that precede language instruction and feel out of place as others ably recite and chant the Hebrew prayers. For the most part, neither my younger children nor I have familiarity with these ancient texts. The melodies do not bring us back to a known place. My son grimaces and looks pained; he clearly does not want to be there.

Questions and doubts flood through me. Why would I push cultural frameworks and institutionalized religion onto my children? What am I teaching them by bringing them to synagogue to sit through services and recite prayers to God? I cringe and feel dishonest as a mother, untrue to my particular Jewish heritage. Am I a fraud? I experience alienation in this tiny subculture of which I am presumed to be an integral member. Once again, and even here, I am not sure that we belong. My son's protests have put me in a soul-searching maternal bind in more than one way. Should I insist that he go? If I force him to attend, he may grow resentful and want nothing to do with his Jewish identity. If I allow him not to go, he may lose connection to the only Jewish institution in the area. There is no option to send him to a Yiddish *shule*; there are no elderly Jewish immigrants from the *shtetls* of Eastern Europe to tell him stories of the past. I teach him some Hebrew at home, and we celebrate the holidays, but will this be enough? The public school he attends, like all the schools in this area, are filled predominantly with Christians; the children talk openly about being thankful for Jesus. Many of his friends (and he himself) attend church regularly and are part of church networks.

I think of my eldest daughter and the fact that in this largely Christian town, there are limited ways to practise being a Jew. And then I think about my youngest child; she loves to go to synagogue, services, and Hebrew classes. At six years old, she is easy going and anxious to learn, so the two of us often go together on Sunday mornings. The rabbi welcomes us warmly and asks my little one if she knows that her name in Hebrew means "to ascend, as in to step up to Israel?" The faces in the temple are friendly and becoming familiar now. My youngest and I have learned to sing along to some of the songs and prayers. The music is pretty and soothing; she smiles at me, and we feel at peace. We feel at home. Perhaps we do belong here.

Unfortunately our peace and sense of calm in the world are easily shattered by ugly external realities: terrorism and anti-Semitic threats have recently hit our small town. After the 2015 shootings in San Bernardino, students of the newly formed Middle Eastern Students Association host an anti-discrimination, anti-violence peace walk and ask me to be a speaker. As a professor of anthropology and as one of the few faculty connected to the Middle East, I accept and am honoured to speak about that which I believe in so strongly. However, as I stand before the crowd and plan to draw on three angles of self—Jewish, anthropologist, and mother—to frame my thoughts, I hesitate. Amid local FBI investigations into the ISIS-pledging terrorists and ongoing threats by local sympathizers, do I really want to go before the crowd and media, boldly proclaiming my Jewish heritage? This is a hard moment for me. Am I the Marrano sister of the poem my brother and I used to read together, where the sister is preparing her matzos hidden deep inside the caves, where she "shall die with a song upon her lips?" I do not feel safe here; I do not want to make my children a target. But I am proud to be Jewish; it informs my values, actions, thoughts, and passions, and I am devoted to modelling this for my students and children. So I give my talk, I quote from the rabbi, and a student tells me afterwards in tears how my words really touched her. Yet I do not take my children to Hebrew school that Sunday, four days after the shooting, because there is no security at the temple.

And so I am left with many questions. What will happen to my American multiethnic, multiracial children as they grow into adulthood and, perhaps, parenthood one day? Will they have Seders with their children and struggle with finding authentic ways to be Jewish? Will it be safe for them to do so? Will they embrace their own version of being Jewish and want to instill Jewish-informed values in their children? Will these questions even arise for them, let alone hold meaning and depth? It is hard to predict. The world of my childhood is gone, yet somehow I believe that they will draw on their own sense of what I have instilled in them. I imagine that they will find unique ways to mother and father their children in progressive, liberal, tolerant, feminist, and Jewish forms—that they will grow up and repair the world, *tikkun olam*. At least that is my hope.

CONCLUSION: A
AM I A "JEWISH MOTHER" AND WHAT DOES THAT MEAN?

Embodying love and hate, hilarity and frustration, our culture has long been familiar with and popularized the image of the "Jewish mother," leading scholars to deconstruct the transforming stereotype and trace the symbolic history of this maternal figure (Antler). Decades ago, Sylvia Rothschild delineated irreconcilable and contrasting images of the "Jewish mother" and the "Modern woman," and scholars have since come to see the evolving caricature as a metaphor for Jewish anxiety and a sense of assimilation into American society (Antler; Prell). In countering and complicating this iconic figure, volumes, such as Siegel's, demonstrate how real women have embodied the Jewish maternal, performed and celebrated traditions, and passed such forms on to their children. As I ponder the relationship between actual, particular Jewish mothers and maternal images, I find myself agreeing with Sered that the latter is "part of the cultural clothing worn by every Jewish woman" (6). I recognize the Jewish mother in my grandmother, mother, and aunts, but I, too, have become some kind of a Jewish mother. Being raised in a community of Jews, I had not fully contemplated the depths of what "being Jewish" meant to me—that is, until I became a mother. Repositioned to a marginalized minority, an oddity to neighbours, I now contemplate my own Jewish story, if and where it fits.

My journey has taken me far from the unwitting and ascribed Jewish culture of childhood, to these intentional and creative paths in search of communal identity and Jewish mothering. In this generational crossing of borders, my children and I have crafted our own forms of Jewish identity that feel authentic, even as they continue to unfold dynamically. Our experiences of being Jewish may entail drawing on relationships forged through the congregation; it may involve singing the prayers that we have recently come to know; it may mean watching funny Jewish videos online at home or looking at photos from the past; it may hold contradictions, ongoing fears of security, and more questions than answers at times. Whatever form it takes, my children have gained a Jewish identity. The implicit has been made explicit and the explicit reinforces that which we feel implicitly. In emphasizing alternative forms of Jewishness and the search for identity, my story illustrates Rubin-Dorsky's claims that in America, Jews have the luxury of seeking definition and that "we have attained the freedom to create ourselves asJews" (90).

With hindsight, it seems inevitable and obvious that being Jewish was going to form a central part of my identity. When I reached my teenage years, I questioned and challenged my parents and the confines of my world. I spread out, travelled, and moved beyond the bubble in which I was raised. Ultimately, however, the sights, sounds, and even smells of this little Jewish world in my memory would forever come to mean home to me. The norms and values of this past community, internalized deep within, became my guide to mothering. In this chapter, I have explored the circumstances and forces that prompted me to cross spiritual borders in response to physical and temporal ones. No doubt the many instances of cultural alienation motivated my transformation. My desire to mother progressive Jewish children is bolstered by the constant reminders of marginalization and encroaching anti-Semitism. Becoming a mother has also led me and my children to seek and find community, identity, and value in Jewish living in unexpected places, including the local synagogue, a fact that surprises no one more than myself. In confronting and exploring the many contradictions, ambiguities, and feminist values that tie my mothering to being Jewish, and being a Jewish feminist to my mothering, I sometimes take a moment to just observe: Yiddish songs and poems by Hannah Senesh at my Passover table with Mexican family, Christian, and atheist friends. I am reconciled to my unique, eclectic, and personal efforts at Jewish mothering. I delight in the unexpected and unfolding path of Jewish feminist mothering, laughing at what a nice Jewish girl like me is doing in a place like this.

NOTES

[1]The Workmen's Circle/Arbeiter Ring was established in 1892 in a tenement on the Lower East Side. It developed over the years from a mutual-aid society for immigrants into a radical activist

organization aimed at promoting secular Jewish education.
[2]As of 2013, 180,000 Hasidic Jews were living in New York City, according to a University of Florida study (Hoover).
[3]Jews typically name their children after a recently deceased family member. My third and fourth children are named after my second daughter who died of SIDS.

WORKS CITED

Antler, Joyce. *You Never Call, You Never Write*. New York: Oxford University Press, 2007. Print.

Berk, Sally Ann. *The Big Little Book of Jewish Wit & Wisdom*. New York: Black Dog & Leventhal Publishers, 2000. Print.

Hoover, Aaron. "As Hasidic Population Grows, Jewish Politics May Shift Right." *UF News*. University of Florida News, 27 Nov. 2006. Web. 15 Dec. 2015.

McKinney, Harriet. "Reflections of a Jewish Mother." *Bridges* 9.1 (2001): 95–97. Print.

O'Reilly, Andrea. *Feminist Mothering*. New York: SUNY series in Feminist Criticism and Theory, 2008. Print.

Prell, Riv-Ellen. *Fighting to Become Americans: Assimilation and the Trouble between Jewish Women and Jewish Men*. Boston: Beacon Press, 1999. Print.

Rothschild, Sylvia. "In Defense of the Jewish Mother." *Off Our Backs* 2.6 (1972): 4-5. Print.

Rubin-Dorsky, Jeffrey. "Philip Roth and American Jewish Identity: The Question of Authenticity." *American Literary History* 13.1 (2001): 79-107. Print.

Sered, Susan. "Introduction: Mothers and Icons." *Nashim: A Journal of Jewish Women's Studies & Gender Issues*. 3 (5760/2000): 6. Web. 15 Dec. 2015.

Siegel, Rachel Josefowitz, Ellen Cole, and Susan Steinberg Oren. *Jewish Mothers Tell Their Stories: Acts of Love and Courage*. New York: Routledge, 2012. Print.

14.
Two Mothers and Two Children

ROSIE ROSENZWEIG

THE NOVICE NUN Kim-Hoa, a striking young beauty holding her palms strong and flat against each other, walks down the centre aisle of the Zen Doa and slowly approaches Thich Nhat Hanh, also known as Thây. I travelled half-way around the world to attend this event. Reliving my own son's recent ordination, the ordination of this lovely Vietnamese would eventually teach me a lot. I would learn even more from watching Kim-Hoa's mother, whose child, like mine, chose the Buddhist monastic path.

My son Ben just completed a three year Buddhist monastic retreat to become a lama in the Tibet Buddhist tradition. My reaction to his choice was much different than that of Kim-Hoa's mother, who was a Buddhist. During his training, I was employed as a Hebrew school teacher, proudly imparting the values of my tradition to the young, yet I felt that I had failed to do this adequately for my own son. Ben recognized my palpable distress and wanted to correct his karma. Knowing what his commitment to Buddhism had set into motion, he suggested that I travel with him to meet the various Buddhist teachers in America, France, India, and Nepal. He hoped that this would alleviate my pain and replace it with a new understanding.

My own mother, whose family of eighty-three souls was murdered in the Holocaust, would have, as they say in Yiddish, a conniption, if she knew that her lovely red-headed grandson had become a Buddhist. Thây's hermitage in France was our first stop on the way to India and Nepal to meet his "root guru" teachers. Their monasteries featured numerous statues of Buddha, which are considered by many Jews to be idols. In my mother's eyes, my son was now worshiping idols, which is a sin. And now, just five years after her demise, I was embarking on a journey with my son that could potentially bear much distress—or, perhaps, the fruit of new wisdom.

Ben was quite clever in his plans; Thây, the aging Vietnamese Zen master, author of more than one hundred books, and founder of a Buddhist University and numerous Buddhist centres, was a poet like me. Ben surmised that I could relate to his easy metaphors and manners. It was auspicious, as the Buddhists often say, that we happened upon an ordination ceremony for a nun and a monk during our visit to Plum Village. This idyllic retreat centre in the south of France was named for the 1250 plum trees planted prior to its purchase in 1982 during the exile foisted on Thây when he advocated for peace rather than side with either North or South Vietnam during the war. Martin Luther King called him "an apostle of peace and nonviolence" in his January 25, 1967 letter[1] to the Nobel Institute nominating Thây for the Nobel Peace Prize.[2] Even now up until his recent stroke, Thây seeks to heal American veterans with post-traumatic stress disorder from the Vietnam War, no matter that his countrymen might have once called them "ugly Americans" for their clumsy searches for the Vietcong.

Now, Kim-Hoa stops to face Thây; her silky black hair sweeps around her face and a long blue tunic covering her silk pants lifts gracefully before coming to a rest. Thây smiles and coaxes her forwards, and the whole *sangha*, or congregation, smiles too—except for one older Vietnamese woman standing next to her husband, both of whom are weeping. This has to be Kim-Hoa's mother, and my own tear ducts open in sympathy. Like this weeping mother, I already said good-bye to the children that my son would never have because of his commitment to the monastic life. Just three months prior, I retrieved Ben from his three-year Buddhist celibate retreat to become a lama in the Nyingma lineage of Vajrayana Tibetan Buddhist tradition. I was still dealing with my distress over my failure as a Jewish mother to guide Ben towards a Jewish future.

I learned from questioning the nuns who lived in Plum Village that Kim-Hoa's family relocated to Germany following the withdrawal of U.S. forces, and it was possible that some of her grandparents suffered as "boat people," fleeing in unsafe crafts to escape the ensuing conflict. These unfortunates were subject to murderous pirates, rapists, and the hazards of the sea; Thây himself pleaded with several governments to rescue the refugees. The Hoa, an ethnic Chinese population of Vietnam who controlled the retail trade of South Vietnam, were subject to the most severe repression and taxation, and I wonder if her family was part of that group. I lived through this era, and the history and my participation in the U.S. anti-war movement, specifically with Women Strike for Peace, flashes through my mind. These folks endured their own Holocaust and survived, as my own parents did, leaving Poland in the nick of time before their families were obliterated.

All this is behind Kim-Hoa now as she takes refuge in the teachings of Buddha, Dharma, and Sangha through her preeminent teacher. At this juncture in my life as a teacher in a Jewish Synagogue School, I find it curious that I am currently in a Buddhist monastery. I am quiet, but I know my own mother would unleash a cry of public mourning if she were here. I envision her now as a proxy voicing my distress. I think about Ben's memorable bar mitzvah, officiated by Rabbi Zalman Schachter-Shalomi, the father of Jewish Renewal, and how the entire congregation applauded my son for his original speech. I surely thought that he would become a rabbi then. In retrospect, however, it seems his interpretation of God's command for Abraham to sacrifice his son Isaac is quite Buddhist in nature. Ben questioned how God could ask Abraham to sacrifice his only son after promising him as many progeny as the stars in the heavens. Ben concluded that to make the future happen, Abraham had to be present in the here and now.

Taken out of my reverie by the sudden conclusion of the ceremony, I watch as Thây leaves in a hush of standing respect, with half the sangha following him. I am drawn to Kim-Hoa and her family as she is stripped of any signs of vanity. Taking turns, her sister nuns begin to shave off her hair. It reminds me of the Orthodox tradition practised by some very observant Jewish brides who ritually shave off their hair before donning the customary marriage wig; however, these brides are promised to only one Jewish man and God, whereas this quiet nun is promising herself to uphold Buddha, Dharma, and the Sangha. My heart is touched as each dark lock falls to the floor, with the honour of shearing the last lock given to the mother, who holds it with great pause. Without the distractions of any material possessions, Kim-Hoa is now ready to begin a four- or five-year path to full ordination. She seems to embody a new serenity with only a brush of black on her scalp and a new vision. In this moment, I briefly understand that my son also sought this serenity when he took his own vows just a few months prior.

Thây's next Dharma talk seems to speak directly to me. He describes how the monastic life allows for more freedom from attachment, how meditation leads to freedom, and how this freedom affects the devotee's entire family. The monastic becomes "an ambassador from the Buddha-land" who will be able to "save the whole family; for if we cannot save our family, then we cannot save other people." The monk or nun has more freedom to be present for the family and will serve as its foundation by inviting confidence and calmly restoring peace through reason and compassion, which is the cornerstone of the Buddhist path. According to Thây, a letter home from a monk or nun can bring liberation through awakened understanding. I consider how my son wrote his grandmother countless times during his three-year monastic retreat; his letters were so full of poetic appreciation for my frail eighty-five-year-old mother that she marvelled repeatedly at his understanding of the world. She continually declared: "Whatever he's learning in that place, he's doing the right thing."

As the talk ends and Kim-Hoa's family circles her for some private time, I need to walk outside. I pass the bamboo grove towards a clearing, and there on the rise before me is the seemingly ageless Thây in his khaki coat and round wool hat. Moving at a purposeful pace, he is leading a multitude in slow walking meditation. He is surrounded by a rhythm of yellow, orange, and mustard robes moving in the breeze; his followers' palms are prayerfully pressed together as they slow their pace to match his. Breathing almost in unison, they walk precisely with their leader in a unified meditation. I find myself altering my breathing pattern to match theirs, as some prior rigidities of mind seem to momentarily loosen their hold on me.

I catch sight of a big-boned Japanese Zen master identified by his black robes with a prominent brown padded fabric breastplate and large sleeves that almost reach his knees; he is tall and muscular and walks with a hard dignity, bearing, and presence. I learn that he was the leader of a German retreat centre where Kim-Hoa's parents settled to heal their memories of war. This black-robed teacher dwarfs the slight-figured Thây, a poet in motion whose energy moves like a calm conscience throughout the community. His movements seem timeless and full of peace, just like the essence of the Jewish Sabbath, which has been described as an island in time. His "peace in every step" reminds me that Shabbat is approaching the very next day and that I purchased a challah bread the day before in the Jewish quarter of Paris to share with my son in Thây's retreat centre. I hope that I can enter into that "island in time" as gracefully as Thây leads this international congregation.

Later in the evening, in the privacy of a sparse bedroom, Ben and I begin the Jewish rituals of Sabbath, which include the three traditional blessings for the children. As I bless him to be like Manasseh and Ephraim, Joseph's sons who kept the faith in Egypt against all odds, I wonder about his future in this new marriage of Judaism and Buddhism that he has entered. And as we break bread and light the candles, I wonder what my future will look like as well. I am confronted with this question again later on in the retreat when, amid the long sitting and walking silences punctuated by Thây's various Dharma talks, I am asked by a group of nuns to take the five vows of Buddhism. I wrestle with many issues during my discussions with them: Jews take vows very seriously, to the point of adding the Hebrew phrase "*b'li neder*" after any promise. This means "without a vow" because one's life depends on keeping one's word. So they consult Thây who agrees to change the term "vows" to "promises" for me. A close reading of the "promises" reveals that they are similar to the Noahide commandments in place before the receiving of the Ten Commandments on Sinai. I have no issue with them, but I do have issue with bowing down to enter into the Order of Interbeing,[3] as Thây named his Zen school. The second Sinai Commandment forbids bowing down before gods other than the One, so I am allowed to take part in the ceremony without bowing down. I am given a Vietnamese name, Nuygem

Thom, meaning the joining together of various paths, which will reflect my shifting beliefs and consciousness in the years to come.

Ultimately, I have come to this retreat to look more deeply into my own Jewish mothering and seek release from the *mea culpa* of blame that I internalized for my son's turning from Judaism. My son is aware of these struggles, so he arranges for us to meet in private with Thây near the end of our two-week visit. Sister True Emptiness, the head nun, organizes the meeting. She resembles the *Rebetzin*, or the chief rabbi's wife, who manages all the details of the kitchen, congregation, children, and followers from the outside world. I am thrilled to meet her because of her role in the Vietnam War as a peace activist, and I remember that Thây led the anti-Vietnam war demonstration in New York where I marched with Ben and his older sister when they were very young. She leads us into an inner chamber, where Thây is busy folding a string hammock, and I am busy handling my backpack, which is heavy with recording devices, Jewish books to give as gifts, a camera, and notebook. Once seated, Ben, mindful of Buddhist etiquette, expresses gratitude for Thây's teachings.

"My mother and I have known much suffering," Ben begins, relating the pain over the many young deaths in my family, "but I have studied your teachings and through your books and tapes, I have been able to appreciate her. I want to thank you for your teachings." This speaks volumes about our troubled relationship to date. He bows. and Thây responds in kind. "My mother has taken the Five Precepts," Ben continues, with Sister True Emptiness rushing to add: "And I have explained to her as you said about the bowing down, the touching of the earth, our source, and she is willing to do it."

"Only if there is no Buddha!" I quickly exclaim, surprised at this misunderstanding. I instantly worry that I have ruined this meeting with my outburst, but I am not willing to relinquish my Jewish beliefs so quickly. Ben, in turn, rushes to explain the history of this belief in Judaism.

"You see," he says, "one of the early Jewish ancestors was Abraham, who was the son of an idol-maker. One day, he destroyed the idols in his father's shop—all but one." Ben continues to tell this Talmud tale of how the Jewish patriarch broke with the local custom of idol worship. When his father asked who destroyed his wares, his son Abraham blamed the one remaining statue. His father declared that impossible because "he is only an image." Abraham challenged him and asked why his father continued to worship him.

I am so pleased and surprised to hear how well Ben remembers the rabbinical commentary on the topic. I am even more surprised at Thây's response: "People have false expectations [about how others] should behave, about how children should behave." As his voice trails off, Ben places his finger on my calf, and very gently presses it to make his point clear. *This* is not the usual commentary on the subject. Thây's comments awake me like a *koan-midrash*—a *koan* being the classic Zen statement that catapults disciples into enlightenment, and a *midrash* being the name for a rabbinical commentary on classic topics. Thây addresses the more significant issue in our mother-son relationship about making our children follow our own image. My eyes open with some new insights here that will begin a process of letting go, something that stereotypical Jewish mothers do not experience very often.

Because it embraces the local Hindu customs of gods, Tibetan Buddhism displays more elaborate statues and stories about the various gods representing the virtuous traits of compassion and focus. These statues will be elaborately displayed in great numbers in each monastery that I subsequently visit. However, they now make me less apprehensive as I begin to understand that each "idol" image represents a virtue to be incorporated by the followers of Buddhism. I still would never bow down before any idol, but I consider how some devotees bowed to me out of respect for being a lama's mother.

The days that stretch out from this moment only serve to solidify this viewpoint. The next stop in this trip involves landing in Kathmandu and meeting Ben's "root guru," Chokyi Nyima Rinpoche. It was his many encounters with this Tibetan Buddhist teacher that influenced Ben to enter his previous three-year monastic retreat in an attempt to understand Buddhism more deeply, and I had long suspected that the Rinpoche was grooming Ben to be a teacher like him. My son also petitioned Chokyi Nyima Rinpoche to arrange a meeting with his elderly father, Tulku Urygen

Rinpoche. I actually make the arduous trek up to Nagi Gompa, a mountain-top monastery, to meet this gentleman. He takes great care to bestow individual teachings on me so that I can understand my son's fascination with this new path. I also have the honour of receiving what devotees call an individual transmission from this Rinpoche. I am cautioned not to share these teachings with anyone because doing so would dissipate the blessings that he bestowed on me. The transmission passes in an instant, although the actual teachings may have lasted for up to two hours.

These teachings, which emphasize the flow of time over lifetimes and the wisdom of patience, seem to flow like a river with no memory of content but with the eternal lesson of timelessness. They are called "pointed teachings for an old woman," because they seem to be a shorthand version of the lengthy books written on the subject and, perhaps, because Buddhism respects the accumulated wisdom of eldering. Later on, I will feel saddened to hear that the Rinpoche passed away, and I will reflect intermittently in the years to come on how I received his teachings, delivered in an even, modulated tone from his sick bed high on a mountain outside of Kathmandu.

These meetings with famous Buddhist teachers of two different traditions blend in wisdom as time goes on. The memory of the weeping Vietnamese mother as she let go of her daughter and her dreams of being a grandparent still appears vividly in my mind. It seems that they actually changed my consciousness and my attitudes towards mothering. Later, as I began years of meditation retreats and meditation groups in various cities, I started to understand how releasing attachments to rigid thinking is reasonable in the context of a larger spiritual understanding of reincarnation and Karma, which are not incompatible with the Kabbalistic teachings of Judaism. This would affect me more deeply as I pursued studies at various Buddhist centres in the Northeast U.S., some academic and some experiential. My reservations about Buddhism were continually answered with much common sense by the many teachers I continued to encounter, and I consequently began to understand my Judaism at a much deeper level. I was motivated to join a Jewish spiritual community in Berkeley, California, called *Chochmat Ha-Lev,* which means "wisdom of the heart," to study

Jewish meditation. I received ordination there, after a three-year low residency program, to become a *Morah ha Hitbodedut*, which means "teacher of Jewish of meditation," and I currently hold weekly meditation groups in my home. I also attend regular long meditation retreats at various Buddhist centres and expect to incorporate Buddhist psychology into my future writings. I believe that, like my son, I have become a Jewish Buddhist or *JuBu*, combining the best of both traditions to understand the other better.

My mothering will never be the same: I could never attach again to those dreams of my son becoming a rabbi and presenting me with many grandchildren. Clearly, I had to let him go to become whomever he chose to be; his life was no longer in my hands, because it was *his* life, not mine that would play out in the future. Indeed, he became just as Thich Nhat Hanh had predicted: the monastic who brought peace to family disputes with his wisdom. He declined the opportunity to follow in his teacher's footsteps and become a guru himself, perhaps because any institutionalized life did not appeal to his sense of independence. He became a householder, which is really a lay Buddhist and a computer guru, and travelled to India and Nepal to train the staff of corporate outsourcing; his sojourn there made him an ideal employee to relate to these nationals, and he uses these travels to visit his teachers. A recent and surprising development saw my son marry a very spiritual Roman Catholic, and I embraced his partner with open arms because of their devotion to each other. I felt relieved and privileged to have another adult child, who became quite devoted to me. Ben, now with greying hair, told me that he decided not to have children in this marriage; he did, however, become the model of a generous uncle to his four nephews. I now realize that it is not the name of the spiritual path that matters but rather the behaviour towards one another that measures our spiritual maturity. As the Dalai Lama has famously stated: "Kindness is my religion."

NOTES

[1]The entire letter is available online at the Washington Mindfulness Community's website (see "Martin Luther King Jr").

[2]More recently, the online Buddhist zine *Lion's Roar* reports that

there was a 2010 petition to nominate him once again for this honour (see "Campaign Strives to Nominate Thich Nhat Hanh").
[3]This name emphasizes the interdependence that all sentient beings have with one another and with the planet earth.

WORKS CITED

"Campaign Strives to Nominate Thich Nhat Hanh for Nobel Peace Prize." *Lion's Roar— Buddhist Wisdom for Our Time*. Lion's Roar Foundation, 4. Jan. 2013. Web. 3 Jan. 2016.

"Martin Luther King, Jr—Letter to the Nobel Institute." *Washington Mindfulness Community Official Website*. N. p., 25 Jan. 1967. Web. 27 Dec. 2015.

15.
"In Your Blood, Live [With Pride, My Daughters]!" (Ezekiel 16)

RABBI DR. HAVIVA NER-DAVID

WHEN I WAS A GIRL growing up in Orthodox Jewish New York suburbia, I read Judy Blume's *Are You There God, It's Me Margaret* (1970). I particularly identified with Margaret's desire to get her period and become a woman, but this was not something I discussed with anyone. Back then, thirty-plus years ago, these things were discussed even less openly than they are today. To be fair, we did have a class in sixth grade Jewish Day School with the school nurse, who showed us how to buckle in (yes, believe it or not, that is how it worked back then!) to diaper-sized "sanitary napkins." My parents also bought me a book called *Where Did I Come From?* (1973), and my mother packed me the necessary supplies should I get my period while in sleep-away camp. I knew that this was a step up from my mother's generation, when girls were slapped when they told their mothers that they got their periods. But the way adults around me dealt with my impending menstruation was discreet enough to send a message of shame nonetheless.

Growing up in an Orthodox Jewish culture complicated an already problematic situation of how to relate to my uterine blood. Not only did I have to contend with general societal menstrual blood taboos, but I also had to confront the more specific ones of my minority religious culture. Each fall, as part of the Torah reading cycle at the beginning of the Jewish New Year, we read the biblical creation story aloud in synagogue. This reminded us women and girls not only of our place in the evolutionary scale but also of how our reproductive powers are a curse and not a blessing. And in services each Friday night, we read the following rabbinic text: "There are three sins for which women die in childbirth: a lack of care with regard to nidah [sexual separation around menstruation], challah [the separation of the dough-offering], and the lighting of the [Shabbat] lamp" (Mishnah, Tractate Shabbat, 2:6).[1]

Later, when I became literate enough in classic rabbinic literature to conduct research on my own, I came across less publicized texts such as this one:

> Why was she given the commandment of menstrual separation? Because she spilled the blood of the First Adam; therefore she was given the commandment of menstrual separation. And why was she given the commandment to sacrifice the first portion of the dough? Because she spoiled the First Adam, who was the first portion of the world; therefore she was given the commandment to sacrifice the first portion of the dough. And why was she given the commandment of lighting the Sabbath lamp? Because she extinguished the soul of the First Adam; therefore she was given the commandment of lighting the Sabbath lamp. (Bereshit Rabah, Parashah 17)

What was I supposed to think and feel about becoming a woman while being bombarded with these messages tying uterine blood to guilt, sin, and punishment? On one hand, I was filled with excitement at the prospect of menarche. On the other hand, I was aware, at least on a subconscious level, that this transition was a complicated one, with conflicting messages of both power and servitude, pride and shame—with, unfortunately, more weight put on the servitude and shame than on the power and pride by my religious tradition.

Years later, when I was engaged to be married, I studied the Jewish religious laws of menstrual separation that require a heterosexual couple to refrain from sex at the sight of any menstrual bleeding. I was especially struck by the ways these laws are practiced today, which are quite different than how they appear in their related biblical passages. First, and most striking, is the fact that, according to the biblical system of ritual purity (*taharah*) and impurity (*tumah*), men and woman are equally subject to the contraction of *tumah*. So how come the people around me only expressed concern about women's ritual impurity? The passage relating to a woman's menstrual impurity appears amid many ritual purity rules that relay how men *and* women can become ritually impure, and what it takes for them to return to purity. It appears in the context of a discussion about ritual impurity contracted by either male *or* female bodily emissions. Uterine blood is only one of the emissions that cause ritual impurity or, *tumah*: "When a woman has a flow, her flow being blood from her body, she shall remain in her ritual impurity seven days; whoever touches her shall be ritually impure until evening" (Leviticus 15:19). As this text illustrates, Leviticus does not forbid contracting *tumah*, so there is no prohibition against touching a woman who is ritually impure. One simply contracts her impurity by doing so.

In Leviticus 15:24, it says that if a man has sexual intercourse with a woman who is menstruating, he contracts the original *tumah*, and will also spend seven days in that ritually impure state. In this case, the man contracts the impurity on the same level that the woman has, as opposed to the lesser degree of *tumah* that he contracts from, for example, simply touching her or sitting on a chair she has sat on. In the more removed case, his ritually impure state lasts only until the evening. In other words, unique to this case of sexual intercourse and *tumah* contagion, the man contracts the woman's *tumah* and is treated as if the blood flow came from his own body, seemingly because he has "touched" the source of the *tumah*, by penetrating the area from which the blood is flowing.

As these passages illustrate, it is not forbidden to be in a state of ritual impurity. However, it is clear from the biblical verses that the preferred state is one of ritual purity. From a practical point of view, ritual impurity primarily affected those who entered the Temple (or Tabernacle in the pre-Temple period) as well as priests, who needed to be pure to eat consecrated food. From the time of the destruction of the Temple and the subsequent cessation of priestly food gifts, ritual impurity has had no practical consequences.

However, there is an additional ramification aside from these Temple-related ones. Other passages show that *tumah* contracted from uterine blood flow is more complex than other forms of ritual impurity, and this notion is reflected in the belief that ritual impurity contracted through sexual intercourse is more severe. For instance, Leviticus provides two lists of forbidden acts (many of them sexual) that prevent one from being *kadosh*, or holy:

> Do not come near a woman during her period of menstrual ritual impurity to uncover her nakedness. (Leviticus 18:19)
>
> If a man lies with a woman during her infirmity [when she is bleeding from her uterus] and reveals her nakedness, he has laid bare her flow, and she has revealed the source of her blood flow; both of them shall be cut off from among their people. (Leviticus 20:18)

Taken together, these verses proscribe sexual relations when a woman is experiencing a blood flow from her uterus. The choice of such an extraordinarily severe punishment in this context intensifies the taboo more than a mere prohibition would.

Leviticus also states that those who contract ritual impurity must wash in order to reverse their status from *tameh* to *tahor*. Proper washing was interpreted by the Rabbis in the Talmudic period in accordance with Leviticus 11:36, which states that a cistern and spring do not contract *tumah*. For them, proper washing required immersion in a *mikveh*, which means a natural body of water, such as a spring, lake, or ocean. If that is not possible, it may also occur in a human-made pit filled with rain water (a cistern) or a rabbinically designed ritual bath. This all explains why women still immerse today after menstruation to reverse their impure status before resuming sexual relations. Yet men do not, even after they contract impurity from seminal emissions, for example. *Tumah* contracted from a uterine flow is, thus, the only ritual impurity that carries along with it a sexual prohibition and is, therefore, the only *tumah* that still has practical ramifications in a non-Temple Jewish reality.

Although this all made sense to me on an intellectual level, it did not justify the *tumah* baggage that was part of my experience as a Jewish girl and woman. The fact that the only *tumah* ritual still enforced today is associated with uterine blood has negatively influenced the perception—by both men and women—of women and their bodies. All *tumah* ideologies and associations after the Temple's destruction have focused exclusively on the bleeding woman; therefore, today, women are erroneously perceived to be the only gender who have the biological capacity to become ritually impure, and the source of that impurity is, ironically, our life-giving wombs. Thus, echoing the biblical creation narrative, the male rabbinic system turned the source of our female power into the source of our female shame.

According to the inner workings of the system of *tumah* and *taharah*, both men and women still to this day contract *tumah*, but it is only women contracting *tumah* from uterine bleeding who are obliged to immerse, since only this *tumah* carries with it a non-Temple-related ramification (i.e., the sexual prohibition). Men have continued to immerse in the *mikveh* throughout the generations—especially in the Kabbalistic circles and Hassidic communities—but not out of obligation. Rather, they have immersed for the spiritual experience; therefore, their immersions are not associated in the collective subconscious with ritual impurity in the way that women's immersions are. Rather, they are associated with spiritual elevation. One could even say that *tumah* consciousness has disappeared today in relation to men so that men can only go higher, whereas women are fated to be brought down spiritually by virtue of our biological fate.[2]

Yet another striking disconnect between biblical verses and the teachings that I received about sexual abstinence during menstruation is apparent in Leviticus 15. The chapter discusses how menstrual impurity creates a week-long period of *tumah* following the first day of a woman's bleeding. In contrast, I was told to keep seven extra "clean" days after my bleeding stopped. These extra days were added during the talmudic period when *nidah*, or regular menstruation, was conflated with an irregular type of uterine blood flow, described in the biblical verses that follow directly after those regarding *nidah*. The text states:

> When a woman has had a discharge of blood for many days, not at the time of her menstrual period, or when she has a discharge beyond her menstrual period, she shall be

> ritually impure, as though at the time of her menstrual period, as long as her flow lasts. Any bedding on which she lies while her flow lasts shall be for her like bedding during her menstrual period; and any object on which she sits shall become ritually impure, as it does during her ritually impure menstrual period. Whoever touches them shall be ritually impure; he shall wash his clothes, bathe in water, and remain ritually impure until evening. When she becomes clean of her discharge, she counts off seven days, and after that, she shall be ritually pure. On the eighth day, she shall take two turtledoves or two pigeons, and bring them to the priest and the entrance to the Tent of Meeting... You shall put the Israelites on guard against their ritual impurity, lest they die through their ritual impurity by defiling my Tabernacle which is among them. (Leviticus 15:19-32)

This passage refers to a woman who experiences an irregular blood flow for many days. When her blood flow stops, she counts another seven bloodless "clean" days, presumably to ensure that the flow has stopped and she is cured of whatever caused this irregularity. At that time, she would bring a sacrificial offering before she could resume worship in the Temple. In Hebrew, the woman experiencing this flow is termed a *zavah* rather than *nidah*.

These related laws, thus, raise a question: what determines whether a flow of blood is considered menstrual, *nidah*, or a non-menstrual, irregular flow, *zivah*, which has stricter rules? That is, how do we decide if the ordinary seven-day separation applies, counting from the first day that the woman sees blood, or if the seven "clean" days must be added to the count? According to the plain interpretation of the text, it seems that the woman herself is the authority in determining if she is experiencing regular menstruation. Timing is of the essence, as is the length of the flow. But the rabbis were apparently not comfortable leaving matters in the hands of women; instead, they set in motion a series of amendments to the biblical rules that created a kind of formula for the woman to determine the nature of her blood flow rather than rely on her instincts and knowledge of her own body.

As such, according to biblical law as interpreted by the rabbis, the *nidah* is automatically in a state of *tumah* for a total of seven days from the time that she starts bleeding. This is the case as long as her flow lasts for seven days or fewer, and as long as it occurs during her typical menstruation time, which is also defined by the rabbis. If her flow lasts for ten or more days, or if she bleeds for three days or more within the eleven days that the rabbis define as atypical, she must wait until her flow stops and then count seven days in which she is "clean" of blood before she can immerse and resume sexual relations. If she bleeds for one or two days only during that eleven day period, she does not have to add seven clean days but simply wait one day to make sure the bleeding has stopped before she can immerse.

Still, it seems that women could not be trusted to implement this rabbinically created system, so even more stringencies were designed to simplify matters. Since having intercourse with a woman who was not careful about keeping these laws is considered a severe infraction, such regulations would ultimately put men's minds at ease. Thus, consider the following text from the Talmud:

> Said Rav Yosef said Rav Yehudah said Rav: Rebbe [Rabbi Yehudah HaNasi] issued an edict in the outskirts: If a woman sees one day of bleeding, she should wait six days plus that one day; if she sees two days of bleeding, she should wait six/five days plus those two days; if she sees three days of bleeding, she should wait seven clean days [plus those three days]. Said Rabbi Zeira: The daughters of Israel were stringent upon themselves; even when they saw a drop of blood the size of a mustard seed, they waited the seven clean days. (BT Nidah 66a)

In the early Talmudic period, Rabbi Judah the Prince launched these new menstrual separation stringencies by declaring that all women experiencing uterine blood flow must regard it within the strictest case scenario. This means that if she bleeds for one or two days, no matter the time in her cycle, she must treat the flow as a regular "*nidah*" period and wait a total of seven days. Similarly, if she bleeds for three or more days, she must wait until the flow stops and then count seven clean days, thus treating the flow as an irregular "*zivah*" flow. Later, Rabbi Zeira added here yet another stricture by completely conflating *nidah* with *zivah* and ruling that any woman who sees even one drop of blood must wait the seven clean days.

The upshot of this development is that the practice traditionally taught today stipulates that any woman who bleeds from her uterus—regardless if it is during her typical menstruation time or whether it is for one day, three days, or fourteen days—must wait a minimum of four days, or until she stops bleeding, if she is of Sephardic descent and five days if she is of Ashkenazi descent. Then she must perform a *hefsek taharah*, which is an internal check to determine if the bleeding has stopped, and wait seven clean days before she immerses in the *mikveh* and resumes sexual relations. In other words, rabbinic law reinterpreted women's healthy menstruation as a sign of irregularity and sickliness.

What does this all say about the rabbis' views on bleeding women? If all women are *zavot*, then our bleeding is not normal; it is sickly, irregular, dangerous, and frightening—even threatening. This stricture, it seems, came mostly as a reaction to and categorization of all uterine blood as unnatural. The rabbis, thus, conflated two experiences that for women are distinct—one being a completely healthy experience and the other signifying a potential health issue. Ultimately, strictures such as these reflect the historical rabbinic fear of women's power and bodies as well as a devaluing of their intellectual capacities and their commitment to the Jewish religious legal system. Their fear of this mysterious blood as well as the severe penalty for having intercourse with an "impure" woman caused them to demand a longer period of abstinence rather than risk having sex with a *nidah* or *zavah*. Moreover, men are permitted by biblical law to marry more than one wife, so for them, the sacrifice was not as great as it is today. Of course, by making the laws stricter, they expanded the time period that women are considered impure and, thus, created an even larger source of "fear" than necessary.

Where does all of what I have outlined above leave me, as a rabbi with four daughters, as well as three sons? I am concerned about all of their perceptions of women, gender, and how these ideologies shape our worldview. Aspects of menstrual separation practices as they developed over time are so deeply entrenched in misogynist interpretations that practising them as per the rabbis' prescription perpetuates ideologies that are harmful to women's psyches and self-images as well as to how men perceive and relate to women. What can I as a mother do to counteract these messages?

I decided to address this important parenting question—with the enthusiastic support of my life partner, Jacob, who is also the father of our seven children—by no longer adhering to the rabbinic interpretation of the menstrual purity separation laws and, instead, by treating my menstrual bleeding as "*nidah*" blood as described in Leviticus. I now wait only seven days from the day my menstrual flow starts before I immerse. When I have irregular menstrual flow, then—and only then—do I apply the rule of adding seven "clean" days. This particularly makes sense to me, since it is difficult to predict bleeding patterns that do not coincide with typical menstruation. I also do this publicly; I do not keep my decision to myself. I write about it, speak about it, and teach other couples about it. I made this decision not only for my own spiritual integrity but to be an example to others as well, especially to my own children.

Still, I had to ask myself if perpetuating sexual abstinence around menstruation was a good idea at all. Although I personally do feel there is a need in our culture to ritualize humanity's relationship with our own mortality—which is, I believe, a potential power of the ritual purity and impurity system when it is observed by both men and women—this cannot be accomplished when women are exclusively compelled to immerse regularly. This tradition projects ideologies of women's spiritual inferiority as well as a fear of women and their uterine blood. Since the destruction of the Temple, ritual menstrual impurity has been specifically understood by Jewish scholars and authorities as well as by the mass culture as being a lower spiritual state, connected to filth and danger—antithetical to the holy. These characteristics have, in turn, been associated with women in general, regardless of their state, because all women are potential bleeders.

This is why I decided to ask Jacob to commit to immersing monthly when I do so; it is a way for us to share this ritual that, in our interpretation, is about renewing our commitment to our relationship rather than about washing away my impurity. And so, each month, we go together to the *mikveh*—whether it be a lake, spring, or ocean, or an artificially created *mikveh* such as the one where I work on Kibbutz Hannaton. As each of us immerses, we once again take that leap of faith in our relationship; it symbolizes that our relationship can survive against the statistical odds by jumping into the abyss that separates all human beings, even those who are most intimately connected. But that abyss represented by the *mikveh*, the living waters, also symbolizes the Divine Spirit of the Primordial Waters, and it is into those waters that we immerse ourselves fully, putting our trust in that Spirit, in ourselves, and in each other. And about this, too, I write and speak and teach, and our children know exactly where we are going, together, as a couple, which is perhaps most important of all.

Still, I was left with the question of rituals around women's bleeding that are not connected to sexual prohibition. Could *mikveh* immersion, despite the *tumah* baggage associated with the ritual, be a way of *celebrating* uterine blood? I began addressing this question by considering my own blood, which I found most symbolic of my own mortality. There is no public ritual to mark miscarriage in Jewish practice, but there is *mikveh* immersion, since one loses considerable uterine blood during the process. So after an emotionally and physically traumatic miscarriage, I decided to mark it with *mikveh* immersion, but I did not leave it at that private mournful act. I followed my post-miscarriage *mikveh* immersion with a sharing circle and prayer service called *Kiddush Levanah*, which is performed once a month to the light of the New Moon, after which I did my own burial ritual of a box of objects that I associated with my lost pregnancy. Immersing in the Living Waters at that particular juncture in my life symbolized for me a personal rebirth into whatever would be the next stage, especially since I believed that was my last chance for having more children. (Unbeknownst to me at the time, Jacob and I would adopt another child and I would give birth to our seventh child at age 42!) For me, this symbolized a submission to whatever would be as well as a reconnection to my essence amid all of the intensity of birthing, parenting, and partnering in building a home and family.

But what about my daughters? How could I fashion for them a positive experience of menarche that would use traditional religious ritual rather than circumvent it? This was a monumental challenge that I, as a feminist woman rabbi, could not ignore. Like miscarriage, this pivotal moment in a woman's life is frequently stigmatized or ignored. It would seem that great shame is attached to menarche, since, at least on a subconscious level, this transition in a young woman's life is seen as the moment when she goes from being *tehorah* (ritually pure) to being *temeah* (ritually impure)—a condition that will only be reversed if she chooses to remain within the traditional norm by immersing in the *mikveh* in the context of marriage. To add insult to injury, the rabbis seemingly do their best to keep young women in the status of "*temeah*," since they want to prevent her from having premarital sex. At a traditional Orthodox *mikveh*, only married women are allowed to immerse, since ritual immersion creates a sexually permissible woman who is allowed to have sex. This is very dangerous as far as the male Orthodox rabbinic establishment is concerned. Female "promiscuity" unleashes a whole array of problems for these rabbis, relating to the continuity of the purity of lineage and souls of the Jewish people. And so, until she is married, a woman is traditionally not given access to this powerful Jewish ritual of spiritual renewal and elevation.[3] The underlying message here is not so difficult to unpack.

It is no wonder, then, that no traditional Jewish ritual exists to positively mark the onset of menstruation. I did not want my daughters to experience menstruation as something impure or dirty but rather as a sign of becoming a woman with the potential power to bring new life into this world. I had read women's accounts of how they experienced the onset of menstruation, and some of these "blood stories" were quite shocking (Lee and Sasser-Coen). I felt responsible for what my own daughters' "blood stories" would be. I did not want to miss this opportunity to positively affect my daughters' relationships with their bodies.

To that end, while attending an interdisciplinary conference in England on menstruation over ten years ago, I participated in a fascinating and eye-opening session with a middle-school teacher at a girls' school. She explained how she has "period parties" for all of the girls in her class as they reach menarche. I immediately loved this idea and returned to Israel excited to implement it in my own family. So when my eleven-year-old daughter Michal (now twenty three years old) got her period for the first time (she was the first in her circle of girlfriends to do so), I asked her what she thought about the idea. I explained to her why I thought it so important that we celebrate and that we do so among her friends. I explained how she could influence others by sharing this experience with them. It seems my argument was convincing enough because Michal agreed. Even she had to admit that a slumber party with a teenage movie, henna tattoos and hair coloring, red foods, and a beading craft project sounded like fun.

We were still living in Jerusalem at the time, where there was no *mikveh* that would allow me to bring my eleven-year-old daughter for immersion. There was no way Michal would agree to immerse outdoors in the nude at that age, so I had to forego my ideal of *mikveh* immersion as part of this "period party." Instead, we blessed Michal by stringing red beads into a necklace and munching on pomegranate seeds and pieces of heart-shaped, blood-red sponge cake. It certainly was a night to remember, which was precisely the point. I am certain that there was not one girl present that night who was not changed in some subtle way by the experience, even if none had a "period party" themselves. (However, one girl's mother, also a rabbi, organized a woman's wisdom circle to mark her daughter's menarche.) And most importantly, Michal will have this as her "blood story" to share with her children, God willing, some day.

My second daughter, Meira, who is now seventeen years old, was already anticipating her period party when she experienced menarche. She had been at Michal's years before and knew what to expect—though for her party, we added a new twist. We had moved to a kibbutz in the Galilee where I founded *Shmaya: A Mikveh for Body, Mind, and Spirit*. We held Meira's party at the ritual bath, and I performed an immersion ritual with Meira to positively mark this life transition. Her friends and her older sister offered her their blessings while we ate and listened to a play list of songs that Michal had carefully selected. Michal also gave her sister a bright red scarf she had knitted for the occasion. The experience was a hit!

Unlike her older sisters who got their periods at age eleven, my third daughter, Hallel, experienced menarche at age thirteen. Jacob and I waited with anticipation for her hormonal swings to subside, just as her older sisters and I waited excitedly to throw her a party. Finally, the day came. But since she was not the first of her friends to get her period, we held a group period party with two of her closest friends, their mothers, and their sisters. I considered this a huge step forwards. Ten years after my oldest daughter had her period party, the event already felt "normal" enough to be simply a fun and meaningful mother-daughter event shared with friends. And, importantly, her friends were there celebrating their own menarche as well.

My youngest daughter, Shefa, who is now five years old, was present at Hallel's period party. She did not know exactly what we were celebrating, but she had a blast beading herself a red and pink necklace, eating pomegranate seeds, heart-shaped chocolates in red wrappers, and beet chips, and feeling like one of the big girls. We made beaded key chains with the Hebrew phrase "Thank You [God in the feminine] for making me a woman," listened to coming of age songs, and performed our immersion rituals. But the biggest source of pride for me was the way my oldest daughters took charge of the event. After having period parties of their own, they knew exactly what to do and understood the importance of the tradition. Laughing, they told Shefa they will come home from wherever they are living when she reaches menarche to throw her a period party, too.

I am pleased that I have been able to counteract some of the negative *tumah* energy my daughters have undoubtedly absorbed from the society around them in regard to their uterine blood, whether by creating rituals for them or me or even by refusing to practice rituals in their traditional forms if they perpetuate negative messages about women's uterine blood. I am especially grateful that I have been able to do this all as a rabbi in a religious context—to stress that the symbol of blood is a life force rather than a source of contamination. I am pleased that my daughters will not feel the need to wrap and hide their pads when they throw them in the garbage or cower in shame when they pay for their tampons at the check-out line or be embarrassed to explain if they are feeling especially emotional because of pre-menstrual hormone swings. I also hope they will not feel the need to mourn miscarriage alone should they ever experience one. This blood is natural and beautiful; it is also one aspect of how we all came into this world—even if it can be uncomfortable and even painful at times. Naming our monthly blood flow as such may also be an act of resistance against the patriarchal powers that be who frame it as an unnatural curse. We should not let them turn their fear of our life-giving powers into our shame or pass this shame onto our daughters. "In Your Blood Live, In Your Blood Live!" said Ezekiel the prophet. And now his prophesy is finally coming true. That is the message I want to pass on to my daughters.

NOTES

[1]When I quote biblical and rabbinic texts throughout this chapter, I am freely translating from the original classical Hebrew and Aramaic and not taking any particular published translation.
[2]Thankfully, this reality is changing now, at least in the liberal Jewish world, with the emergence of a fast-growing movement to reclaim and reframe *mikveh* as a non-gendered ritual related to spiritual renewal, healing, and marking transitions rather than washing away impurity, for both men and women.
[3]However, as noted in the note above, this is changing as *mikveh* is being reclaimed and reframed as a non-gendered transition, transformation, spiritual cleansing, preparation, and healing ritual in the liberal Jewish world.

WORKS CITED

Blume, Judy. *Are You There, God? It's Me Margaret.* New York: Random House, 1970. Print.

Lee, Janet and Sasser-Coen, Jennifer. *Blood Stories: Menarche and the Politics of the Female Body in Contemporary U.S. Society.* New York: Routledge, 1996. Print.

16.
Joy Unspeakable (or, a Beautiful Day)

KATHRYN BELL

Restore to me the joy of your salvation and grant me a willing spirit, to sustain me. (New International Version, Ps. 51.12)

I HAVE NOT YET made myself coffee. I have managed to roughly herd three sleepy-eyed children out of warm beds and onto chilly kitchen floors. I stand, poised for duty, but with a heart-and-soul sigh. My toes are inches from the dog mess; rags are in hand. The groan of my heavy heart holds my body hostage with hesitation. Joy seems far, unreachable now.

Free-Girl's homework waits unchecked while she dances, in front of the mirror, oblivious to the urgency of the morning. Proud-Baby, helpless and hungry, cries from his highchair. Dimple-Boy cannot find his lunch bag or his green cereal bowl... and he cannot hope to find his shoes, socks, and jacket on his own either. No one is eating breakfast. The dogs are pacing, prancing, frenetic; their toenails are tippy tapping in tense pleading, asking to be let out in skittish desperation, with embarrassed tails.

Our morning is scattered and rushed because my ring, a small stone from my grandmother, is lost and haunting me with its absence. I took too much time to search for it—first under pillows and blankets, then in the night-table and under the bed, and finally in my hair and even desperately in the bathroom sink. I stopped the alarm again and again to search further and deeper and more frantically, and so I am responsible for our morning's butterfly effect. Every snooze I tapped to silence the reminders of time passing seemed to flap proverbial butterfly wings, leading us to this chaotic morning—the perfect storm of joylessness.

My unadorned finger reminds me of the space my grandmother once filled. I feel that if only I could find the ring, I could set this day right. I would have my grandmother and her quiet faith inaudibly reflecting in the glint of the heirloom I wear daily, reminding me to follow the same path she did. In quietly loving and serving, she spoke more strongly to me with her weekday grace-filled actions than the fleeting words of most Sunday pulpit preaching.

As a newborn, I was given my grandmother's middle name as my own: Ann, meaning *grace*. I would later give the middle name Grace to my daughter, in her honour. It was my grandmother who cradled my young child-self in her big, soft lap and taught me that I was of intrinsic value and securely loved by sending me with the secret message in Afrikaans "*ek is 'n mooi meisie*"[1] to garner sweets from my grandfather. In grade school, it was my grandmother who helped my heart deeply understand the truth of the old hymns, the amazing grace, telling me stories of growing up in South Africa and their family coming to Canada to find refuge from mounting tensions and injustice. It was my grandmother who brushed my long preteen hair into a ponytail, telling me I had "such a pretty neck" and erasing so many body image concerns growing inside me and erupting like the acne on my face.

My grandmother was a province away when I was a teenager, but she always called or wrote to assure me that she prayed for me daily. She encouraged me as a young first-time mother to really befriend my lost cousin—also a young first-time mother—before I knew it was really the best thing for *both* of us, and it would lead years later to a deep soul friendship and renewal of faith. Our first family road trip, including a long car and ferry ride, was to visit my grandmother so she could pick beach rocks with her two-year-old great-granddaughter and whisper a blessing while she put her warm hands around my swollen womb, which was growing the great-grandson she would never meet earth side.

Her daily prayers for me filled my mother heart and spirit with love. But without the ring, I am forgetting this. How fleeting faith can feel when I try to do it all on my own.

I am consumed by the anti-joy… and I see now that it is spreading.

My ears echo with my own barking, "Just let those dogs outside before they make another mess!" I cringe at the sight of Dimple-Boy's dimple-less face as he cracks the backdoor open and calls the canines, the crisp air cutting into the kitchen. My eyes brim to spill. My mother soul is aching for the chance to start over. My body finally folds down, defeated, to clean the dog-mess.

And, suddenly, Dimple-Boy calls to me (the never-ceasing call for maternal attention, the asking for parts of me I did not know I had to give); he demands of me, "Mom! MOM! Come and see this beautiful day!"

Barely audible, the still, small, pleading quiet voice says to me softly, "go to him."

My heart calls out wordlessly, to my grandmother and our God. No words, just a reaching. Maybe I am not alone?

My eyes will not leave the warm dog-puddle, the yellow blemish spreading across the floor and demanding to be blotted. Proud-Baby screams, still helpless and hungry in his highchair, and fills my flushed ears with mother guilt and shame. Free-Girl chatters to herself loudly in the round bathroom mirror in front of the pedestal sink, her reflection rapt with attentiveness. She is spinning and twisting, singing and intoning nonsense; her drivel imprisons my thoughts, making me slow to process. I cannot help but consider the pedestal she puts me on and how I deserve to be in dog-puddles today. In a brief instant, I think about how she is a reflection of me—my heart on my sleeve in the world—but today I am merely irked by her flitting. It pains me, deeply. The noise around me is deafening; Dimple-Boy—flashing teeth, smile, and those dimples!—calls me again, "Mom, MOM! You have to come see this *beautiful day*!" My face is blank, undimpled; I feel numb. And *even louder still*, the quiet voice is pleading…

Exasperated, I give *in*. I give *in* to the dimpled call and give *in* to the still, quiet-voice. In the giving *in*, the other sounds fade; by giving *in*, I am refusing to give *up*. I leave the rags to fall into the mess and, stepping wide, I go to him who calls me with such desperation. I go to look out the window at the beautiful day; I go, hoping my choice to be there for my son will give me the joy I long for. Standing next to him, Proud-Baby's ignored cries nagging my ears, my eyes search the sky, the day, for the beauty, but the day is ordinary, and my heart is completely unmoved. My brief hope for redemption of this morning fades, and I feel alone in the grey; I feel my heart give *up*.

"Isn't it a beautiful day, Mom?" Dimple-Boy gasps out again, uncontained, taking hold of my hand with his and tugging softly.

I silently search anew the grey-tinged clouds, renewing my diligence to find the beauty for his sake. I hunt urgently for hints and hues of beauty in pink or a whisper of purple, candy-cotton clouds or even emerging orange promises of a sunny day. But the cold grey stares back at me starkly, and I see no heavenly brushstrokes of joy. As I turn to look into his eyes, I am desperately searching inside myself for an answer to give my son. On a whim perhaps, or in response to the still, silent prompting, I leave my hard, proud shell, and stepping freely, I go to Him who calls me with such inspiration. In that moment, my heart reconnects with my faith, and I know without a doubt that I am not alone.

And, suddenly, I see *the beautiful day.* We, the God of my faith and I with my grandmother-shaped mother heart, have defeated the anti-joy, blotted it up and kept it from spreading. The beautiful day is shining up at me from the dimpled face so full of *joy unspeakable* at dull clouds and new mornings, as a canvas not yet painted. I see love in his face and am witness to the pure and radiant joy that he is longing to share with me. My heart and soul sing, and my face beams to reflect his. I gasp out "It is! It is a beautiful day God made for us!" as I tussle his golden hair. Free-Girl suddenly joins us, twirling next to me. Proud-Baby hushes with the shift of our attention. The dogs ask to come in, and I slide the door open again. I am so humbly thankful for this unexpected joy moment.

Meanwhile, the ring waits for me to find at a later time; I have a feeling of assurance that I will reunite with my grandmother after my time in this world. In the meantime, I will look for the joy, given *in* these spirit things that are mine for such a short time, here in motherhood and in quiet faith, in simply serving and serving simply, in whispered prayers of daily love, and somewhere beyond anything that is I or a beautiful day in this world. *Ek is 'n mooi meisie!*

NOTES

[1]I had thought this meant "may I have candy please," because my grandfather would often give me sweets to share with grandma when I repeated the phrase. But it translates to "I am a lovely/pretty girl."

About the Contributors

Kathryn Bell, MC, is a master's in counselling graduate from the Graduate Centre in Applied Psychology, Athabasca University. She, with her husband, is raising her young children in Alberta and is both working and publishing in the field. She enjoys volunteering, hobby photography, gardening, and supporting new or young mothers.

Bridget Boland is a writer, certified shamanic energetic healer, doula, and former attorney. Her novel *The Doula* was published by Simon and Schuster in 2012. Bridget's writing has appeared in *Conde Nast Women's Sports and Fitness*, *YogaChicago*, and *The Essential Chicago*. Excerpts from her work have won the Writers League of Texas Memoir Prize, and the Surrey Writers Conference Nonfiction Award. She holds an MFA in creative writing from the School of the Art Institute of Chicago and a JD from Loyola University of Chicago.

Deidre Hill Butler, PhD, is an associate professor of sociology and director of Africana studies at Union College in Schenectady, New York (USA). Dr. Hill Butler research examines intersections of race, gender, and place from perspectives of black women. Dr. Hill Butler recently curated a community engaged photo exhibit "Revitalized Community: Bordeaux Since the 2010 flood" at the newly renovated Bordeaux Branch of the Nashville, Tennessee, public library. The photo exhibit is part of a manuscript chronicling how the Bordeaux neighbourhood of Nashville is rebuilding since a devastating 2010 flood through the activism of community mothers active in residential groups. Dr. Hill Butler's other current work examines how black stepmothers negotiate their roles in American families. She and her partner, Alan Sr., are parents of two young sons and she is the bonus (step) mother to four young adults.

Elvira Casal received her PhD in English from Vanderbilt in 1993. She is a full professor and associate chair of the English Department at Middle Tennessee State University. She is a member of the Women's Studies Council and President's Commission on the Status of Women at MTSU. Her current research examines nineteenth-century woman novelists. She has published on various topics, including mothers in Jane Austen's work.

Ann W. Duncan (PhD, University of Virginia) is associate professor of religion at Goucher College in Baltimore, Maryland. Her research and teaching focus on intersections of religion and public life, including religion and politics, new religious movements, the religious "nones," and motherhood and American Christianity. She is co-editor of *Church-State Issues in America Today* (Praeger, 2009) and the forthcoming *"The Universe is Indifferent": Theology, Philosophy, and Mad Men* (Cascade, 2016).

Florence Pasche Guignard pursues interdisciplinary research that engages issues at the intersection of religion, ritual, gender, embodiment, and material culture, and integrates approaches from motherhood studies and media studies. After completing her PhD in the study of religions at the University of Lausanne (Switzerland), she joined the Department for the Study of Religion at the University of Toronto as a postdoctoral researcher with a fellowship from the Swiss National Science Foundation. She has taught at the Department of Historical Studies of the University of Toronto Mississauga. She is currently affiliated with the University of Fribourg (Switzerland).

Rannveig Haga holds a PhD in History of Religions at Uppsala University. She has conducted ethnographic research among Somalis in Dubai, Somaliland, Sweden, and Finland. Her main research interests include women's agency, Islam and parenting, and epistemic justice. She is currently working on two research projects related to the Somali diaspora funded by The Baltic Sea Foundation and The Swedish Research Council. Haga is the author of *Tradition as Resource: Transnational Somali Women Traders Facing the Reality of Civil War* (Uppsala University Press 2009). Her latest publication is in the edited book *Making European Muslims* (Routledge 2014).

Sharon Lang (PhD Harvard) is a professor of anthropology at the University of Redlands, who teaches courses on Jewish culture and identity, the Israeli-Palestinian conflict, the anthropology of mothering, and cross-cultural dance. She is the author of *Sharaf Politics* (Routledge) and several articles on SIDS published in the *Journal for Research on Mothering*. She is also the president of the Guild for Infant Survival (Inland Empire) and the vice-president of the Jewish Peace Lobby.

Dr. Emily McAvan is a queer, Jewish mother. Her work centres on the interaction between religion and literature. Her first book, *The Postmodern Sacred* (McFarland 2012), is an examination of the religious iconography of science fiction and fantasy.

Emily Hunter McGowin has a PhD in theology from the University of Dayton. Her dissertation, "As for Me and My House: The Theology of the Family in the American Quiverfull Movement," is an ethnographic and theological study of Quiverfull families. Her other writings have been published in *New Blackfriars* and *Baptist History and Heritage*.

Rabbi Dr. Haviva Ner-David is a writer and rabbi, who lives on Kibbutz Hannaton in the Lower Galilee with her husband and seven children. She is founding chair of *Shmaya: A Mikveh for Mind, Body, and Spirit (*the only mikveh in Israel open to all who want to immerse and for whatever purpose and in whatever manner they choose), where she is a mikveh consultant and guide. She is author of two memoirs, most recently *Chanah's Voice: A Rabbi Wrestles with Gender, Commandment and the Women's Rituals of*

Baking, Bathing and Brightening (Ben Yehuda Press, 2014). Rabbi Dr. Ner-David is currently working on a novel and a third memoir, and is looking forwards to the publication of her next book, *Getting (and Staying) Married Jewishly: A Workbook and Guide for Engaged Couples* (due to be published by Ben Yehuda Press in 2017). The first woman to publicly receive rabbinic ordination from an orthodox rabbi (in 2006), she was ordained ten years later as an inter-spiritual minister at One Spirit Inter-spiritual Seminary and now calls herself a post-denominational inter-spiritual rabbi.

Therese Novotny teaches at Marquette University in Milwaukee, Wisconsin. Her dissertation, "Julian of Norwich: Voicing the Vernacular," focuses on medieval studies with a particular interest in medieval women and the paths they took toward self-expression and literacy. Her research examines the formal and informal means women used to gain access to an education and participate in a male-dominant culture. She studies the rich reservoir of rhetorical models readily available to women in unexpected places, namely in non-textual forms, in oral discourse, and visual art. She also researches the efforts women have made to enter public discourse through secular and religious avenues. Prior to her academic career, she worked in public relations in Milwaukee.

Sarah-Jane Page is lecturer in sociology at Aston University, Birmingham, UK. Her main research interests encompass investigating religion through the lens of sexuality and gender in previous projects, including exploring clergy motherhood in the Anglican Church, clergy husbands, and religious young adults' attitudes and experiences of sexuality. She has published in journals, such as *Feminist Review*, *Journal of Beliefs and Values*, *Feminist Theology*, and *Gender, Work and Organization*. She has co-authored a book (with Andrew Yip) titled *Religious and Sexual Identities* (Ashgate, 2013).

Vanessa Reimer holds a PhD in gender, feminist and women's studies from York University (Toronto, Canada). She is the co-editor of Demeter Press collections *Mother of Invention: How Our Mothers Influenced Us as Feminist Academics and Activists* (Reimer and Sahagian 2013) and *The Mother-Blame Game* (Reimer and Sahagian 2015). Her research interests include feminist studies in religion, girlhood, and mothering.

Rosie Rosenzweig is a resident scholar at Brandeis University's Women's Studies Research Center. She is the author of "A Jewish Mother in Shangri-la," which explores her journey to meet her son's Buddhist teachers in America, France, India, and Nepal. After interviewing over forty women artists, she is currently writing a book about creativity.

Zairunisha is a Ph.D. scholar in the Centre for Philosophy, School of Social Sciences at Jawaharlal Nehru University, Delhi, India. She is presently working for a thesis on motherhood, reproductive technology, and feminist bioethics. She has published articles titled "Problem of Personal Identity and its Criterion" and "Impact of Reproductive Technology on Women's Lives in New Delhi" in national and international journals. She has also presented papers on motherhood in various nation and international conferences. As an assistant professor, she has taught courses in philosophy at Indrapratha College for Women, University of Delhi, Delhi, India from 2011 to 2015.